Skills, Not Just Diplomas

Skills, Not Just Diplomas
*Managing Education for Results
in Eastern Europe and Central Asia*

Lars Sondergaard and Mamta Murthi
with Dina Abu-Ghaida, Christian Bodewig, and Jan Rutkowski

THE WORLD BANK
Washington, D.C.

© 2012 The International Bank for Reconstruction and Development / The World Bank
1818 H Street NW
Washington DC 20433
Telephone: 202-473-1000
Internet: www.worldbank.org

All rights reserved

1 2 3 4 :: 14 13 12 11

This volume is a product of the staff of the International Bank for Reconstruction and Development / The World Bank. The findings, interpretations, and conclusions expressed in this volume do not necessarily reflect the views of the Executive Directors of The World Bank or the governments they represent.

The World Bank does not guarantee the accuracy of the data included in this work. The boundaries, colors, denominations, and other information shown on any map in this work do not imply any judgement on the part of The World Bank concerning the legal status of any territory or the endorsement or acceptance of such boundaries.

Rights and Permissions
The material in this publication is copyrighted. Copying and/or transmitting portions or all of this work without permission may be a violation of applicable law. The International Bank for Reconstruction and Development / The World Bank encourages dissemination of its work and will normally grant permission to reproduce portions of the work promptly.

For permission to photocopy or reprint any part of this work, please send a request with complete information to the Copyright Clearance Center Inc., 222 Rosewood Drive, Danvers, MA 01923, USA; telephone: 978-750-8400; fax: 978-750-4470; Internet: www.copyright.com.

All other queries on rights and licenses, including subsidiary rights, should be addressed to the Office of the Publisher, The World Bank, 1818 H Street NW, Washington, DC 20433, USA; fax: 202-522-2422; e-mail: pubrights@worldbank.org.

ISBN: 978-0-8213-8096-3
eISBN: 978-0-8213-8097-0
DOI: 10.1596/978-0-8213-8096-3

Library of Congress Cataloging-in-Publication data has been requested.

Cover photo: The graduating class of 2007, Alexandru Ioan Cuza University, Iași, Romania, march to their commencement ceremony. © Mediafax Foto/Liviu Chirica.

Contents

Foreword		*xv*
Acknowledgments		*xix*
Abbreviations		*xxi*
Overview		**1**
	The Skills Challenge	2
	Why Are Skills an Emerging Problem if Education Systems Are Delivering?	4
	Priority Areas for Action	7
	Managing Education Systems for Results	9
	Build the Foundations of Adult Learning Systems	14
	Conclusion	14
	Notes	15
Chapter 1	**The Demand for Skills in ECA**	**17**
	Background: The Demand for Highly Skilled Labor in the Global Knowledge Economy	18
	Demand for Skilled Labor Has Risen in the ECA Region	20
	Unemployment Patterns in ECA Countries Confirm the Demand for Skilled Labor	25

	Wages Have Risen for Skilled Labor	31
	Lack of Needed Skills Is Impeding Enterprise Growth	36
	Skills Mismatch in the ECA Region	39
	Summary	41
	Notes	43
Chapter 2	**Education and the Supply of Skills to the ECA Market**	**47**
	Background: The Global Knowledge Economy Requires Lifelong Learning	48
	Formal Education in ECA Countries: High Attainment and Good Quality Relative to Current Income Levels	50
	Why Are Skills Emerging as a Problem if Education Systems Are Delivering?	52
	Students May Not Be Acquiring the Right Skills	63
	Adult Learning Is Limited in the Region	65
	Summary	77
	Annex 2A: Education Systems in ECA Today	80
	Notes	87
Chapter 3	**Resolving the Skills Shortage in the ECA Region: A Policy Framework**	**89**
	Operating in the Dark: Ministries Know Too Little to Effectively Manage the Education Sector	90
	Legacy of Central Planning	96
	Inefficient Use of Funds	103
	Addressing the Skills Challenge	108
	Summary	111
	Notes	112
Chapter 4	**Managing for Results at the Pre-University Level of Education**	**115**
	Track Student Learning and Employment Outcomes	116
	Expand Autonomy in Exchange for Accountability for Results	120

	Improve the Efficiency of Resource Use	126
	Summary	136
	Notes	138
Chapter 5	**Managing for Results in the Tertiary Education Sector**	**139**
	Introduce Learning Assessments and Track Employment Outcomes	140
	Strengthen Accountability	152
	Introduce Performance-Based Financing and Encourage Private Funding Resources	159
	Summary	162
	Notes	163
Chapter 6	**Advancing Adult Learning in ECA**	**165**
	Building the Foundations for Adult Learning Systems	166
	Promote Autonomy and Accountability of both Public and Private Providers	172
	Ensure the Efficiency of Sector Financing	175
	Continued Government Role in Retraining and Education for the Unemployed	183
	Priorities for Adult Education and Training Systems in ECA Countries	187
	Summary	191
	Notes	191
Chapter 7	**Extended Summary: The Path for Education Reforms in the ECA Region**	**193**
	The Skills Challenge in the ECA Region	194
	Why Are Skills an Emerging Problem if Education Systems Are Delivering?	197
	Priority Areas for Action	203
	Managing Education Systems for Results	207
	Build the Foundations of Adult Learning Systems	219
	Summary	220
	Notes	222
References		**225**

Boxes

2.1	Defining "Skills," "Competencies," and Other Terms	49
2.2	Testing for Reading Competency in the Programme for International Student Assessment (PISA)	55
2.3	Turkey: Many Students Fail to Acquire Even the Most Basic Proficiencies	57
2.4	Russia: Building Higher-Order Skills Is Proving Difficult	59
2.5	The History of Vocational Education in the ECA Region	64
2.6	Two Forms of Adult Learning	69
3.1	The Value of Standardized External Student Assessments in ECA Countries	94
3.2	Detailed Regulations Set Norms Even for Education Facilities in the ECA Region	99
4.1	Using Data to Measure Gaps and Design Better Policies: Three Examples	118
4.2	Eliminating Class Size Norms in Denmark	124
4.3	Rethinking Secondary Education	125
4.4	Per Student Funding Formula: Recognizing the Varied Costs of Providing Education	128
4.5	Rationalizing Class Sizes in Bulgaria	133
4.6	Developing New Teacher Policies	135
5.1	The Difficulty of Measuring Competencies at the Tertiary Level	142
5.2	Decentralization of the University Sector in Romania	146
5.3	Introducing Businesslike Leadership and Management in Lithuanian Universities	149
5.4	Using External Watchdogs to Shed Light on Integrity Problems	155
5.5	Two Approaches to Strengthening Accountability	157
6.1	Lifelong Learning Strategy of the Czech Republic	167
6.2	Policy Tools for Advancing Adult Learning in the United Kingdom	169
6.3	Market Failures that Impede Adult Learning	176
6.4	Supporting Small and Medium Enterprises to Participate in Training	181
6.5	Second-Chance and Remedial Education	184
7.1	Higher-Order Skills for the World of Work in the 21st Century	199
7.2	A Large Proportion of Students Are Failing	201

7.3	Options for Making Schools More Accountable for Learning Outcomes	213

Figures

O.1	Analysis of Reading Competency of 15-Year-Old Students on the PISA 2009	3
O.2	Distribution of Firms in ECA Region that Consider Worker Skills a "Major" or "Very Severe" Constraint, 2008	4
O.3	Primary School Student-Teacher Ratios in ECA Compared to Other Regions of the World, 1990–2008	8
O.4	Status of Measuring and Using Data on Student Learning Outcomes in the ECA Region, 2009	10
1.1	Trends in Routine and Nonroutine Tasks of U.S. Labor Force, 1960–2002	19
1.2	Worker Responses to Survey on Working Conditions in Europe, 2005	20
1.3	Job Creation and Destruction Rates for Selected Occupations in Georgia, 2007	22
1.4	Job Creation and Destruction Rates for Selected Occupations in Ukraine, 2007	23
1.5	Changes in Occupational Share of Total Employment in Selected ECA Countries, Various Years	24
1.6	Yearly Outflow Rates from Employment to Jobs by Occupation in Two Subregions of ECA, 2006	27
1.7	Unemployment-to-Vacancy Ratio by Occupation in Croatia, the Czech Republic, and Ukraine, Various Years	28
1.8	Labor Shortages and Surpluses by Level of Educational Attainment, Selected ECA Countries	29
1.9	Returns to Schooling in Selected ECA Transition Countries, Various Years	32
1.10	Wage Premia by Level of Education in Hungary, 1986–2004	33
1.11	Wage Premia by Education Level in the Russian Federation and Turkey	34
1.12	Premia by Occupation Relative to Elementary Occupations in Various ECA Countries	35
1.13	Wage Growth by Occupation in Bulgaria and Poland, 1996–2006	37

1.14	Employers' Perceptions of Worker Skills as a Constraint to Growth, Various ECA Countries	38
1.15	Time Needed by Firms to Hire Specific Workers, by ECA Subregion, 2005	40
1.16	Employers' Valuation of Workers' Knowledge and Skills in Kazakhstan and Poland	42
2.1	Gross Enrollment Rates in Tertiary Education, by World Bank Region	51
2.2	Assessing a Skill—Reading Performance in the Fourth Grade: PIRLS Performance of ECA Countries, 2001 and 2006	53
2.3	Analysis of Reading Competency of 15-Year-Old Students on the PISA 2009	54
2.4	Assessing a Competency—Reading Level at Age 15: Share of Students Scoring Level 1 or Below on Reading Section of PISA 2009	56
B2.3	Distribution of PISA 2006 Math Scores by Type of School in Turkey	57
2.5	Students Aware of Bribery for Grade or Exam in their Faculty	62
B2.5	Global Comparison of Average Vocational Enrollment of Upper Secondary Students by Region, 1989, 1999, and 2007	64
2.6	Share of Upper Secondary Students Enrolled in Vocational Programs in ECA Countries over Time	66
2.7	Share of ECA Firms that Offer Formal Training Programs for Permanent, Full-Time Employees, 2008	70
2.8	Employee- and Firm-level Data on Worker Participation in CVET Courses, EU10 and other EU Member States	72
2.9	Training Length and Percentage of Employees Participating in CVET Courses, EU10 and EU27	73
2.10	ECA Firms that Offer Formal Training to Employees, by Employee Category, 2005	74
2.11	Large and Small Firms that Offer Training to Skilled Employees, ECA, EU, and United Kingdom, 2005	76
2.12	Adult Education and Training Program Participants in EU, 2007	78
3.1	Educational Background of 25–34-year-olds in the ECA Region, 2006	91

3.2	Learning to Use Data to Drive Education Policy	95
3.3	Status of Measuring and Using Data on Student Learning Outcomes in the ECA Region, 2009	96
3.4	Relationship between Primary School Test Scores, Adult Education Levels, and Per Student Spending in Two Municipalities of Poland	100
3.5	Relationship between Primary School Test Scores, Average Class Size, and Per Student Spending in Two Municipalities of Poland	101
3.6	Dynamics of the 6- to 12-year-old Population in the ECA Region, 1990–2006	104
3.7	Primary School Student-Teacher Ratios in ECA Compared to Other Regions of the World, 1990–2008	105
3.8	Real Per Student Expenditure Compared to TIMSS Math Scores in Romania, 1999–2008	106
3.9	Percentage of Students with a Teacher Over 50 Years Old in ECA Countries, Selected Years	107
3.10	Progress Towards Results-based Education Financing in the ECA Region, 2010	110
B4.4	Groupings of Bulgarian Municipalities, Together with Baseline Per Student Financing Amounts and Adjustment Coefficients, 2007	128
4.1	Comparison of Average Size of Primary School Classes Worldwide, Various Years	131
4.2	Average Class Size in Large Primary and Secondary Schools in Nine ECA Countries, Various Years	132
B4.5A	Estimated Number of Public School Closures in Bulgaria from 1991–92 through 2008–09	134
B4.5B	Average Class Size and Student-Teacher Ratios in Bulgaria, 2000–08	134
5.1	Progress on Implementing Quality-Assurance Mechanisms: The Bologna Scorecard	158
B6.3	Barriers to the Expansion of Adult Education and Training in the ECA Region	177
6.1	Employment Placement Rates by Type of Retraining, Turkey, 2008	186
6.2	Adult Education and Training Priorities in the ECA Region	187

7.1	Assessing a Skill—Reading Performance in the Fourth Grade: PIRLS Performance of ECA Countries, 2001 and 2006	196
7.2	Analysis of Reading Competency of 15-Year-Old Students on the PISA 2009	197
7.3	Distribution of Firms in ECA Region That Consider Worker Skills a "Major" or "Very Severe" Constraint, 2008	198
7.4	Worker Responses to Survey on Working Conditions in Europe, 2005	200
7.5	Students Report Unofficial Payments Are "Usually" or "Always" Needed in Public Technical Colleges and Universities, 2006	203
7.6	Primary School Student-Teacher Ratios in ECA Compared to Other Regions of the World, 1990–2008	205
7.7	Comparison of Average Size of Primary School Classes Worldwide, Various Years	206
7.8	Percentage of Students with a Teacher Over 50 Years Old in ECA Countries, Selected Years	207
7.9	Status of Measuring and Using Data on Student Learning Outcomes in the ECA Region, 2009	209
7.10	Progress Towards Results-based Education Financing in the ECA Region, 2009	217

Tables

1.1	Unemployment Rates by Educational Attainment and ECA Subregion, 2006	25
2.1	Time Needed to Find First Job by Level of Educational Attainment in Serbia and Ukraine	67
2.2	Training Participants as Share of Participants in Active Labor Market Policies and of Total Unemployed, EU27 and EU10, 2006	77
2A.1	Duration of Education in ECA Countries, Various Years	80
2A.2	ECA Country Results on International Assessments since 1995	85
3.1	Information Collected from Tracer Study of Dutch University Graduates, 2007	97
B4.1	Learning Gaps between Roma and Non-Roma Students in Serbia, as Measured by PISA 2006 and 2009 Results	118

B5.3	Summary of Changes	150
5.1	Tools for Strengthening Basic Academic and Fiscal Integrity in University-Level Institutions	154
5.2	Three Models of Performance-Based Funding	161
6.1	Recommended Policy Framework for Adult Education and Training in the ECA Region	189
B7.2	Proportion of 15-Year-Old Students in ECA Who Achieved Only Basic Reading Competency on PISA 2009	201
7.1	Information Collected from Tracer Study of Dutch University Graduates, 2007	211
7.2	Tools for Strengthening Academic and Fiscal Integrity in University-Level Institutions	215

Foreword

It is no secret that good education lies at the heart of economic growth and development. At the same time, improving the quality and relevance of education is enormously difficult not least because there is no one single policy measure that will do so effectively. This book contributes to our understanding of how to improve education by examining the recent experience of the countries of Eastern Europe and the former Soviet Union.

Fabled for uniform access and high quality of education 20 years ago, the countries in this region have struggled to maintain their reputation. Three factors have contributed to the slide in quality and relevance. First, one of the legacies of central planning is that the countries pay too much attention to the measurement of inputs into learning—such as the number of schools and the number of teachers—and not enough to outcomes. Indeed, they have been late in developing systems to assess how much students are learning and whether learning is leading to employment. In this sense, their education systems operate in the dark, which makes policy making extremely difficult. Second, the system of management, also a vestige of the past, limits the ability of schools to improve the learning environment for students, as well of municipalities that may want a different mix of programs to meet local labor market needs. As with assessment, the countries have been slow to embrace the governance and accountability reforms that are now part of the landscape of education systems the world over. These limitations to autonomy and accountability for outcomes have reduced the energy and the incentives for improvements from within the system, contributing to a shortage of skills. Indeed, firm complaints about the shortage of relevant skills for expansion and growth have risen to a crescendo in most countries. Finally, the systems increasingly allocate resources where they are not needed. For example, the sharp decline in student numbers in the past 20 years has not resulted in a commensurate decline in the number of classrooms and teachers. As a result, resources are increasingly tied up in buildings and teachers where they may be better spent elsewhere. Most of these limitations are found not just in schools but extend to higher education and to training.

The result of these limitations is that the quality and relevance of education in the countries in the region is increasingly questionable. A large proportion of students finish lower secondary school with a minimal command of literacy and numeracy. Their failure to learn even the basics is not picked up early enough by assessment systems, nor are schools and municipalities given sufficient incentives to ensure that all students learn the basics. The systems are also struggling with imparting higher order skills beyond the basics, for which well-motivated and high-quality teachers are critically needed but which few school systems are able to attract, given the low pay and historical overstaffing. And without the vision or resources to make vocational and technical education an attractive option for students—indeed, this remains one of the most unreformed subsectors of the education system—quality has eroded and students have shied away from this form of education, possibly contributing to the widespread shortage of vocational and technical skills now found in these countries.

This book makes the case that improving the quality and relevance of education requires a fundamental change of approach to education in the countries of the region. To start with, education systems need to "turn the lights on" and take seriously the measurement of what students actually learn as opposed to measurement of the inputs into the education process on the implicit assumption that learning follows. This assessment needs to inform both teaching and policy making. Policy makers also need to move away from controlling inputs and processes and instead increase the emphasis on incentives to improve student learning, whether in school or in higher education. And, finally, for these reforms to be financially feasible, current spending on education needs to be used much more effectively. In particular, countries in the region cannot afford to maintain one of the lowest class sizes in the world while heating and lighting half-empty buildings when resources are needed elsewhere.

It is our sincere hope that this book will stimulate debate about how to improve education and training both for the countries under discussion and in the world at large, and thereby encourage action to help realize prosperity for all.

>   Philippe Le Houerou
>   Vice President
>   Europe and Central Asia Region
>   World Bank
>   Washington, D.C.

Acknowledgments

This study was managed by Lars Sondergaard, who authored chapters 3 and 4, and Mamta Murthi, who authored the Overview and chapter 7. Jan Rutkowski authored chapter 1; Dina Abu-Ghaida authored chapter 2 with inputs from and Christian Bodewig and Lars Sondergaard; Lars Sondergaard authored chapter 4 with inputs from Alex Usher; and Christian Bodewig authored chapter 6 with inputs from Sarojini Hirshleifer. Dina Abu-Ghaida co-managed the study in its early stages with Lars Sondergaard.

The book grew out of a regional research program launched and supported by Europe and Central Asia's Chief Economist's office, and during the writing of the book, two chief economists helped shape it: Pradeep Mitra and Indermit Gill. The authors are grateful to both for their guidance and support in writing this book.

The book is underpinned by significant contributions, including background papers, by Michael Mertaugh, Alex Usher, Iveta Silova, Andras Benedek, Algerlynn Gill, Rostislav Kapelyushnikov, and Hakan Ercan, and one jointly by Jerzy Wiśniewski, Maciej Jakubowski, Harry Anthony Patrinos, and Emilio Ernesto Porta. We also thank Juan Manuel Moreno and Nina Arnhold for reading and providing comments on various drafts and helping to shape the book's main messages, and Algerlynn Gill for her excellent research assistance and inputs into several of the book's chapters. In addition, Nadezhda Lepeshko and Carmen Laurente helped prepare graphs and figures for the document. The book also benefitted from the excellent editorial work of Peggy McInerny and Patricia Carley. Larry Forgy provided editorial assistance on chapter 1.

We also benefitted from valuable comments from our peer reviewers: Richard Murnane, Amit Dar, Bernard Hugonnier, Halsey Rogers, and Manfred Wallenborn. And we benefitted from inputs, comments, and suggestions from numerous colleagues, including Mohamed Ihsan Ajwad, Gordon Betcherman, Mary Canning, Isak Froumin, Sachiko Kataoka, Arvo Kuddo, Toby Linden, Lily Mulatu, Bojana Naceva, Reehana Rifat Raza, Alberto Rodriguez, Marcelo Selowski, Jan Sadlak, Jamil Salmi, Luis Crouch, and countless others. Any and all errors that remain in this volume are the sole responsibility of the authors.

Abbreviations

AES	Adult Education Survey
AHELO	Assessment of Higher Education Learning Outcomes
ALG	adult learning grant
ALMP	active labor market policy
ARACIS	Romanian Agency for Quality Assurance in Higher Education
BEEPS	Business Environment and Enterprise Performance Survey
BGN	Bulgarian currency (lev)
CHE	Center for Higher Education Development
CIS	Commonwealth of Independent States
CISSTAT	Interstate Statistical Committee of the Commonwealth of Independent States
CNEAA	Romanian Council for Accreditation
CONVEyT	(Mexico) National Council of Education for Life and Work
Crostat	Republic of Croatia Central Bureau of Statistics
CVETS	Continuing Vocational Education and Training Survey

EBRD	European Bank for Reconstruction and Development
EC	European Commission
ECA	Europe and Central Asia
ECTA	European Credit Transfer and Accumulation System
EHEA	European Higher Education Area
EMIS	Education Management and Information System
ENQA	European Network of Quality Assurance
ESF	European Social Fund
ESG	European Standards and Guidelines
ESU	European Students Union
EU	European Union
EU10/10+1	EU10 comprises Bulgaria, the Czech Republic, Estonia, Hungary, Latvia, Lithuania, Poland, Romania, the Slovak Republic and Slovenia. EU10+1 adds Croatia.
EU15	Austria, Belgium, Denmark, Finland, France, Germany, Greece, Ireland, Italy, Luxembourg, the Netherlands, Portugal, Spain, Sweden, and the United Kingdom
EU27	Austria, Belgium, Bulgaria, Cyprus, the Czech Republic, Denmark, Estonia, Finland, France, Germany, Greece, Hungary, Ireland, Italy, Latvia, Lithuania, Luxemburg, Malta, the Netherlands, Poland, Portugal, Romania, the Slovak Republic, Slovenia, Spain, Sweden, and the United Kingdom
EUA	European University Association
EURASHE	European Association of Institutions of Higher Learning
GDP	gross domestic product
HEGESCO	Higher Education as a Generator of Strategic Competences Project
HRDF	(Malaysia) Human Resource Development Fund
IEA	International Association for the Evaluation of Educational Achievements
ICT	information and communication technology
ILA	Individual Learning Account
ISCED	International Standard Classification of Education

ISCO-88	International Standard Classification of Occupations 1988, International Labour Organization
LFS	Labor Force Survey
LITS	Life in Transition Survey (jointly conducted by EBRD and World Bank)
LSC	(UK) Learning and Skills Council
LSMS	Living Standards and Measurement Survey
MERI	(Romania) Ministry of Education Research and Innovation
MES	Ministry of Education and Science
MOF	Ministry of Finance
MTEF	Medium-Term Expenditure Framework
NAVET	(Bulgaria) National Agency for Vocational Education and Training
NGO	nongovernmental organization
NQF	National Qualifications Framework
NVQ	National Vocational Qualification System
OECD	Organisation for Economic Co-operation and Development
PB	performance budgeting
PETS	Public Expenditure Tracking Survey
PIAAC	Program for International Assessment of Adult Competencies, OECD
PISA	Programme for International Student Assessment, OECD
PIRLS	Progress in International Reading Literacy Study
PPP	purchasing power parity
SEE	South Eastern Europe (for the purposes of this report, Albania, Bosnia and Herzegovina, Croatia, the former Yugoslav Republic of Macedonia, Montenegro, and Serbia)
SIMCE	Sistema de Medicion de la Calidad Education
SME	small and medium enterprise
SSC	(UK) Sector Skills Councils
TALIS	Teaching and Learning International Survey
TIMSS	Trends in International Mathematics and Science Study
UNECE	United Nations Commission for Europe
UNICEF	United Nations Children's Fund

UNESCO	United Nations Educational, Scientific and Cultural Organization
UNESCO-CEPES	Centre Européan pour l'Enseignement Supérieur (European Centre for Higher Education), UNESCO, Bucharest
VCOT	Vermont Classroom Observation Tool
VET	vocational education and training

Country abbreviations used in figures and tables:

ALB	Albania
ARM	Armenia
AUT	Austria
AZE	Azerbaijan
BEL	Belgium
BGR	Bulgaria
BIH	Bosnia and Herzegovina
BLR	Belarus
CYP	Cyprus
CZE	Czech Republic
DEU	Germany
DNK	Denmark
ESP	Spain
EST	Estonia
FIN	Finland
FRA	France
GBR	United Kingdom
GEO	Georgia
GRC	Greece
HRV	Croatia
HUN	Hungary
IRL	Ireland
ISL	Iceland
ITA	Italy
KAZ	Kazakhstan
KGZ	Kyrgyz Republic
LTU	Lithuania
LUX	Luxembourg
LVA	Latvia
MDA	Moldova
MKD	Macedonia, former Yugoslav Republic of

MLT	Malta
NLD	the Netherlands
NOR	Norway
POL	Poland
PRT	Portugal
ROU	Romania
RUS	Russian Federation
SRB	Serbia
SVK	the Slovak Republic
SVN	Slovenia
SWE	Sweden
TJK	Tajikistan
TKM	Turkmenistan
TUR	Turkey
UKR	Ukraine
UZB	Uzbekistan

Note: These three-letter country codes are part of the International Organization for Standardization (ISO) 3166 standard to represent countries.

Overview

The countries of Europe and Central Asia (ECA)[1] are currently emerging from the deepest recession suffered by any developing region. Post-crisis conditions are very different from those of preceding years. Financial resources are more limited and more expensive, and export growth is restrained by potentially slower growth in destination countries. Restoring and sustaining growth in this context require reforms that boost competitiveness and increase labor productivity. Such reforms are all the more important given the shrinking of the working-age population in many countries of the region.

Earlier boom years in the ECA region exposed significant bottlenecks to growth, particularly with respect to the skills of the labor force (Mitra et al. 2010). Paradoxically, for a region with relatively high and expanding educational attainment (as measured by the number of years of completed schooling) and relatively high-quality education in the early years of schooling, a shortage of worker skills has emerged as one of the most important constraints to firm expansion. This book seeks to answer the following questions: Why do ECA firms increasingly complain that they cannot find graduates with the right skills? What can ECA countries do to close the skills gap?

When trying to answer these questions, this book faces a fundamental problem: data exist on the number of students who graduate (i.e., how many diplomas are issued) in ECA countries, but internationally comparable data on whether graduates of upper secondary and tertiary institutions (from which the bulk of ECA graduates now enter the labor market) have the right skills and competencies for the job market do not exist.

This book uses a range of different data sources to argue that the skills problem in the ECA region relates more to the quality and relevance of the education provided in ECA countries than to problems of access. A central argument of the book is that ministries of education are constrained in a number of ways from effectively managing their education and training sectors. The three most important and interrelated impediments to improving quality and relevance are the lack of systematic data on key skills-related performance issues (i.e., how much students are learning and whether they are finding jobs after they graduate), the legacy of central planning, and inefficient use of resources.

Lack of data on student learning and employment outcomes makes it difficult for education ministries to address the legacy of central planning, which emphasizes centralized management based on inputs. Ministries of education in the region continue to micromanage the sector using detailed norms and regulations. This input-oriented style of management leads to the inefficient use of resources and results in a rigid education sector—not the type of flexible sector needed by ECA to create modern, skilled workforces. This book highlights how these constraints manifest themselves and then presents ways of overcoming them, relying on the experience of ECA countries that have successfully addressed them, together with international experience. Recommendations are presented in separate chapters for pre-university, tertiary, and adult education.

The Skills Challenge

The ECA region had a well-regarded education system before the transition. While the intervening years have taken some of the shine off this reputation, these countries continue to have strong achievements. Notably, enrollments are high at all levels of education. The communist legacy is particularly visible in low-income countries in the region, which have the highest secondary enrollments in the world for their income level. Tertiary enrollments, which have grown rapidly in the past two decades, are also high relative to income levels, with the exception of a few low-income Commonwealth of Independent States (CIS) countries, such as Azerbaijan and Uzbekistan.

The ECA region is reasonably successful not only in terms of enrollment rates, but also in terms of providing quality education in the early grades. In particular, in international tests that measure student competencies in primary and lower secondary education, students in many (but not all) ECA countries outperform their peers in countries with the same income level (see figure O.1). For instance, students in Estonia, where gross domestic product (GDP) per capita was $21,644[2] in 2008, outperformed their peers in Denmark, Sweden, Iceland, and Austria—where per capita income is almost twice as high—on the mathematics part of the 2009 Programme for International Student Assessment (PISA). The picture for educational quality within the ECA region is varied, however, as more than several countries, such as Bulgaria, Romania, Montenegro, Azerbaijan, and the Kyrgyz Republic, have students (in the early grades) that underperform relative to their income level.

In spite of these positive achievements of ECA education systems, the European Bank for Reconstruction and Development (EBRD)–World Bank Business Environment and Enterprise Performance Surveys (BEEPS) show that ECA firms' perception of skills constraints changed dramatically around 2005.[3] By 2008, skilled labor shortages had become the second most commonly reported constraint to growth in the BEEPS survey across all countries in the region, second only to tax rates (see figure O.2). On average, 30 percent of firms considered education and skills to

Figure O.1 Analysis of Reading Competency of 15-Year-Old Students on the PISA 2009

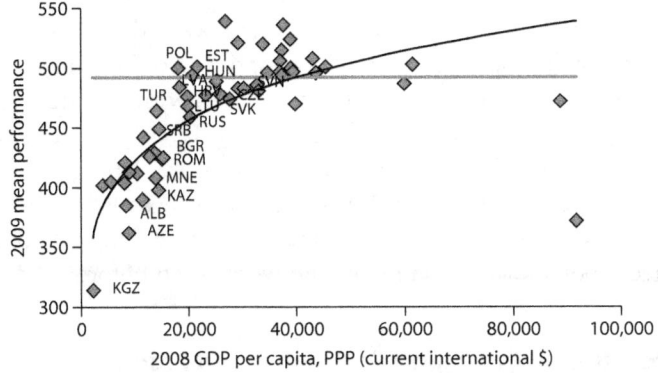

Source: PISA 2009 Database and World Bank staff calculations based on World Development Indicators Database.
Note: PISA = Programme for International Student Assessment. The figure shows a regression line representing countries' predicted PISA reading scores based solely on GDP per capita, compared to the Organisation for Economic Co-operation and Development mean reading score (horizontal line) and GDP per capita in 2008. See "Abbreviations" for a key to country abbreviations.

Figure O.2 Distribution of Firms in ECA Region that Consider Worker Skills a "Major" or "Very Severe" Constraint, 2008

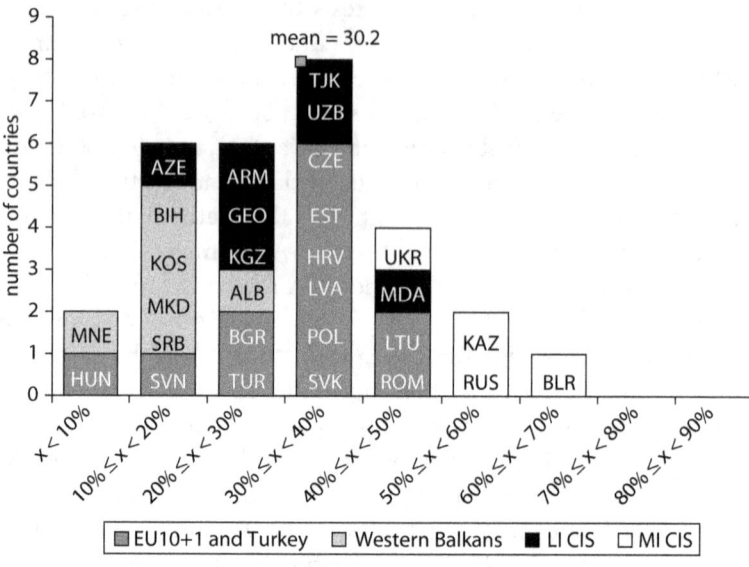

Source: Authors' calculations based on BEEPS 2008.
Note: LI = low-income, MI = middle-income, x = % of firms (in respective countries) that consider education as an obstacle. Figure shows data obtained from the fourth round of the BEEPS carried out in 2008–09, which covered approximately 11,800 enterprises in 29 countries. See "Abbreviations" for a key to country abbreviations.

be a major or severe constraint in 2008. The highest proportion of firms reporting constraints were found among the middle-income CIS countries, where upwards of 40 percent of firms were dissatisfied with the availability of skilled workers. A smaller proportion of firms in the Western Balkans reported similar levels of dissatisfaction, with significant variability in the dissatisfaction levels of firms in the EU10+1 (European Union 10+1) countries and Turkey (BEEPS dataset 2008). While the recession may have provided something of a respite from these labor shortages, as the economies in the region recover, labor demand will tighten once again and skilled labor shortages will likely be worse than before.

Why Are Skills an Emerging Problem if Education Systems Are Delivering?

Despite generally high average enrollment and attainment rates, as well as respectable quality education (where measured, at the early grade level) for their income level, ECA countries' growth is constrained by skills shortages. This is a puzzle that cannot be fully resolved, mainly because crucial information is missing. Put simply, there is no internationally comparable information on the quality of upper secondary or tertiary education or the relevance of education at these levels—information that would indicate whether graduates have the right skills for the modern job market

There are international assessments that provide information on student competencies up to the age of 15 (usually the end of lower secondary education), but this is not an age when most people in the region are entering the job market. Beyond these early-stage assessments, no comprehensive, fully reliable information exists on student competencies. What is more, the information on student competencies that is available relates only to fundamental cognitive skills, not behavioral skills—involving such issues as work ethic and teamwork—which are emphasized by employers. For policy makers to better understand the causes of the emerging skills bottleneck—and how to address it—this informational gap needs to be closed. Given the lack of data on the skills of new labor market entrants, the book's conclusions are necessarily based only on the data that are obtainable.

Two problems related to quality seem particularly acute in the ECA region: too many students are failing, and education systems have difficulties imparting problem-solving skills. In terms of the many students that fail, PISA 2009 data show that all ECA countries (except a handful of new EU member states) have very large proportions of 15-year-olds who have such poor numeracy and literacy skills that their success in the modern workplace is highly doubtful. As work becomes more demanding even for this group, their poor skills will become more apparent. Although ECA countries perform strongly on international assessments that measure students at the primary level (grade 4), their performance is weaker on assessments of students around the end of lower secondary education (grade 8). These results suggest that their education systems are adept at imparting basic skills, but have problems imparting higher order skills such as problem solving—the very skills that firms increasingly seek.

More troubling, the quality of education in the ECA region also does not show signs of consistent improvement. In fact, up to 2006 it appeared to be getting worse in many countries. Rather than narrowing the gap between their scores and Organisation for Economic Co-operation and Development (OECD) mean scores, many ECA countries that participate in international learning assessments at this level—which are likely the better-managed countries—either seemed stuck or had regressed in terms of their scores. It is probable, moreover, that the situation is even worse in ECA countries that do not participate in efforts to measure and compare the academic performance of their students. Encouragingly, the latest round of PISA (2009) may have marked a turning point for 11 ECA countries that showed improvements compared to their 2006 performance (including significant increases in Bulgaria, Romania, Serbia, the Kyrgyz Republic, and Turkey). However, seven ECA countries continued the downward slide observed previously with a deterioration compared to their 2006 performance.

The quality of upper secondary and tertiary education in the region is also unlikely to have improved, although lack of data makes it hard to confirm this contention. Since educational quality is not showing consistent improvement at the lower secondary level, this weakness is probably mirrored at the upper secondary level (albeit with a lag). Enrollments at the tertiary level used to be tightly controlled and reserved for the few, best performers. In the past two decades, however, enrollments have doubled, tripled, or quadrupled, but without the benefit of the quality assurance mechanisms needed for the many new programs, institutions, and types of students, and without the kind of information required for parents and students to make informed choices. As a result, it is unclear if the expansion of the system has been accompanied by growing quality.

Graduates of upper secondary and tertiary education may also be graduating with the wrong set of skills. During the early years of the transition, the vocational school system—which once produced more than half of all secondary graduates in most ECA countries—collapsed very quickly. Voting with their feet, students have left vocational schools in favor of general secondary education and the prospect of pursuing a tertiary degree. It may be that the pendulum has swung too far in one direction, however, as employers assert that it is now hard to find graduates with technical skills. Yet, until the region's vocational schools are reformed to ensure that they can produce graduates with appropriate skills, it may be too soon to be encouraging students to return to this sector.

The contribution of education to the skills gap is not only a story of the uncertain quality and relevance of formal education. It also involves too little progress in providing workers with options for further training. Growing evidence shows that continuous adult education and training fosters employment and greater productivity. The development of this sector should accordingly be central to the region's economic growth agenda, particularly in more advanced ECA countries and countries that are facing a significant demographic decline—a decline that suggests that labor force participation and individual productivity will have to increase in order to generate higher rates of economic growth. Yet many of these countries have only started to prepare for an expansion of the adult training sector, needed not only to compete in the global economy, but also to address the lag effects of the transition to market economies. In light of growing employer demands for greater skills, adult education and training in ECA countries can no longer be ignored.

Priority Areas for Action

As noted at the outset, three major impediments are inhibiting the creation of flexible and responsive education systems in the ECA region. First, these systems have been operating "in the dark" because they design policies and take management decisions without systematically collecting and analyzing data on the learning and employment outcomes of students and graduates. Second, the legacy of central planning has kept the management of school systems highly centralized, with central policy makers intensely involved in operational details. While virtually all OECD countries have embraced performance-oriented management in education since the 1980s (see OECD 2004)—albeit at different speeds—most ECA countries continue to use management practices that focus on compliance with detailed regulations and financing schemes based on inputs, not outputs. This means that most local education authorities and school principals lack the autonomy and authority to make crucial management decisions for their own institutions, including how much and what type of vocational content students can choose from and how many teachers to employ. As a result, the system is inflexible and does not respond either to labor market needs or changes in student numbers.

Third, education systems in the ECA region use financial resources highly inefficiently. Nowhere is this more apparent than in the preuniversity sector, where few countries have adjusted teacher staffing levels in response to falling student numbers over the past 20 years. Consequently, student-teacher ratios have fallen sharply (and per student costs have risen)—more so than in any other region in the world (see figure O.3). This implies that scarce resources are tied up in paying meager salaries to too many staff members and heating half-empty buildings.

To be fair, these impediments affect ECA countries differently and vary accordingly to the level of education. However, no ECA country

Figure O.3 Primary School Student-Teacher Ratios in ECA Compared to Other Regions of the World, 1990–2008

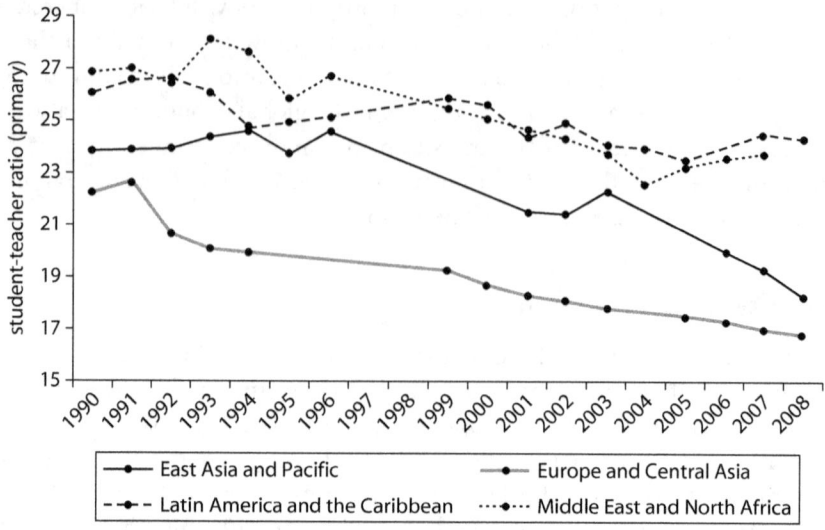

Sources: EdStats database, plus authors' linear interpolations for missing years.
Note: Actual data are marked with dots. One of the problems with international data on student-teacher ratios (in both the World Bank's EdStats database and the other international education databases) is that it is unclear whether or not data for a particular country are reported on a full-time equivalent basis.

has fully escaped the legacy of central planning.[4] That system focused on controlling inputs—that is, it checked whether local actors were in compliance with detailed norms for all inputs. Education ministries remained uninformed, however, about whether students acquired skills and competencies.

In terms of how these impediments affect the different levels of education, they are most clearly apparent at the pre-university level, which absorbs two-thirds of total education funding in the ECA region. The same three impediments affect tertiary education in a slightly different way, as this sector has already undergone significant reform over the past 20 years, during which time it has doubled or tripled in size in many countries (see chapter 5). Because most ECA countries do not yet have adult education sectors in the modern sense, these impediments cannot be fairly characterized as problems of this sector. However, the policy recommendations offered in this book do apply to adult education and offer ideas and principles for how this subsector could be developed and managed in the region (see chapter 6).

Managing Education Systems for Results

To address the three impediments outlined above, countries in the ECA region need to manage their education systems for results. First and foremost, they need to collect more information on "performance," that is, on what students are learning, what jobs they are finding, and what salaries graduates are earning. In addition, ECA countries could benefit from following the lead of OECD countries and several developing countries and replace input-oriented management of the education sector with performance-oriented management. This change implies devolving more autonomy to frontline providers and putting in place accountability mechanisms—for instance, in the form of performance contracts and performance-based budgeting—that emphasize performance and not compliance with norms. With a greater availability of performance data and with frontline providers empowered with greater decision-making power, the preconditions will be in place for education systems in the region to become both more responsive to labor market needs and more efficient.

Focus Attention on Learning and Employment Outcomes

Countries in the ECA region would benefit from greater measurement of student learning and employment outcomes, information that they can then use to design better policies. There is significant consensus on the key skills and competencies that education is expected to deliver, as well as standardized tests to measure them.[5] Many countries in the region already participate in international assessments, but have moved more slowly than other regions in generating useful information from national assessments. Although all school systems in the region have some kind of national assessment system, many are in the early stages of development (see figure O.4) and there is very little evidence to date that ECA countries are using these assessments to inform policy. Rather, national assessments continue to be seen as a certification mechanism, one that confirms a student has gained a mastery of a predetermined curriculum, thus enabling a diploma to be issued or the student to progress to upper secondary or tertiary education. Student assessments are rarely seen as an opportunity to identify the strengths and weaknesses of an education system.

When students graduate, ministries of education in the ECA region do not systematically collect, analyze, and disseminate information on their employment outcomes. Such information is, however, critical for policy

Figure O.4 Status of Measuring and Using Data on Student Learning Outcomes in the ECA Region, 2009

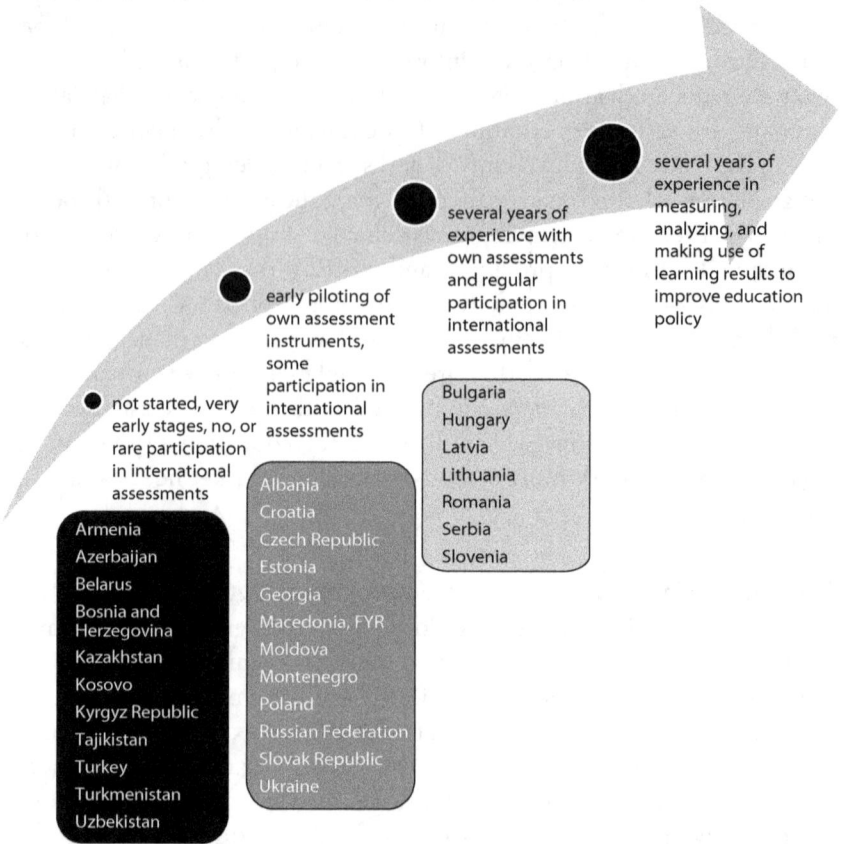

Sources: Authors' assessments based on data from UNICEF (2007, table 2.1); the extent of countries' participation in PISA, Progress in International Literacy Study (PIRLS) and Trends in International Mathematics and Science Study (TIMSS) since 1995; and inputs from World Bank country experts. The UNICEF data is drawn from "Table 2.1: Status of Reforms of Assessment and Examination Systems, 2006," regarding "Introduction of other school exams or assessments (e.g. basic school)" and "Introduction of sample-based national assessment." In this table, UNICEF scores the progress of countries on a range of 0 to 4, with 0 representing "not planned or started" and 4 representing "operational." In addition, the figure uses World Bank staff compilations on the number of international assessments in which each country has participated.

makers and higher education institutions because it helps them detect which programs and fields of study are in high demand among employers. Moreover, this data can help students make better choices about which university and field of study to pursue. Again, some member countries of the OECD (including Hungary, Italy, and the Netherlands), together with Romania, provide examples in this area for others to emulate.

Introduce Autonomy and Accountability Based on Results
Overcoming the legacy of central planning involves moving away from detailed norms and instead holding actors accountable for *performance* (or results). At the central level, this implies that policy makers in the ECA region would relinquish certain duties and assume others so that education systems may innovate and improve student learning outcomes. The opportunity before central governments in these countries is to move away from managing schools and classrooms and focus instead on setting goals, policies, and standards; defining responsibilities; mobilizing financial resources; ensuring political consensus; targeting poor and excluded students; and monitoring and evaluating service delivery and system quality.

Extending autonomy throughout education systems means placing authority and responsibility in the hands of the people most able to innovate and improve the quality of education: local managers and education authorities (see Osborne and Gaebler 1992). It also means holding these actors accountable for improving the learning outcomes of the bulk of their students. Aligning the incentives of these stakeholders with the student learning outcomes desired by policy makers requires education ministries to set overall performance goals; articulate who is responsible and accountable to whom and for what; and ensure that these responsibilities are agreed, accepted, and understood.

At the pre-university level, policy makers can expand the autonomy of lower-level actors in the school system by granting them greater decision-making power over school operations and budgets and relaxing norms on class sizes. Greater autonomy is particularly needed in vocational education and training, where programs and institutes need the ability to expand or contract course offerings in response to student and employer demand, not rigid governmental norms.

Simultaneously, policy makers will need to implement a range of accountability mechanisms to hold schools accountable for results. Potential mechanisms include the creation of school councils that involve parents and local communities in school decision-making processes; requiring schools to prepare school development plans that outline each school's strengths and weaknesses, together with an action plan for making improvements; preparing "school scorecards" that include basic indicators on a school's performance; as well sanctioning low-performing schools and rewarding high-performing schools. Here, however, it is important to define a high-performing school as one that delivers improved learning outcomes to all types of students, including those from low-income and minority households.

Significant improvements in the direction of greater autonomy and accountability will, however, be difficult to achieve in the school system unless policy makers in the region address the demoralization of the teaching force, an effort that will involve resolution of serious overstaffing and improving the pay, professional development, and work conditions of teachers.

At the tertiary level, greater autonomy and effective accountability are equally critical. The first part of this equation has been carried out in a number of countries in the region—mainly the new EU member states and, to a lesser degree, the countries of South Eastern Europe as well as the Russian Federation and Ukraine—which have already granted tertiary providers considerable autonomy. These countries, while continuing to make needed improvements in the devolution of managerial authority, must now face the primary (but not exclusive) challenge of improving academic and fiscal integrity in the sector by introducing stronger accountability mechanisms. Other countries in the region, especially Belarus and most of the low-income CIS states, have yet to change how their tertiary education systems are managed. These countries face the simultaneous challenges of enhancing university autonomy while developing accountability mechanisms and introducing performance-based financing. Regarding the need to monitor and evaluate system delivery and quality, all countries in the region lag behind; in other words, all need to make greater efforts to "turn on the lights" by vastly improving their data collection on student learning and educational outcomes.

Even though fundamental integrity problems remain widespread in the university sector, it is important that ECA policy makers refrain from attempting to resolve these problems *before* they devolve authority to universities and introduce flexible financing. The group of ECA countries that have not yet initiated tertiary reforms need to introduce autonomy and accountability as mutually reinforcing policy instruments. Policy makers in these countries need not simply transfer autonomy to static, traditional universities, but can instead mandate that increased autonomy be accompanied by more "businesslike" and accountable leadership and management.

In view of the relatively weak institutional capacity in the region—including somewhat newly established or nonexistent quality assurance agencies—policy makers may need to employ many different, complementary tools to strengthen accountability for results. These tools include rankings, tracer studies, and creation of an enabling environment to facilitate the growth of the private sector. Counting on a quality assurance agency to quickly establish the capacity needed to externally monitor a rapidly growing sector is risky—this kind of agency needs to be part of the solution, but not the only response.

Improve the Efficiency of Resource Use through Performance-based Financing

Managing school systems for performance means moving away from inflexible line-item budgeting towards greater use of delegated budgets, with incentives for maintaining enrollment and attendance (i.e., per student financing—a path on which the majority of ECA countries have already embarked). More flexible, smarter financing in the form of block grants (i.e., contract- or performance-based) can also provide funding to institutions in return for meeting agreed learning outcomes. Not only does this type of financing give local education managers much-needed flexibility that input-based budgets do not permit, it keeps them focused on student results.

In addition to performance-based financing, improving financial efficiency at the pre-university level will require creating incentives for larger class sizes, encouraging school optimization, and addressing the issue of overstaffing. At the tertiary level, several ECA countries (for example, Poland and Romania) have already adopted per student financing, shifting their focus away from inputs and toward results. The remainder of countries in the region will need to introduce performance-based financing to improve the efficiency of spending in this sector.

If ECA countries want to simultaneously raise participation rates and increase the quality of tertiary education, more private resources will also be needed—the cost pressures facing higher education in the region are simply too great. Mobilizing private resources will help strengthen results-oriented outcomes in the tertiary sector in two fundamental ways: (1) by increasing competition, as more nimble and innovative private providers help bring innovations to public providers, and (2) by increasing students' connection to the education process. When students and parents pay tuition fees—whether to a public or a private provider—they are generally more demanding about the quality and relevance of the education provided. There is no single ideal level of funding for higher education, and no single ideal mix of public and private funding sources. Different countries will make different kinds of trade-offs.

Build the Foundations of Adult Learning Systems

Unlike pre-university and university education, adult education systems are largely nonexistent in most ECA countries. Building such systems will require shifting away from government-defined programs towards a well-regulated market of private and public providers that deliver training services to both working and unemployed adults. Governments in the region will, however, continue to play a role in education and training for the unemployed, often by contracting private providers to deliver needed services. Policies that address market failures in this sector are especially important to lay the groundwork for effective adult education systems. In general, successful systems require a high degree of coordination and partnership between government agencies and the private sector, as well as giving the demand side of training—that is, businesses and individuals—a strong voice in determining training policy. Once a solid adult learning sector is established, governments can then "steer" it by monitoring data on program quality, promoting autonomy in return for accountability, and improving the efficiency of government financing in the sector.

Expanding adult learning is a priority for advanced economies in the region that are facing a demographic decline. Their challenge is to ensure that existing coordination mechanisms function well and that regulation and financing are used to facilitate the emergence of a private sector-oriented adult education and training market. The principal priority of less advanced economies in the region experiencing a demographic decline (i.e., many of those in South Eastern Europe and the middle-income CIS countries) is to introduce a policy framework for adult learning and create the tools needed to implement this strategy (e.g., coordination mechanisms, plus initial steps toward regulation). For the less advanced economies in the region that are not facing a demographic decline (i.e., those of low-income CIS countries and Albania), it may be more productive to limit efforts to establish policy frameworks and coordination mechanisms for this sector. For many countries, participating in the OECD's Programme for International Assessment of Adult Competencies (PIAAC) would be an important first step in understanding the current skills and competencies of their work forces.

Conclusion

It will take time to steer education systems in the ECA region away from a focus on inputs toward a focus on delivering a quality education to the majority of students. Waiting to begin this process will only cause countries to fall farther behind in delivering the skills their economies need to compete in a global economy. Overall, much greater measurement of student learning outcomes is needed at all levels of education if policy makers are to understand the strengths and weaknesses of their respective systems and design effective policies to improve them. If the role of central governments is redefined to focus on strategic policy, system goals, and regulation, central policy makers will be freed to use incentives to manage lower-level actors to meet goals and then measure the results.

In schools, this process will involve greater use of per capita financing, more autonomy, and greater accountability for learning outcomes. At the level of higher education, strengthening national quality assurance mechanisms is needed to improve the accountability of education providers, as is greater dissemination of information on learning and employment outcomes (e.g., results from tracer studies, or university rankings) to inform student choice. In addition, existing financing incentives will need strengthening through the introduction of more performance-based budgeting and, where warranted, greater institutional autonomy. Although adult learning systems are critically important for the region, their priority in individual ECA countries will depend on economic and demographic conditions and other, perhaps more pressing education challenges. All countries in the region can, however, begin to develop a coherent strategy for adult education and training.

Notes

1. The countries included in the Europe and Central Asia (ECA) region include Albania, Armenia, Azerbaijan, Belarus, Bosnia and Herzegovina, Bulgaria, Croatia, Czech Republic, Estonia, Georgia, Hungary, Kazakhstan, Kosovo, Kyrgyz Republic, Latvia, Lithuania, the former Yugoslav Republic of Macedonia, Moldova, Montenegro, Poland, Romania, the Russian Federation, Serbia, the Slovak Republic, Slovenia, Tajikistan, Turkey, Turkmenistan, Ukraine, and Uzbekistan.
2. Adjusted for Purchasing Power Parity, or PPP.
3. The EBRD–World Bank Business Environment and Enterprise Performance Surveys (BEEPS) provide successive snapshots of the self-reported constraints to expansion by firms in the ECA region. The surveys were conducted in virtually all ECA countries in 1999, 2002, 2005, and 2008. Survey samples are constructed by random sampling from the national registry of firms (or equivalent) and cover both industry and service sectors.

4. It should be noted that Turkey does not have a socialist past, but does operate "in the dark" to a large extent and has not made the performance-oriented management reforms of other OECD countries. The expenditure efficiency issues are, however, different in nature. See World Bank 2005a.
5. While the use of learning assessments is not uncontroversial, testing methodologies have improved in recent years, making these tests better and more useful for assessing student learning than was previously the case.

CHAPTER 1

The Demand for Skills in ECA

Throughout the world there has been an increase in the demand for skilled labor in what is now a global knowledge economy. More specifically, the demand for skills related to complex communication and nonroutine cognitive tasks has increased, while the demand for routine and manual skills has declined. Employment trends in the region encompassing Eastern Europe and Central Asia (ECA) reflect this new reality: jobs have been shifting significantly from unskilled to skilled labor and the wages of highly skilled workers have dramatically improved over the past 20 years. This shift parallels an economic transition that has involved intensive enterprise restructuring as countries moved from centrally planned to market-based economies. New skills have come into demand, as employment has been allocated away from declining industries and firms toward expanding ones. In addition, there has been a large-scale shift of jobs from agriculture and, to a lesser extent, industry towards the service sector.

This evolution in the labor market is at the heart of major changes in employment outlook throughout the region. The movement toward greater use of skilled labor has in turn produced relatively greater unemployment for low-skilled workers. Wages of highly skilled white collar workers have also grown at a much faster rate than those of less-skilled manual workers. As a result, returns to education and professional skills—that is, their value on the marketplace—have sharply increased during the transition. The parallel upward movement of employment and wages points to a shift in demand rather than supply as the main cause of these trends.

Research indicates that this change in demand has not been adequately met by an adjustment in the supply of skills, resulting in a kind of skills "mismatch" throughout the region. In fact, many modern firms in ECA countries view the lack of necessary skills among potential workers as a major impediment to their operations and development. These needed skills include not just the ability to apply knowledge and solve tasks, but also the ability to work as part of a team—just one example of the type of behavioral skills increasingly desired by employers.

This chapter describes the evolution and patterns of demand for skills in the entire ECA region (see "Abbreviations" for a list of country groupings used in this report. The notion of "labor demand" has different meanings in different ECA subregions because of vast differences in income level and the degree of formality of the labor market. While in many of the new member states of the European Union (EU), wage (-dependent) employment represents a large share of total employment, in other countries (e.g., the Western Balkans or Commonwealth of Independent States [CIS] members), it represents a lower fraction (about 30–40 percent). Furthermore, a substantial part of wage employment in many subregions is in the public service sector. Accordingly, the results presented in this chapter for wage workers refer to a considerably larger part of some subregions than others.

Background: The Demand for Highly Skilled Labor in the Global Knowledge Economy

There is no question that skilled labor is increasingly in demand in today's modern economies. Skills requiring expert, inventive thinking are sought after and skills involving repetitive tasks are not. In the United States, for example, the task content of the work done by the labor force has changed greatly over the past 40 years. As shown in figure 1.1, the proportion of the U.S. labor force employed in occupations that make intensive use of nonroutine cognitive tasks—both interactive and analytic—has increased substantially since 1960. In contrast, the percentage of the labor force employed in occupations involving routine cognitive and

Figure 1.1 Trends in Routine and Nonroutine Tasks of U.S. Labor Force, 1960–2002

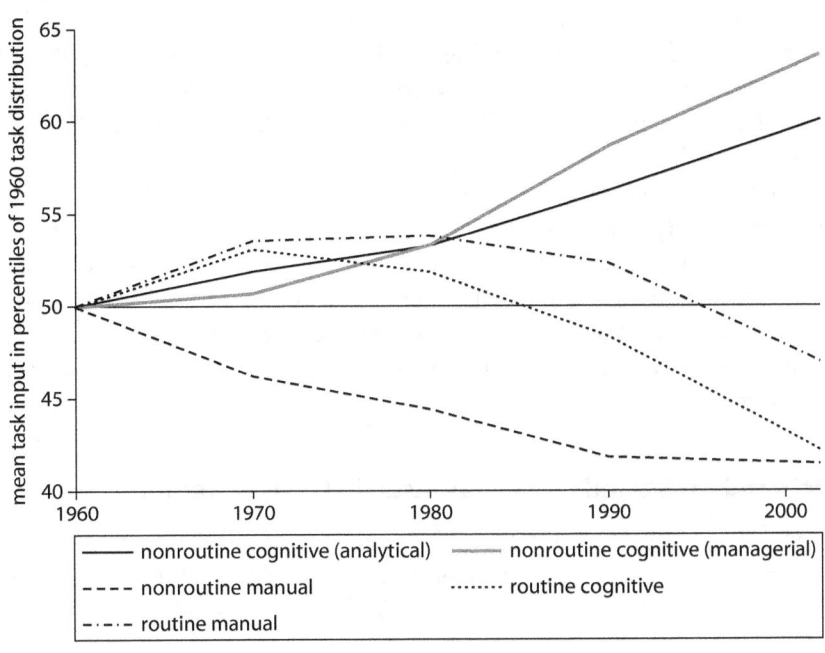

Source: Autor, Levy, and Murnane 2003. With data updated to 2002 by David Autor.

manual tasks, as well as nonroutine manual activities, has declined (Autor, Levy, and Murnane 2003).

There are three labor market ramifications of the shift in employment from routine and manual tasks towards nonroutine cognitive tasks. First, employment structure changes: a growing proportion of the labor force is employed in jobs requiring higher-level, nonroutine skills (see Levy and Murnane 2004). Second, wage structure changes: wage inequality rises due to an increase in the skill premium; in particular, the wage gap between low- and highly skilled workers widens. Third, unemployment rises among less-skilled workers following the elimination of routine jobs.

Technological development also spurs change in how work is organized, which itself can lead to higher-skill needs. Computer technology, for example, has contributed to the shift away from the so-called Taylorist organization of labor (characterized by mass production and bureaucratic controls) to high-performance work practices (characterized by decentralized decision making, just-in-time operations, teamwork, and multitasking (EC 2008; OECD 1999b). U.S. data on firms that adopted information and communication technology show, for example, that increases in the demand for highly skilled workers can be attributed more to the requirements of new work organization than to the introduction of new technology itself (Breshnan, Brynjolfsson, and Hitt 2002), a process that has been termed "skill-biased organizational change."[1]

Workers in today's economies are increasingly required to solve complex and unexpected tasks in their jobs, which involve fewer and fewer simple, predictable activities. In addition, workers must be able to master changing technologies and make sense of large amounts of information. Figure 1.2 shows the complexities of this new working environment, as expressed by worker responses to questions about the nature of their employment.

Demand for Skilled Labor Has Risen in the ECA Region

This section focuses on two measurable aspects of skills in the ECA region from a labor market perspective:[2] educational attainment and

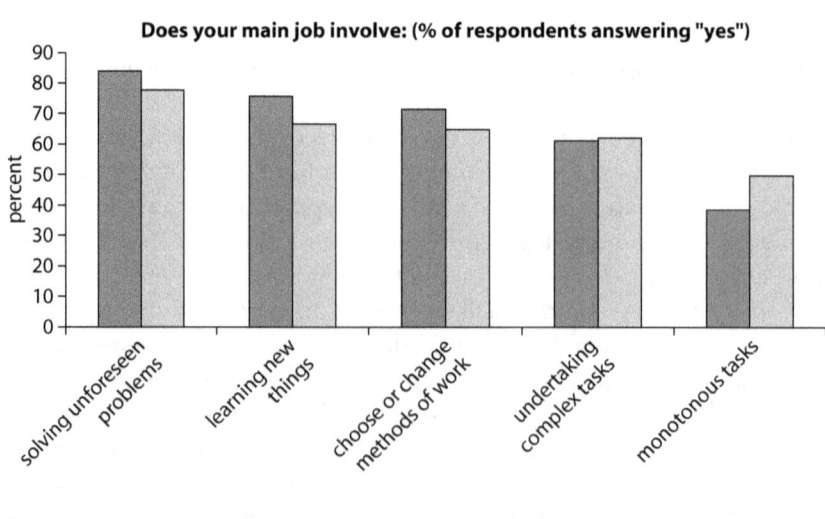

Figure 1.2 Worker Responses to Survey on Working Conditions in Europe, 2005

Source: Authors' calculations based on data obtained from Eurofound 2007.

occupation. The more educated a worker, the more skilled he or she is assumed to be. It is taken for granted that some occupations (e.g., manager or professional) require higher-level skills than others (e.g., service worker, salesperson, machine operator). Education levels cannot be mapped directly to occupations and skills, but education levels and occupations can shed light on the demand for skills in a given labor market. The text that follows relies on the International Standard Classification of Occupations, known as ISCO-88 rev. 3, to classify various types of employment in ECA countries.[3]

While data are not available that would allow the kind of analysis presented in figure 1.1 for the ECA region, a wide range of proximate data points to similar trends there. Shifts in demand in favor of more skilled labor have been reinforced in ECA by the transition from plan to market. Turkey, although not a transition economy, has also experienced deep structural changes associated with economic modernization and rapid growth that have brought about changes in the demand for skills.

The economic transition in the region has been associated with significant job flows between sectors, with labor moving to the service sector, largely from agriculture and, to a lesser degree, from industry. In reality, this transition simply removed institutional barriers to a natural restructuring process associated with economic development. For example, in Estonia, service sector employment as a share of total employment increased by 18 percentage points from 1990 to 2007; in the Slovak Republic, by 12 percentage points from 1994 to 2007; in Moldova, by 13 percentage points over the seven-year period, 2000 to 2007; and in the Kyrgyz Republic, by 5 percentage points in just four years. In Turkey, again, not a transition economy, the share of services in the national economy increased by 15 percentage points between 1990 and 2006. In all cases, increases in service employment as a share of total employment were accompanied by some drop in the share of employment in industry, but mainly by a sharp drop in the share of employment in agriculture.

There has also been significant job reallocation among enterprises within the same industry in ECA countries (Rutkowski and Scarpetta 2005). In fact, job reallocation rates in transition economies exceed those in developed countries (Bartelsman, Haltivanger, and Scarpetta 2004). This reallocation can be attributed in some measure to firm turnover (i.e., the entry and exit of firms), particularly in transition economies. For example, in a number of ECA countries for which firm-level data are available, newly established firms account for between 25 and 50 percent of total job creation, exceeding the share common in developed countries (Rutkowski and Scarpetta 2005).

Looking at employment structure by occupation provides a straightforward measure of the skill content of labor demand. In most ECA countries, employment has shifted away from less skilled occupations towards more skilled occupations. In particular, there has been a shift from blue- to white-collar occupations, as well as an increase in the skill content of employment in both kinds of work. The typical pattern of change in occupational structure has included (1) a substantial fall in demand for agricultural skills, (2) a fall in demand for manual labor, both skilled and unskilled, (3) a rise in demand for service sector occupations, and finally, (4) a surge in demand for professional skills.

Figure 1.3 shows the occupational profile (and, by implication, skill profile) of newly created jobs versus jobs being destroyed in Georgia in 2007. As seen in the figure, a gradual but measured shift from industry to services is occurring, with many jobs destroyed and few created for such manual labor-oriented professions as technicians and machine operators. Viewed in terms of labor demand, workers in these occupations saw the demand for their skills fall. At the same time, few jobs were

Figure 1.3 Job Creation and Destruction Rates for Selected Occupations in Georgia, 2007

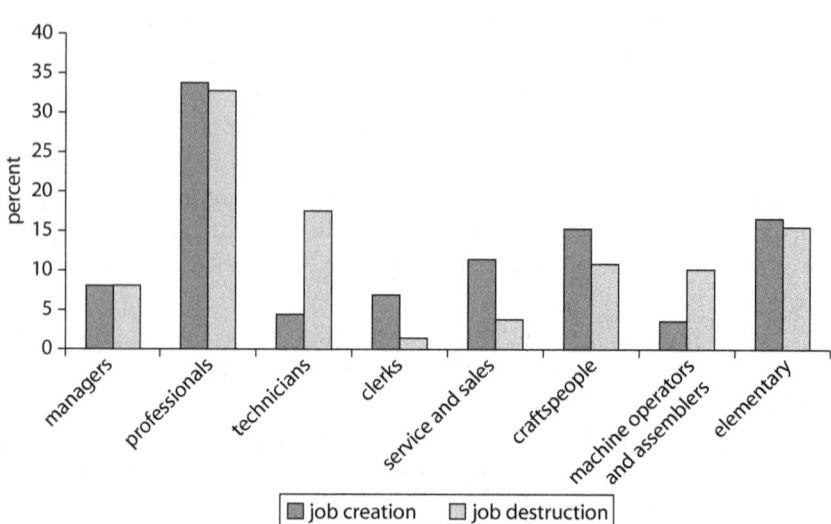

Source: Data obtained during a labor market survey of Georgian firms in 2007. The survey is discussed in greater detail in Rutkowski 2008b.

destroyed and many were created for service workers and salespeople, who thus saw the demand for their skills rise.

The pattern of job reallocation was somewhat different in Ukraine (see figure 1.4). In 2007, demand shifted away from unskilled towards skilled manual labor. The job destruction rate exceeded the job creation rate for elementary occupations;[4] consequently, the share of jobs requiring elementary skills decreased. At the same time, the job creation rate exceeded the job destruction rate for skilled manual occupations, meaning the share of skilled manual jobs increased. There was also a decline in professional employment in Ukraine.

Figure 1.5 shows patterns of change in the occupational structure of employment across the ECA region over a longer time series, patterns that are especially well illustrated by the panels for Poland (panel a) and Russian Federation (panel d). Within the broad trend of the shift from unskilled to skilled labor, there are numerous country-specific exceptions. A diverse group of countries, from Romania to Turkey to the Kyrgyz Republic, saw increases in the demand for manual labor (not decreases), but these increases were for skilled manual labor. Some countries (e.g., the former Yugoslav Republic of Macedonia) saw a sharp increase in the

Figure 1.4 Job Creation and Destruction Rates for Selected Occupations in Ukraine, 2007

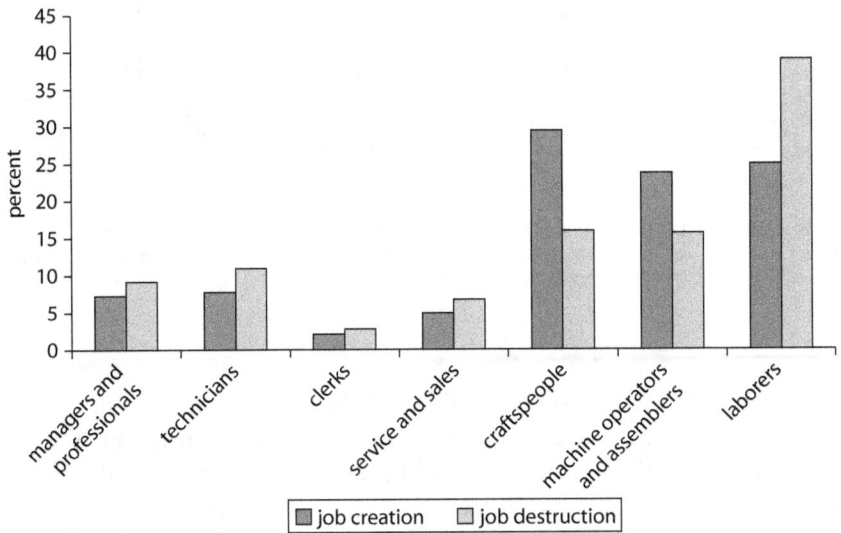

Sources: Ukraine Labor Demand Survey (World Bank 2009); Bank staff calculations.

Figure 1.5 Changes in Occupational Share of Total Employment in Selected ECA Countries, Various Years

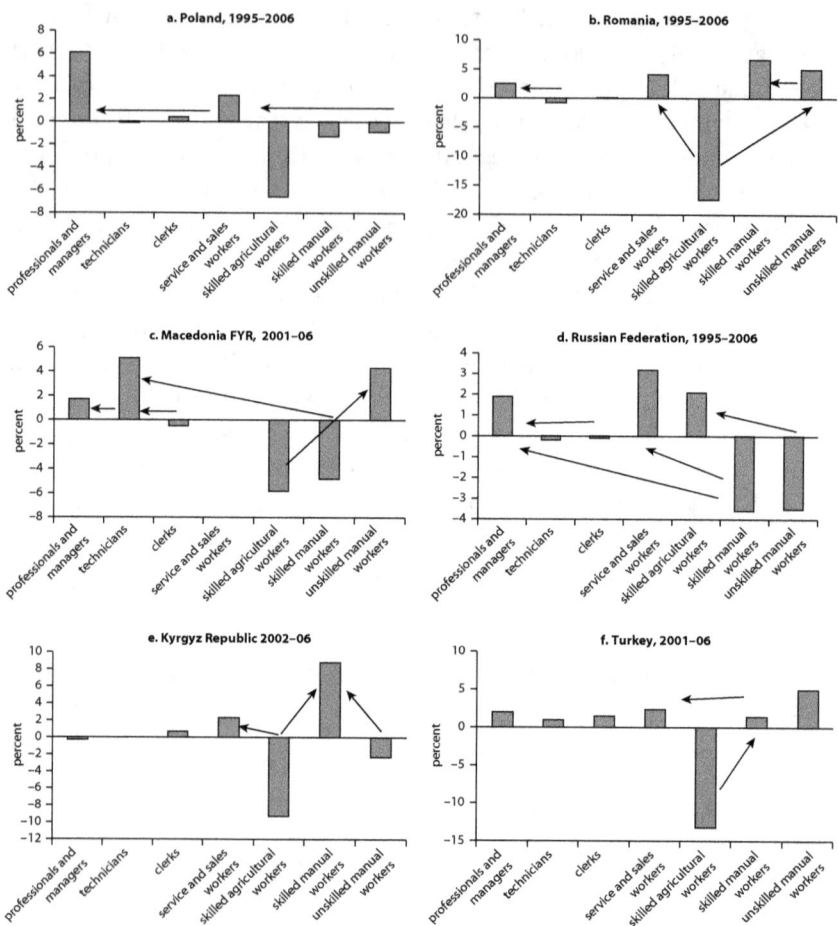

Sources: UNECE SD, Labour Force and Wages; Eurostat SD, Labour Market; World Bank staff calculations.
Note: The arrows in each panel suggest *hypothetical* movements of workers between occupations (i.e., possible movements of labor between different occupations during this time period).

demand for medium-level professional skills (e.g., technicians and associate professionals), and a rise in unskilled manual employment. Others (e.g., Georgia and Ukraine) saw a fall in the share of professional occupations. These variations notwithstanding, the overall picture is one of a rising demand for skilled labor. The limited number of existing studies on the demand for skills in transition economies also confirms this picture.[5]

Unemployment Patterns in ECA Countries Confirm the Demand for Skilled Labor

Increased demand for skilled labor is also evident in the pattern of unemployment and exit from unemployment found in the ECA region.[6] Table 1.1 presents unemployment rates by educational attainment by subregion.[7] As a rule, the unemployment rate is highest among workers with only a basic education, except in Turkey and the middle-income CIS countries. The relatively low unemployment rate among workers with this level of education can be attributed to the fact that many of these workers are employed in agriculture.

By contrast, the unemployment rate is by far the lowest among workers with a tertiary education in all ECA subregions. In fact, it is roughly half that of workers with a general secondary education. In all subregions, workers who finish school with vocational or technical skills are less likely to be unemployed than workers with general secondary skills (Turkey being an exception).[8] The difference is particularly pronounced in middle-income CIS countries, where the unemployment rate among workers with a vocational or technical education is half that among workers with a general secondary education.

Table 1.1 Unemployment Rates by Educational Attainment and ECA Subregion, 2006
(percent)

	Education level			
Country group	Primary or less	Secondary general	Secondary vocational and/or technical[a]	Tertiary
EU10 + 1	22.1	12.4	9.6	5.8
SEE	32.0	24.5	22.7	12.5
Middle-income CIS	7.2	14.2	7.2	5.0
Low-income CIS	29.7	26.1	22.3	16.2
Turkey	15.8	20.0	25.0	9.4

Sources: EBRD-World Bank 2006; authors' calculations.
Note: See "Abbreviations" for a key to country groupings. Unemployment rates estimated using data from the EBRD-World Bank Life in Transition Survey (LITS) may differ from official country data because of methodological differences.
a. The category of "secondary technical/vocational education" used by the LITS combines two different subcategories: (1) workers who completed secondary technical school (4–5 years of courses leading to a secondary school diploma), and (2) workers who received basic vocational training (1–3 years of courses, which do not lead to a secondary school diploma). Evidence from countries for which the more detailed breakdown is available indicates that the employment chances of workers with secondary technical education are significantly better than that of workers with basic vocational training. For example, in Poland the unemployment rate among workers with basic vocational training tends to be one-third higher than that among workers with secondary technical education. This may be due to the inferior quality of training received during the shorter courses, or to a sorting process whereby students who are less able or come from a disadvantaged background tend to self-select into schools that offer basic vocational training rather than the more demanding secondary technical schools.

The high demand for professional and technical skills in the ECA region is also evident when one looks at the movement of workers from unemployment to jobs. Professionals and technicians across countries in the region have by far the highest chances of escaping unemployment and finding a new job. Figure 1.6 depicts outflow rates from unemployment to employment for two ECA subregions: the EU10+1 (European Union+1) countries and low-income CIS countries (the pattern prevailing in middle-income CIS and South Eastern Europe (SEE) countries is similar to that in the EU10+1 group).

In the EU10+1 countries, the escape rate from unemployment is highest among professionals and technicians, followed by medium-skilled white- and blue-collar workers. It is lowest among unskilled and agricultural workers. In low-income CIS countries, the pattern is somewhat different: medium-skilled, blue-collar agricultural workers have better chances of finding a job than do medium-skilled white-collar workers. But workers in more skilled occupations nevertheless find jobs more easily than those in less-skilled occupations.

The poor employment prospects of less-skilled workers in the region are also evident from the unemployment-to-vacancy (U/V) ratio, which is high for less-skilled workers and low for highly skilled workers. Data on the U/V ratio for Croatia, the Czech Republic, and Ukraine illustrate the point (see figure 1.7). Job opportunities for different occupations are quite similar in these three countries: the number of unemployed professionals and technicians (skill levels 3 and 4, respectively, in the ISCO-88 framework) per vacancy is low and that of unemployed unskilled workers (skill level 1) is high. Employment chances are also relatively good for skilled manual workers, especially craft workers (skill level 2). But job prospects are limited for white-collar workers with medium-level skills (e.g., clerks, service workers, salespeople). The demand for white-collar labor with medium-level skills is limited relative to supply, while the demand for blue-collar labor with mid-level skills is high relative to supply.

Putting together the information on employment presented in the previous section with the data on unemployment presented in this section, it is possible to obtain an estimate of shortages and surpluses in the economies of the ECA region, particularly by comparing the relative shares of employment and unemployment of different educational groups. Figure 1.8 shows that in countries as diverse as Croatia, Poland, Russia, Uzbekistan, and Tajikistan (listed in order of gross national income [GNI] per capita), there is a shortage of workers with professional or technical qualifications and a surplus of workers with

Figure 1.6 Yearly Outflow Rates from Employment to Jobs by Occupation in Two Subregions of ECA, 2006

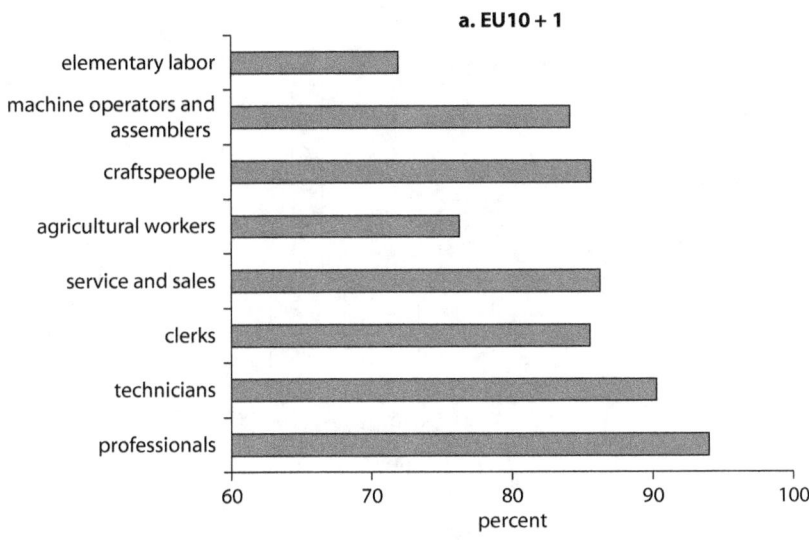

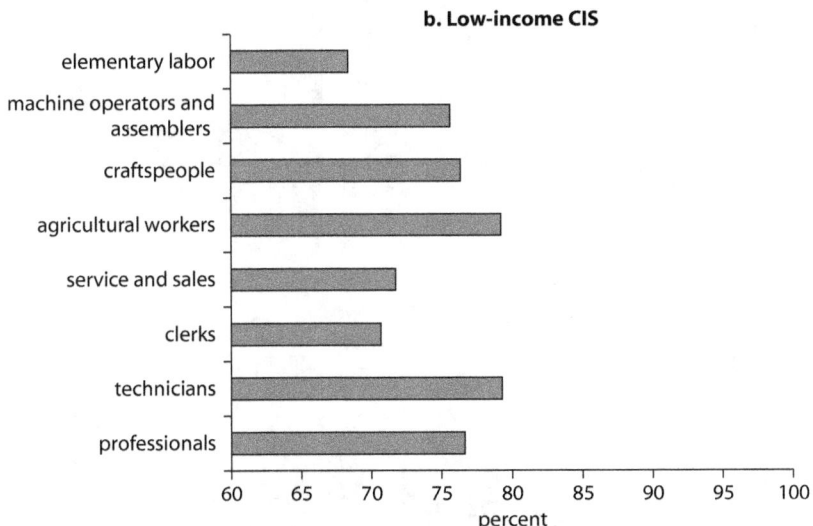

Sources: EBRD–World Bank 2006; World Bank staff calculations.
Note: The yearly outflow rate from unemployment to jobs is the number of workers who were employed during the reference week, but unemployed one year earlier expressed as a percentage of all unemployed.

Figure 1.7   Unemployment-to-Vacancy Ratio by Occupation in Croatia, the Czech Republic, and Ukraine, Various Years

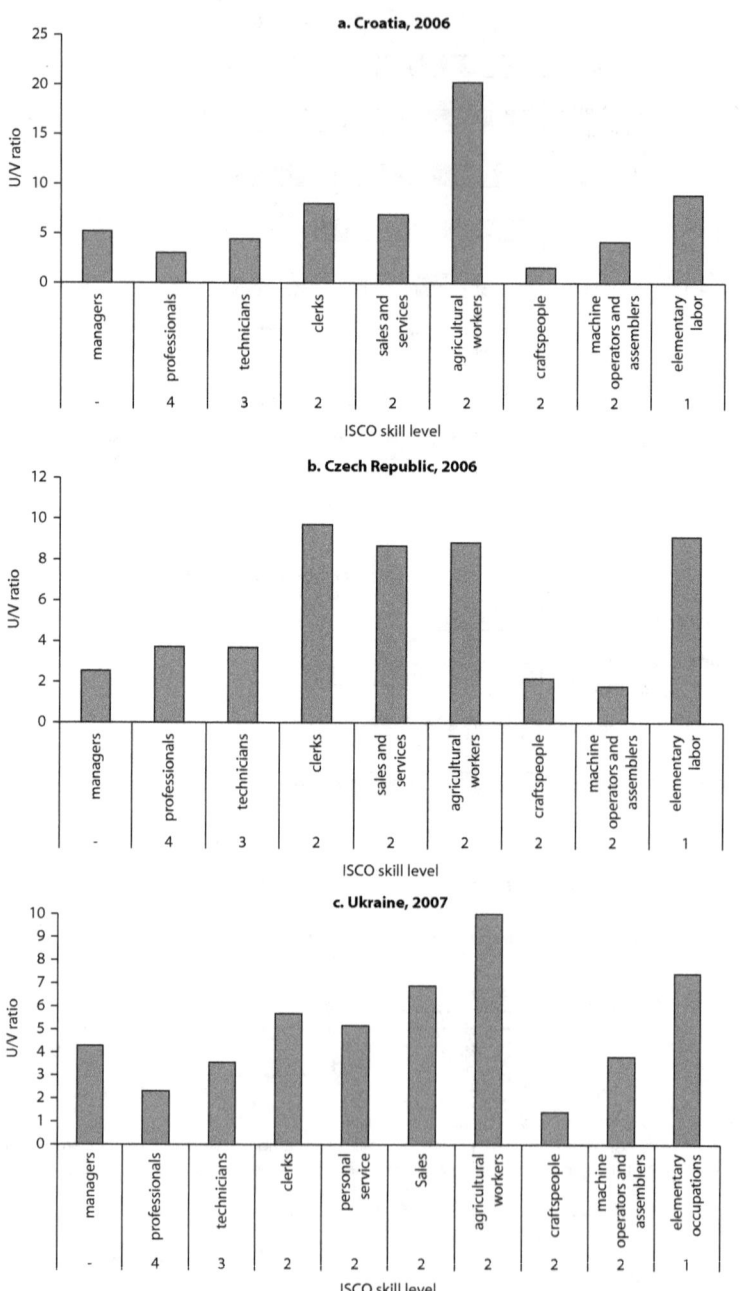

Sources: Data provided by the Croatian Employment Service for 2006, Ministry of Labour and Social Affairs of the Czech Republic for 2006, and Ukraine State Employment Service for 2007; authors' calculations.

Figure 1.8 Labor Shortages and Surpluses by Level of Educational Attainment, Selected ECA Countries

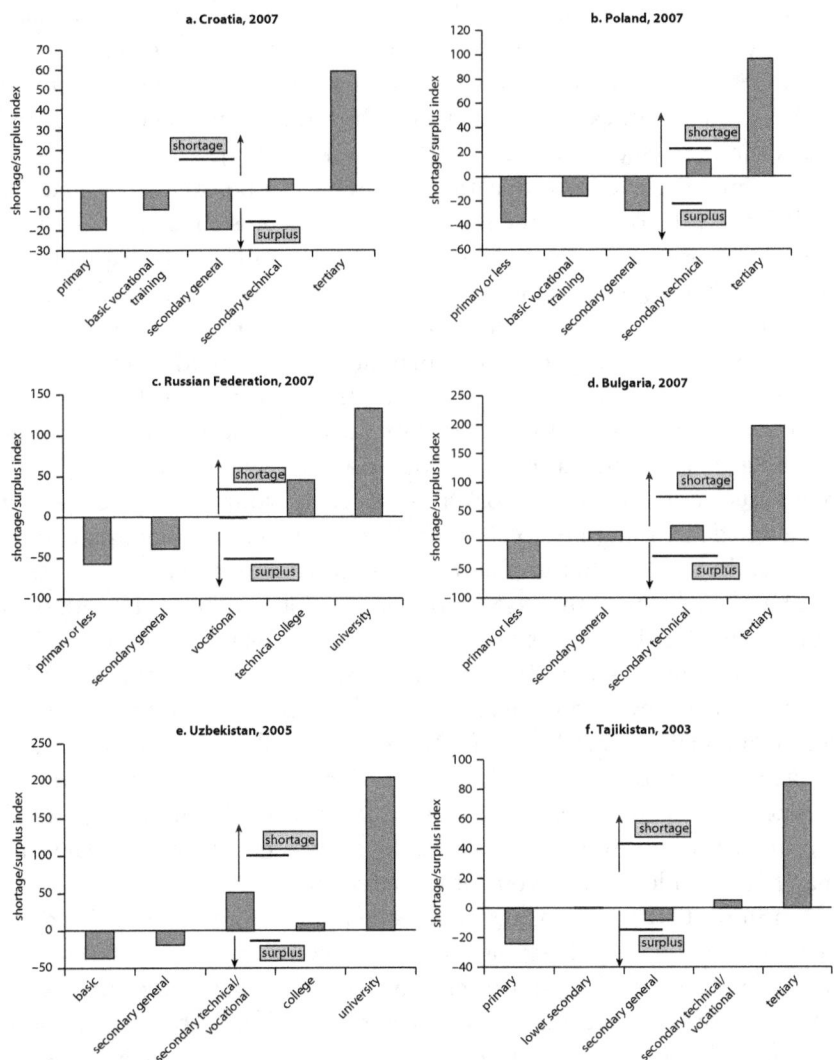

Sources: Crostat 2007; Bulgaria 2007; Poland 2007; Russian Federation 2007; World Bank 2005b, 2003a; authors' calculations.
Note: The skill shortage or surplus index is calculated as $(e/u-1)*100$, where e and u are respectively employment and unemployment shares of a given occupational group.

basic skills. This pattern is common in most ECA countries, regardless of their income level or progress in the transition towards a market economy. In addition to the skills mismatch between educational categories, there is also a mismatch within educational categories in certain countries. For example, a study of Croatia found that among workers with a tertiary education, there was a shortage of engineers and a surplus of lawyers and art designers (Rutkowski 2008a).

It is important to note that there continues to be excess demand for skilled manual workers at the same time that there is an excess supply of unskilled workers, medium-skilled nonmanual workers, and agricultural workers. There is some evidence that the excess demand for skilled manual workers is the result of a shrinking supply of workers in this category.

The relative shortage of skilled manual workers could have occurred in three ways. First, as seen in figure 1.5, there has been a shift in occupational structure away from skilled manual occupations in some countries (e.g., Poland, Russia, and FYR Macedonia). Given poor employment prospects at home, some workers—especially younger workers—may have decided to migrate to Western Europe, where employment prospects and wages are better. There is substantial anecdotal evidence that this has actually been the case for the populations of the EU10 countries (especially after EU accession in 2004 allowed for greater labor mobility). Poland and Ukraine (the first a member of the EU, the second a nonmember) provide good examples of the widespread outmigration of skilled manual workers.[9] Second, the supply of skilled manual workers is likely to have declined due to a shift from vocational towards general secondary education that has occurred in most ECA countries (Poland is again a relevant example). Finally, older workers with vocational skills may have decided to drop out of the labor force.

An important question is whether the apparent simultaneous excess demand for some workers and excess supply of others is the result of friction in labor market adjustments, or whether it has a structural component. While structural unemployment is difficult to assess, there appears to be significant long-term unemployment in the region concentrated among low-skilled workers, often leading to poverty and social exclusion (Alam et al. 2005). Retraining is often ineffective because the skill requirements of newly created jobs differ significantly from those of the jobs that were destroyed.[10] Some degree of friction in the labor market is customary, but the skill profile of labor demand is changing fairly rapidly in ECA countries due to both technological progress and the adoption of new production processes. There are thus good reasons to believe there is a structural component to the labor surpluses and shortages observed in the region.

The ability of the labor market—and the education system—to respond to this disequilibrium is a question of market signals and institutions. Among potential issues are whether wages are sufficiently flexible to adjust to changing demand and supply conditions, labor market information on job prospects by type of education and occupation is available, educational institutions can adjust program offerings to the needs of the labor market, and employment services can effectively match workers to available jobs. The next sections examine whether labor market signals (via returns to education) reflect the underlying changes in labor demand in the region and whether employers are able to attract workers with the right skills.

Wages Have Risen for Skilled Labor

Changes in the demand for skills are certainly reflected in the movement of wages. Given the supply of skills, an increase in demand for certain skills manifests as an increase in the relative wages of workers who possess these skills. In the majority of ECA countries, the returns to education have sharply increased and are presently comparable to those observed in developed market economies. However, as shown in figure 1.9, returns to education are still relatively low in some of the less advanced, slower-reforming transition countries. The evolution of the occupational wage structure unambiguously points to an increase in wage premia for white-collar skills, particularly professional and managerial skills.

Figure 1.9 reveals that ECA countries in the early 2000s could be divided into three groups: a small group where returns to schooling were high by international standards, a dominant group where returns were moderate, and a small but nonnegligible group where returns were low. There is a clear association between the degree of progress of economic transition to a market economy and the level of returns to schooling in these countries (Flabbi, Paternostro, and Tiongson 2007). The high-returns group included advanced transition economies (e.g., Hungary and Poland), while the low-returns group included mainly less advanced economies (e.g., Romania, Tajikistan, and Ukraine).[11] As a rule, countries where returns to education were high were those where employment had already shifted towards more skilled occupations, whereas countries where they were low were those where there had been less of a shift. At that time, the rates of returns to education in

Figure 1.9 Returns to Schooling in Selected ECA Transition Countries, Various Years

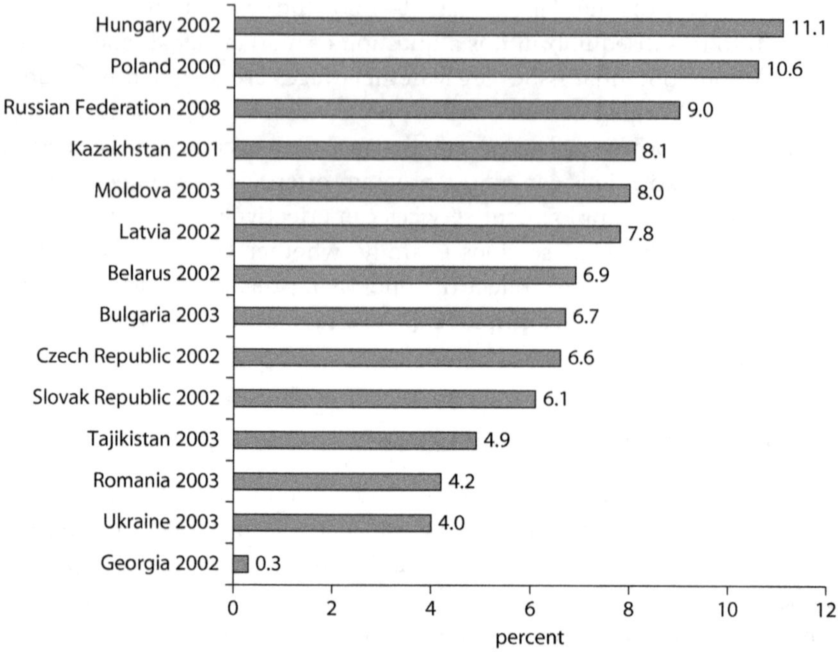

Country	Percent
Hungary 2002	11.1
Poland 2000	10.6
Russian Federation 2008	9.0
Kazakhstan 2001	8.1
Moldova 2003	8.0
Latvia 2002	7.8
Belarus 2002	6.9
Bulgaria 2003	6.7
Czech Republic 2002	6.6
Slovak Republic 2002	6.1
Tajikistan 2003	4.9
Romania 2003	4.2
Ukraine 2003	4.0
Georgia 2002	0.3

Sources: Patrinos 2008 (Ukraine); Kapelyushnikov 2008 (Russia) and Yemtsov, Cnobloch, and Mete 2006 (Belarus, Bulgaria, Georgia, Hungary, Moldova, Poland, Romania, and Tajikistan).
Note: Average return per a year of additional education estimated based on a Mincerian wage regression of the form: $\ln w = a + \rho s + \beta_0 x + \beta_1 x^2 + \gamma z + \varepsilon$; where w represents the wage of an individual, s denotes years of schooling, x denotes labor market experience (years), z is a vector of other individual and job characteristics (e.g., gender, industry, etc.), and ε is an error term, which *inter alia* captures unmeasured differences in innate ability. The parameter ρ represents the return to one year of schooling.

most ECA economies were broadly comparable with those of developed economies (about 7.5 percent), but substantially lower than those of developing economies (where the rate is above 10 percent; Psacharopulos and Patrinos 2004).

The increase in returns to schooling during the economic transition in the region has been driven by a surge in returns to tertiary education.[12] Wage premia to tertiary education have increased dramatically, while those to secondary education have remained roughly stable.[13] This is well illustrated by the example of Hungary (see figure 1.10), where the wage premium to university education more than doubled in the wake of the transition. At the same time, the premium to secondary education (both general and technical) rose only slightly higher than it

Figure 1.10 Wage Premia by Level of Education in Hungary, 1986–2004

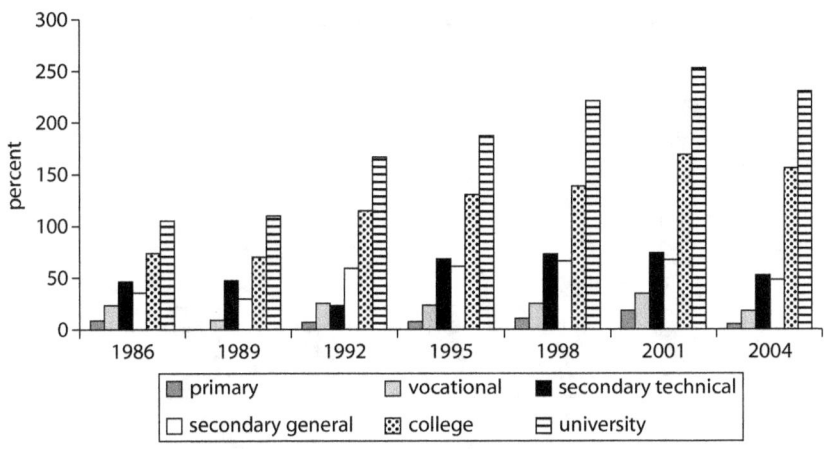

Sources: Campos and Jolliffe 2007; authors' calculations.
Note: Wage premia are relative to uncompleted primary education.

was before the transition. Similar trends occurred in other EU10+1 countries (Rutkowski 1996a, 2001). Although time series data for other ECA countries are not available, it seems fair to assume that the increase in the wage premium to university education was a decisive factor in other countries, too. The sharp increase in returns to tertiary education is consistent with the growth in demand for highly professional skills documented earlier in this chapter.

While in most ECA countries workers with a tertiary education earn considerably higher salaries than workers with a secondary education, returns to secondary education are limited. Figure 1.11 illustrates this trend for Russia and Turkey. In Russia, an average worker with a university education earns over twice as much as a worker with only primary education and nearly 60 percent more than a worker with general secondary education.[14] In turn, a worker with general upper-level secondary education earns only 20 percent more than a worker with less education. Differences in the wage premia by type of secondary school are virtually negligible. A very similar pattern prevails in Turkey.

The shift in demand for skills during the economic transition produced a new wage structure that is remarkably similar across ECA economies (see figure 1.12). Using the average wage of workers in elementary occupations as a reference, managers earn 3.5–4.5 times as much; professionals, 2.5–3.0 times more; technicians, about 2 times more; and skilled

Figure 1.11 Wage Premia by Education Level in the Russian Federation and Turkey

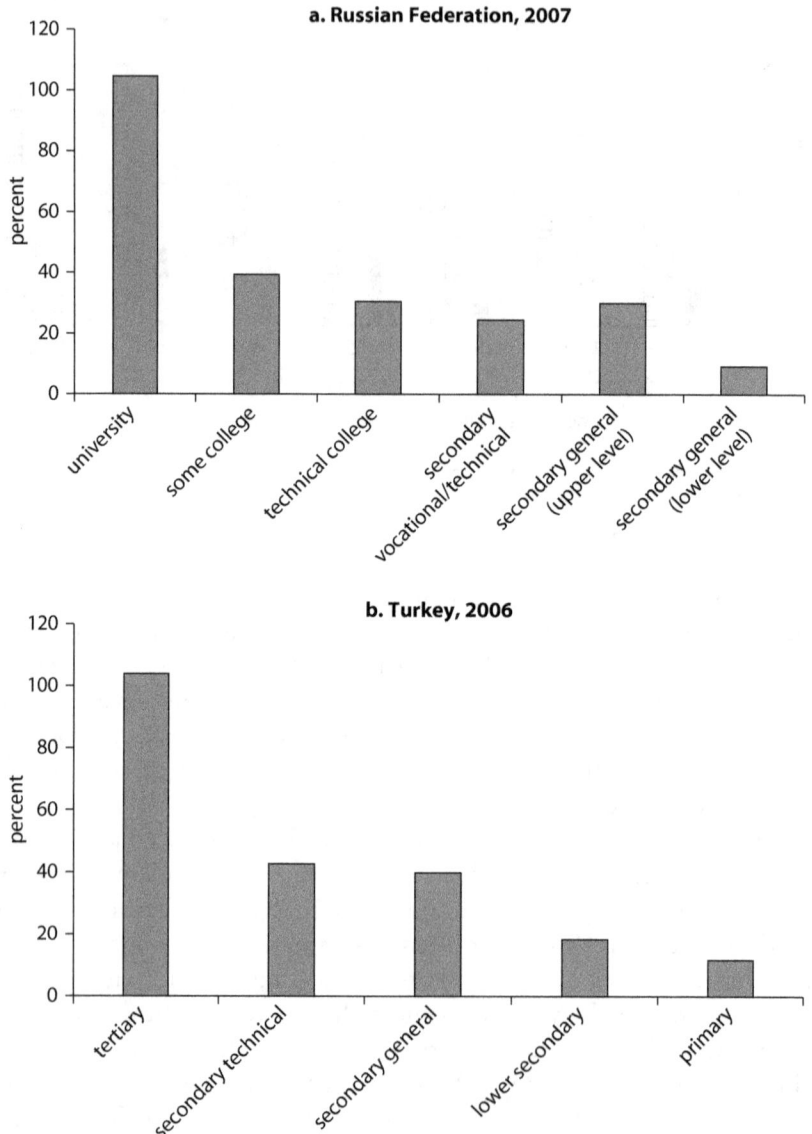

Sources: Kapelyushnikov 2008 (Russian Federation); Ercan 2008 (Turkey); authors' calculations.

Figure 1.12 Premia by Occupation Relative to Elementary Occupations in Various ECA Countries

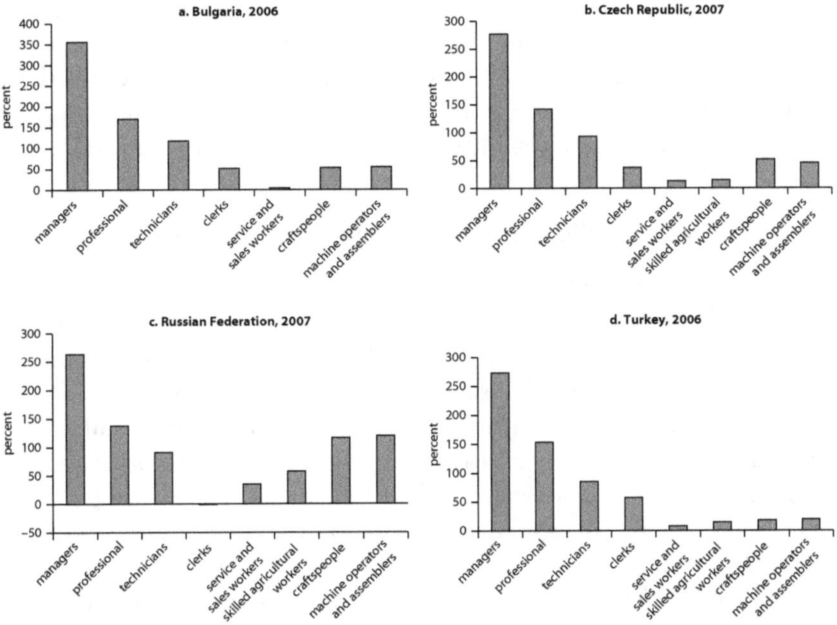

Sources: Eurostat, Labor Market Statistics (database) (Bulgaria and Czech Republic); Ercan 2008 (Turkey); Kapelyushnikov 2008 (Russia); World Bank staff calculations.

manual workers and clerks, about 1.5 times more. Service workers and salespeople earn only slightly more—some 10 percent—than workers in elementary occupations. While patterns across most ECA countries are similar, the relative wage status of skilled manual workers is much better in Russia than in the EU10 countries. Concomitantly, the relative wage status of professionals and technicians is worse in Russia. Moreover, there are no returns to clerical skills in Russia; clerks earn on average the same wage as laborers. Thus the occupational wage structure in Russia is biased towards skilled manual labor; as such, it is closer to that prevailing under central planning. A similar pattern also prevails in Ukraine (World Bank 2009b).[15]

In addition to the current variance in wages across job categories, there is evidence that wage rates are diverging over time. In most ECA countries for which data are available, workers in occupations requiring highly skilled labor (e.g., managers, professionals, and technicians) saw their relative wages increase, while workers in occupations requiring medium- and lower-level skills (especially manual skills) saw their relative wages fall. Thus the wage differential between highly skilled white-collar workers and less skilled white- and blue-collar workers has substantially widened. Figure 1.13 illustrates this trend in Bulgaria and Poland.[16] The wage status of highly skilled white-collar workers in these countries has substantially improved, while that of less skilled workers (both white- and blue-collar) has deteriorated during the transition.

Lack of Needed Skills Is Impeding Enterprise Growth

The preceding sections documented the shift in labor demand in ECA countries from less to more skilled labor within both blue- and white-collar occupations. In addition, demand has shifted notably from blue- to white-collar occupations. These changes, which have resulted in high rates of return to investment in skills in the region, are the result of two simultaneous changes: an increase in demand for skilled workers arising from skill-biased technological and organizational change and (in the transition economies) factors specific to the transition from a centrally planned to a market economy.

Available evidence suggests that the supply of skills has adjusted fairly slowly to the changes in demand. Many firms in ECA, especially modern and growing firms, now see the skills of available workers as a major obstacle to their operations and growth. The strongest evidence for this perception comes from the findings of the Business Environment and Enterprise Performance Surveys (BEEPS) conducted by the European Bank for Reconstruction and Development (EBRD) and the World Bank.[17] For the first time since BEEPS was launched in 1999, workers' education and skills were recently identified by employers as one of the top constraints to firm growth.[18]

In fact, worker skills were not typically identified by firms as a constraint until 2005; other constraints (e.g., taxes and business environment) were deemed more important. However, during the most recent round of BEEPS, conducted in 2008, lack of skilled manpower moved up to become the second-most common constraint on growth cited by firms. Indeed, by 2008 the traditional strengths of ECA countries—good endowments of infrastructure and skills—appear to have eroded (Mitra, Selowsky, and Zalduendo 2010).

Panel a of figure 1.14 shows the distribution of ECA countries according to the level of dissatisfaction with workers' education and skills among local firms. On average, 30 percent of firms considered these

Figure 1.13 Wage Growth by Occupation in Bulgaria and Poland, 1996–2006
(average wage growth = 1)

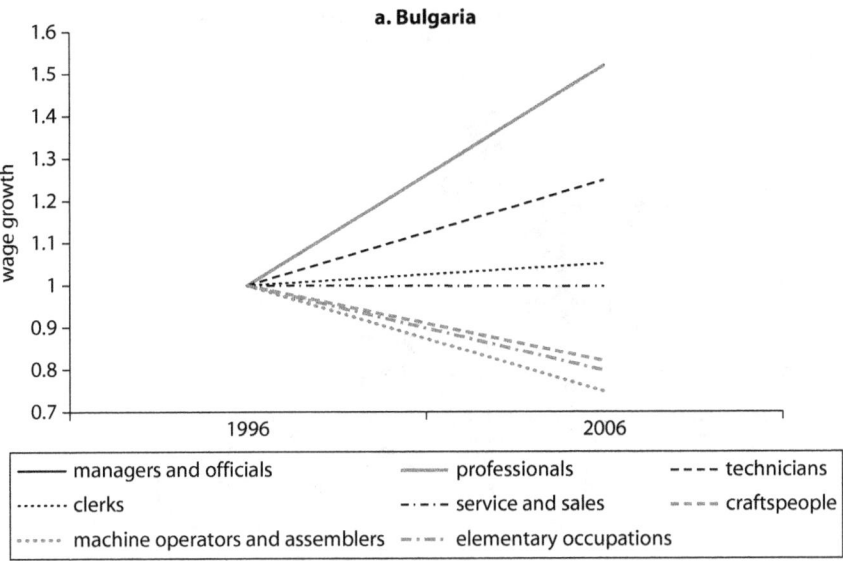

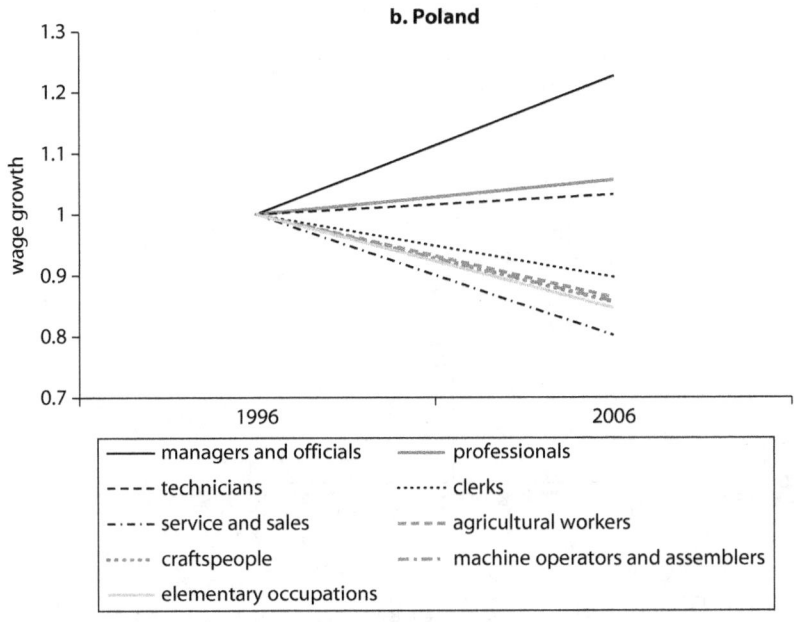

Sources: Eurostat, Labor Market Statistics (database); World Bank staff calculations.

Figure 1.14 Employers' Perceptions of Worker Skills as a Constraint to Growth, Various ECA Countries

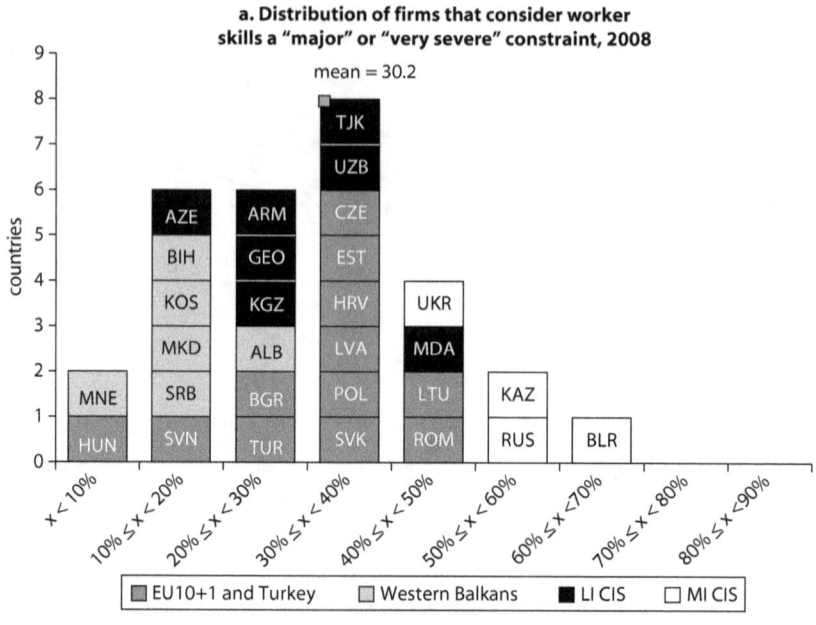

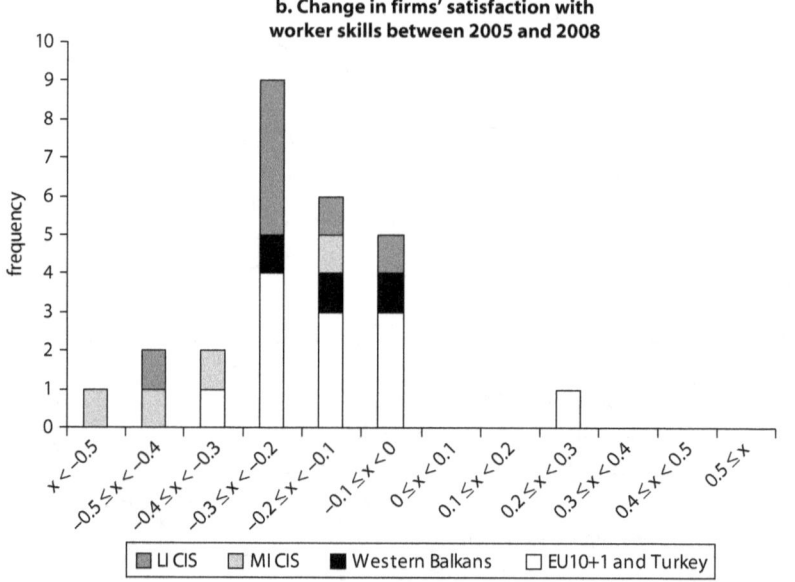

Sources: BEEPS 2008; Mitra, Selowsky, and Zalduendo 2010.
Note: LI = low-income, MI = middle-income. See "Abbreviations" for country abbreviations and groupings.

factors to be a major or severe constraint to their operations and growth. The greatest dissatisfaction was among middle-income CIS countries, where more than 40 percent of firms were dissatisfied. In contrast, relatively less dissatisfaction was reported by firms in the Western Balkan countries and significant variability was reported in the EU10+1 countries.

Worker skills are particularly likely to become a binding constraint during periods of rapid economic growth. As might then be expected, the percentage of firms for which the availability of the "right" workers was either *no obstacle* or a *minor obstacle* decreased during the period between 2005 and 2008 due to strong economic growth in the region. Panel b of figure 1.14 depicts the difference in percentage of satisfied firms between 2005 and 2008 regarding the suitability of the skills and education of workers for doing business. A negative value (along the x axis) assigned to a particular country indicates a decline in the percentage of satisfied firms over this period. For example, if the share of satisfied firms in country A declined by 25 percent between 2005 and 2008, then country A would be positioned in the –0.2 to –0.3 percent range of the x-axis. As this panel shows, all ECA countries, with the exception of one EU member state, experienced a decline in the share of satisfied firms between 2005 and 2008. The worst deterioration in the availability of skills relative to demand took place in the middle-income CIS countries. But even in a large number of new EU members and other CIS countries, the reduction in satisfied firms was between 0.2 and 0.3 (or 20–30 percent of all firms).

As might be expected, modern firms suffer more from skills shortages than do traditional ones.[19] Across the ECA region, modern companies find it more difficult to recruit workers with the required qualifications than do traditional firms, particularly professional and skilled manual workers. For example, in the EU10+1 countries in 2005, modern firms needed, on average, five weeks to hire a professional worker, while traditional firms needed fewer than three weeks (see panel a of figure 1.15). In low-income CIS countries, the search for a skilled manual worker among modern firms was, on average, one week longer than that of traditional enterprises (see panel b of figure 1.15).

Skills Mismatch in the ECA Region

As the previous sections have documented, there is a skills mismatch in the ECA region. Unless it is addressed, governments in the region will be

Figure 1.15 Time Needed by Firms to Hire Specific Workers, by ECA Subregion, 2005

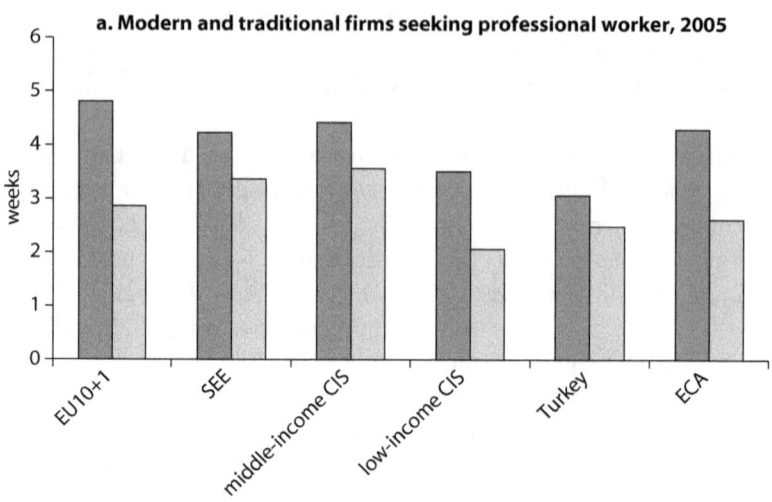

Sources: EBRD-World Bank 2005; World Bank staff calculations.
Note: See "Abbreviations" for country abbreviations and groupings.

unable to facilitate either the growth of firms or a reduction in structural unemployment. Why the skills mismatch exists is a subject of intense inquiry.[20] Although evidence indicates that many factors are involved, this book focuses on one possible cause: education and training institutions in the region provide inappropriate types of skills to their graduates.

There are several ways in which the skills mismatch can be related to the education and training of graduates in ECA countries. First, graduates may not have the necessary technical skills to do the jobs that employers have to offer. This is not solely a matter of educational attainment, that is, of completing a certain level of education. It is also a matter of whether students have the skills needed on the job—the relevant knowledge, the ability to apply that knowledge, and the know-how to complete tasks and solve problems—when they graduate. In addition, the relevance of the education received by graduates is also important. That is, students may be studying the wrong things. Second, graduates of education and training systems in the region may lack the necessary behavioral (or soft) skills needed by employers, such as job attitudes and teamwork skills. There is widespread evidence from across the ECA region that firms seek graduates who not only have knowledge as well as technical and general skills, but who also have behavioral skills. For instance, recent surveys of employers in Kazakhstan (panel a of figure 1.16) and Poland (panel b of figure 1.16) show that firms value such behavioral skills as highly (in some instances, more highly) as knowledge and routine cognitive skills (e.g., mathematics and computer skills)—important as the latter may be.[21]

Before turning to the ways in which education and training systems fall short of delivering the right skills, it is worth noting that one possible reason for the continued identification of skills as a bottleneck to growth in the ECA region is unreasonable expectations on the part of ECA firms. A recent comparison of firms' expectations of new workers in the United Kingdom and Poland, for example, showed that Polish employers expected young workers to possess advanced vocational job-specific skills, while their U.K. counterparts preferred workers who had reached an adequate level of literacy and numeracy, without necessarily having fully developed, job-specific vocational skills (World Bank 2010b). The report concluded that: "The expectations of Polish employers will probably have to change, and they will have to assume a greater role in the financing and provision of vocational training to their workforce" (World Bank 2010b).

Summary

The demand for highly skilled labor has increased in most if not all ECA countries. This profound change in demand stems from the opening of their economies to international competition and the consequent

Figure 1.16 Employers' Valuation of Workers' Knowledge and Skills in Kazakhstan and Poland

(percentage of firms reporting as "very important")

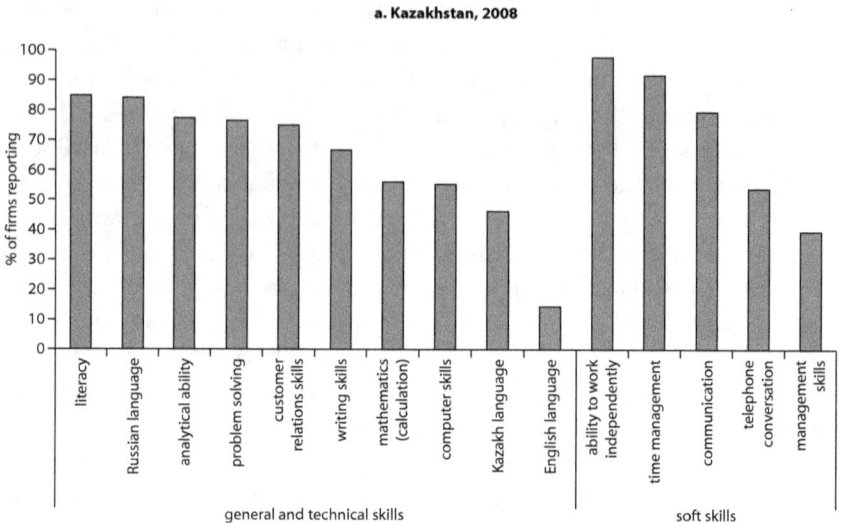

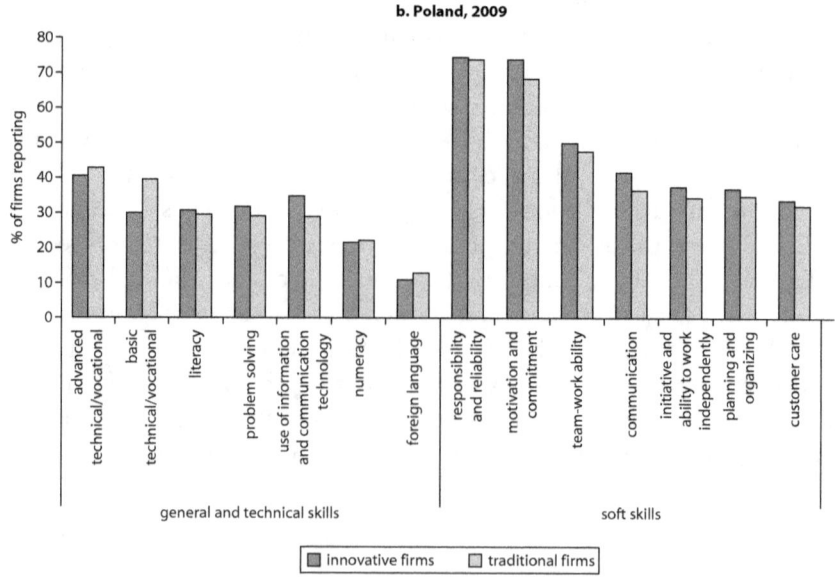

Sources: Ivaschenko 2008; World Bank 2010b.

Firms were categorized as "innovative" if in the year preceding the survey they introduced innovations, otherwise they were categorized as "traditional."

far-reaching reallocation of labor that took place. New firms have entered the market, new economic activities have emerged, and new jobs have been created, calling for different skills than those required previously. As economies have shifted, the service sector has expanded, while the agricultural and, to a lesser degree, industrial sectors have shrunk. Firms have changed the skills composition of their workforces to raise productivity and improve competitiveness; as a result, labor demand has shifted away from lower-skilled toward higher-skilled occupations.

This change in employment structure is most pronounced in the countries of Central Europe, but is visible in some form everywhere in the ECA region. Simultaneously, returns to education have increased and the wages of highly skilled professional workers have greatly improved, while those of lesser-skilled workers have deteriorated. Consequently, the job prospects of better-educated, highly skilled workers have expanded dramatically. Unemployment and low-paid employment in the region is accordingly concentrated among less educated and less skilled workers, a group whose job opportunities are increasingly limited in most ECA countries.

All of these changes have put added strains on education and training systems in the region, which are expected to prepare workers for changed and changing labor markets, but which do not appear geared to meet those labor market needs. The next chapter looks at the supply of skills to the labor market in ECA countries in more detail. Given that skills shortages have become a major constraint to firm growth in many ECA countries, whatever changes have occurred on the supply side appear to have been insufficient. The next chapter tries to explain why.

Notes

1. Alternatively, upgrading the education of the workforce may itself be a factor that leads to increased demand for higher-level skills. That is, the increase in demand for such skills may reflect an increase in the supply of these skills, a process known as endogenous skill-biased technological change. Acemoğlu (1998) argues that a high proportion of skilled workers in the labor force implies a large market size for skill-complementary technologies, meaning that the productivity of skilled workers will be upgraded faster. In this model, an increase in the supply of skills over the long run induces skill-biased technological change, which shifts the relative demand for skills (EC 2008).
2. Chapter 2 discusses skills from an education and training perspective.

3. In this book, high-level white-collar (i.e., nonmanual) skills refer to ISCO-88 groups 1 and 2, and high-level order blue-collar (manual) skills refer to ISCO-88 groups 6, 7, and 8. Low-level, nonmanual skills refer to ISCO-88 groups 4 and 5, and low-level manual skills refer to ISCO-88 group 9. See ILO (1988).
4. Elementary occupations consist of simple and routine tasks that mainly require the use of hand-held tools and often some physical effort.
5. Peter (2003) analyzes skill-biased changes in wages and employment in the Russian economy during the transition. Commander and Köllő (2004) examine the evolution of demand for skills in Hungary, Romania, and Russia. Bartlett (2007) examines the demand for skills in the Western Balkans, and Rutkowski (2008b) and the World Bank (2009b) document the skills mismatch in Georgia and Ukraine, respectively.
6. At the beginning of the transition, the rising unemployment rates of low-skilled workers likely in part reflected the hidden unemployment of these workers—that is, workers whom the state claimed to be employed but who were in fact superfluous to production. With the transition to a more market-based economy, this de facto unemployment was essentially unmasked, rather than created. However, by 2011, the rising unemployment rates of low-skilled workers is more likely a reflection of actual shifts in demand for labor rather than a continued unmasking of hidden unemployment.
7. Unemployment statistics by educational attainment can be difficult to interpret because the determination of whether a respondent is in the labor force affects both the numerator and the denominator of the unemployment rate. If a larger share of workers with vocational secondary education are judged to be "discouraged workers" and out of the work force, this may lead to a lower unemployment rate for workers in this category, even if a smaller share of them are employed. The more appropriate statistic to use for judging the match between terminal level of education and employment status is the employment rate (employed share of graduates with the specific education level) and not the unemployment rate. Such calculations can be done if countries start tracking their graduates using "graduate tracer studies," as recommended in this book.
8. It can be argued that the better employment outcomes of workers with technical secondary education compared with those of workers with general secondary education reflect the different composition of both groups. One hypothesis is that due to the selection process, graduates of general secondary schools who do not proceed to tertiary education are less able, on average, than the graduates of secondary technical schools. However, this hypothesis remains to be tested. Another possibility is that workers with technical secondary education are in a different age cohort—one that received a better education—than workers with general secondary

education. Yet available evidence indicates that the cohort effect is small and thus unlikely to account for the differences between the two educational groups.
9. While not under the scope of this book, it should be noted that migration has had a significant effect on labor trends in the region. A recent World Bank study examines both migration and remittances in the region. See Mansoor and Quillin 2007.
10. Surveys of demand for skills that were carried out in Poland and FYR Macedonia in 2009 indicated that most newly created jobs require professional or nonmanual skills, while most jobs that were destroyed required manual skills. This obviously limits the scope for retraining (Rutkowski 2010; World Bank 2010b).
11. The low returns to schooling for these countries is presumably in part a legacy of the socialist period, when education levels were much higher than would be predicted for their level of development, a situation that holds down wages during the time when the economic structure is catching up to education levels.
12. As figure 1.9 suggests, much of the increase in these returns was concentrated in the early years of the transition. A few countries, typically those with lower returns, show a flatter trajectory.
13. The terms "premia" and "returns" to education are used here interchangeably. However, strictly speaking, they are not synonymous. Returns to education take into account both wage premia and private costs of obtaining education. Accordingly, premia could have increased without private returns increasing as dramatically.
14. These estimates do not control for other factors that affect wages, such as labor market experience, gender, location, and so forth.
15. This finding likely reflects the legacy of central planning and a noncompetitive wage setting, especially in enterprises fully or partly owned by the state, in both countries.
16. In some countries in the region there were deviations from the overall trend presented here. For example, salaries of professionals in the Czech Republic decreased slightly in relative terms between 1996 and 2007. Similarly, in Estonia and the Slovak Republic, the relative wages of managers fell slightly during the same period. The slight fall in the relative wages of professionals and managers that occurred in the mid-2000s likely represents an adjustment to the increase in the supply of the relevant skills that occurred in response to growing demand.
17. BEEPS, a joint initiative of the EBRD and the World Bank, collects firm-level data on a broad range of issues concerning the business environment and the performance of firms, including labor and workforce skills.

18. The most common constraint identified by firms in the region was the tax regime.
19. Firms were categorized as "modern" if they used the Internet in interactions with their clients and suppliers, and "traditional" if they did not. Clearly, use of the Internet is only a proxy for modern technology.
20. Some degree of skills mismatch is natural and unavoidable in every growing and restructuring economy due to adjustment costs and the delayed response of national educational systems. Especially in the context of fast-changing technology, changes in the skill structure of the labor supply tend to lag behind those of labor demand, even in a well-performing labor market.
21. Surveys of the demand for skills in Poland and FYR Macedonia that were carried out in 2009 provide additional empirical support to the claim that employers value job attitudes and behavioral skills at least as much as academic or technical and/or vocational skills. At the same time, both Polish and Macedonian employers complain that many recent school graduates and young workers are lacking "soft" skills (Rutkowski 2010; World Bank 2010b).

CHAPTER 2

Education and the Supply of Skills to the ECA Market

The skills gap described in the previous chapter represents something of a puzzle from the perspective of the education and training sector in the ECA region. ECA countries have had very high educational attainment rates for decades and, over the past 20 years, have experienced a rapid expansion of tertiary enrollment. In addition, these countries deliver quality education (where it is measured) at the elementary and lower secondary levels comparable to that of their peers at the same income level. Given these conditions, why do ECA firms increasingly complain that they cannot find graduates with the right skills?

In answering this question, there is a fundamental problem: data are available on the number of students who graduate (i.e., how many diplomas are issued) in ECA countries, but internationally comparable data on the quality and relevance of upper secondary and tertiary institutions do not exist. Data gaps are even more acute with regard to the education and training received by adults outside of the formal education system. Only a few of the new EU member states track the extent of such training (in terms of participation rates and hours of training); data on the quality and relevance of this type of training, however, do not exist anywhere.

While the data gaps make it impossible to provide a definitive answer to the skills puzzle, this study is able to point to fundamental weaknesses in the ECA region's education systems that almost certainly contribute to the skills gaps observed in chapter 1. Addressing these shortcomings may not fully close these gaps, but it will create more flexible and better-managed education systems, which will, in turn, increase the likelihood that young people will graduate with—and adult workers will be able to acquire—the skills in demand today. Moreover, it is clearly a priority that ECA countries address the information deficits that are currently forestalling a more comprehensive—and satisfying—answer to the puzzle above.

Although the education offered in many ECA countries is respectable for their level of income, it does not appear to be good enough (or of the right relevance) to meet the rising demand for skills in the region. Two problems related to quality seem particularly acute: too many students are failing and education systems have difficulties imparting problem-solving skills. Educational quality, moreover, is not demonstrating reliable progress. It is not improving at the lower secondary level, a weakness that is probably mirrored at the upper secondary level (albeit with a lag). Enrollments at the tertiary level have doubled, tripled, or quadrupled in the past two decades, but this occurred in an environment where quality assurance mechanisms are very weak, indicating that quality in this sector is also unlikely to have improved. The skills gap can also be explained by too little progress in providing workers with options for continuous training, despite evidence that such training fosters employment and greater productivity. The development of the adult training sector should accordingly be central to the region's medium-term economic growth agenda.

Background: The Global Knowledge Economy Requires Lifelong Learning

To prepare students for the global knowledge economy, education systems must build human capital, which the OECD defines as "the knowledge, skills, competencies, and other attributes embodied in individuals that are relevant to personal, social, and economic well-being" (OECD 1999a). The framework for education is thus one of lifelong learning in which the new knowledge and skills needed for successful adaptation to changing circumstances are continuously acquired over the life cycle. This framework, and the key competencies needed to function in today's complex societies, are elaborated in the OECD's "Definition and Selection of Key Competences" (DeSeCo) project (OECD 2005b),[1] which identifies three broad clusters of competencies:

The ability to use tools interactively, including the ability to use language, symbols, text, knowledge, information, and technology. This requires more than having access to a tool and the technical skills required to handle it (e.g., the skills needed to read a text or use software). Rather, individuals also need to create and adapt knowledge and skills, which require a familiarity with the tool itself, as well as an understanding of how it changes the way one can interact with the world and how it can be used to accomplish broader goals.

The ability to interact in heterogeneous groups, including the ability to relate well to others, cooperate and work in teams, and manage and resolve conflicts. As societies become more fragmented and more diverse, it becomes important to manage interpersonal relationships well, which benefits both individuals and their abilities to build new forms of cooperation.

Box 2.1

Defining "Skills," "Competencies," and Other Terms

This book utilizes a range of education and learning concepts that were used to develop the European Qualifications Framework for Lifelong Learning of the EU. There, certain key terms are defined as follows:

- *Skills:* the ability to apply knowledge and use know-how to complete tasks and solve problems. Skills may be cognitive (involving the use of logical, intuitive, and creative thinking) or practical (involving manual dexterity and the use of methods, materials, tools, and instruments).
- *Competence* (or *competency):* the proven ability to use knowledge; skills; and personal, social, and methodological abilities in work or study situations and in professional and personal development. Competence may be described in terms of responsibility and autonomy.
- *Learning outcomes:* statements of what a learner knows, understands, and is able to do on completion of a learning process, defined in terms of knowledge, skills, and competencies.
- *Qualifications:* a formal assessment and validation by a competency body that determines an individual has achieved learning outcomes in conformance with given standards.
- *Knowledge:* the outcome of the assimilation of information through learning. Knowledge is the body of facts, principles, theories, and practices related to a field of work or study. It can be theoretical or factual or both.

Source: EU 2008.

The ability to act autonomously, including the ability to form and conduct life plans and personal projects, as well as to assert rights, interests, limits, and needs. Acting autonomously does not mean functioning in social isolation. Instead, individuals must act autonomously in order to participate effectively in the development of society and function well in different spheres of life, including the workplace, family life, and social life.

To develop the higher-level competencies in demand among contemporary employers, students must become able to organize and regulate their own learning, learn both independently and in groups, and overcome difficulties in the learning process. This versatility requires that they become aware of their own thinking processes, as well as their learning strategies and methods. What they acquire from school and university education is the cognitive and motivational prerequisite for successful learning in future life, with adult education and training helping refresh and build on these foundations.

Education and training systems today are assessed against their ability to develop the above-described competencies in their students. Clearly, such systems must first provide individuals *access* to schooling and training, as measured by years of education of recent graduates, current enrollment trends, and the share of working-age adults who participate in adult learning programs. Schooling must, moreover, be of sufficient *quality* in order for it to result in actual learning, or the acquisition of knowledge and skills (sometimes referred to as educational outcomes) by students. Various national and international student assessment instruments have been developed precisely to measure these learning outcomes. Finally, an education system must be able to impart the more complex competencies described above in graduates at all levels; that is, it must impart education that is *relevant* with respect to labor market demands and social conditions.

Formal Education in ECA Countries: High Attainment and Good Quality Relative to Current Income Levels

Starting from a high base, the ECA region has generally seen a significant improvement in educational attainment since the start of the transition toward market economies in the early 1990s. ECA countries went into the transition with an average of at least eight years of compulsory education; by 2006, this number had increased to nine years, corresponding roughly to the primary and lower secondary cycle (see annex 2A, table 2A.1). This increase closed the gap between most ECA and high-income OECD countries in terms of average years of education.

The most rapid growth in attainment has taken place at the tertiary level, albeit with considerable variation across the region. In fact, the increase in tertiary enrollment rates over the period 1999–2006 is higher for ECA countries (from below 40 percent to almost 50 percent) than for either high-income countries or the East Asia or Latin America regions. This growth has occurred across the region over the past decade, although Turkey and the South Eastern European and low-income CIS countries are trailing the EU10+1 and middle-income CIS countries. Gross tertiary enrollment rates in the ECA region as a whole demonstrate a pattern similar to those in secondary education: a dip in the mid-1990s, followed by a strong rebound. For the period 1990–2006 overall, the level of gross tertiary enrollments in the region were second only to the high-income countries (see figure 2.1).

ECA countries not only do well in terms of attainment, they also deliver relatively good-quality education, especially in the early grades. Indeed, many younger students in the region outperform their Western European peers in reading at the fourth-grade level. For example, students from the majority of participating ECA countries scored above the scale average[2] on the Progress in International Reading Literacy Study (PIRLS) in both 2001 and 2006. There are, however, important

Figure 2.1 Gross Enrollment Rates in Tertiary Education, by World Bank Region
(percent)

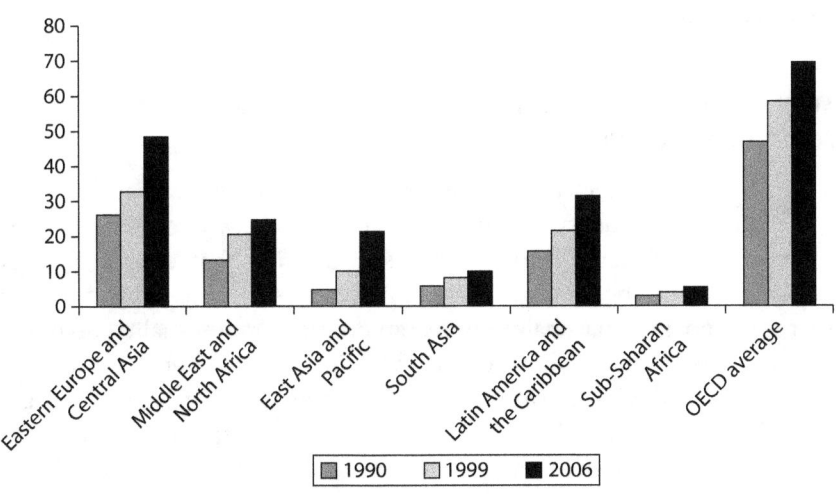

Source: Edstats Database.
Note: In the case of South Asia, the figure for 1999 is actually for 2000.

variations across the ECA region. Countries that have not joined the EU, for example, scored below the average, with the marked exception of the Russian Federation, which scored well above the average and demonstrated the greatest improvement between 2001 and 2006 (see figure 2.2). This strong performance in reading at the fourth-grade level indicates that schools in ECA countries are very capable of providing a quality education at the early stages.

Many—but not all—ECA countries continue to do well on international assessments of reading at or near the end of lower secondary education (e.g., Programme for International Student Assessment [PISA], Trends in International Mathematics and Science Study [TIMSS]) relative to the performance of other countries at the same income level.[3] Figure 2.3 provides a scatter plot of 2008 per capita GDP against the PISA 2009 reading scores of countries participating in PISA (with ECA countries highlighted by their letter acronyms). The figure shows a positive relationship between the two values, suggesting that 15-year-olds in countries with higher national incomes tend to perform better on the reading component of the PISA. Significantly, the ECA region seems divided. Certain countries (mainly the new EU member states but also Turkey and Serbia) lie above the regression line, indicating that the reading performance of their students is better than would be predicted on the basis of GDP per capita alone. Others lie below the regression line, including Romania, Montenegro, Bulgaria, Azerbaijan, and the Kyrgyz Republic. Students in these countries scored lower on the reading component of PISA than their national per capita GDP would have predicted.

Why Are Skills Emerging as a Problem if Education Systems Are Delivering?

Given high attainment levels, booming tertiary enrollments, and respectable educational quality at lower education levels, why are firms in the ECA region still complaining? This is a question that cannot be fully resolved, mainly because crucial information is missing. Unfortunately, there are no internationally comparable data on the quality of upper secondary or tertiary education or the relevance of education at these levels—information that would indicate whether graduates have the right skills for the modern job market There are international assessments on student competencies up to the age of 15 (usually the end of lower secondary education), but few seek jobs at that age. Beyond these early-stage assessments, no wide-ranging, fully reliable information exists on

Figure 2.2 Assessing a Skill—Reading Performance in the Fourth Grade: PIRLS Performance of ECA Countries, 2001 and 2006

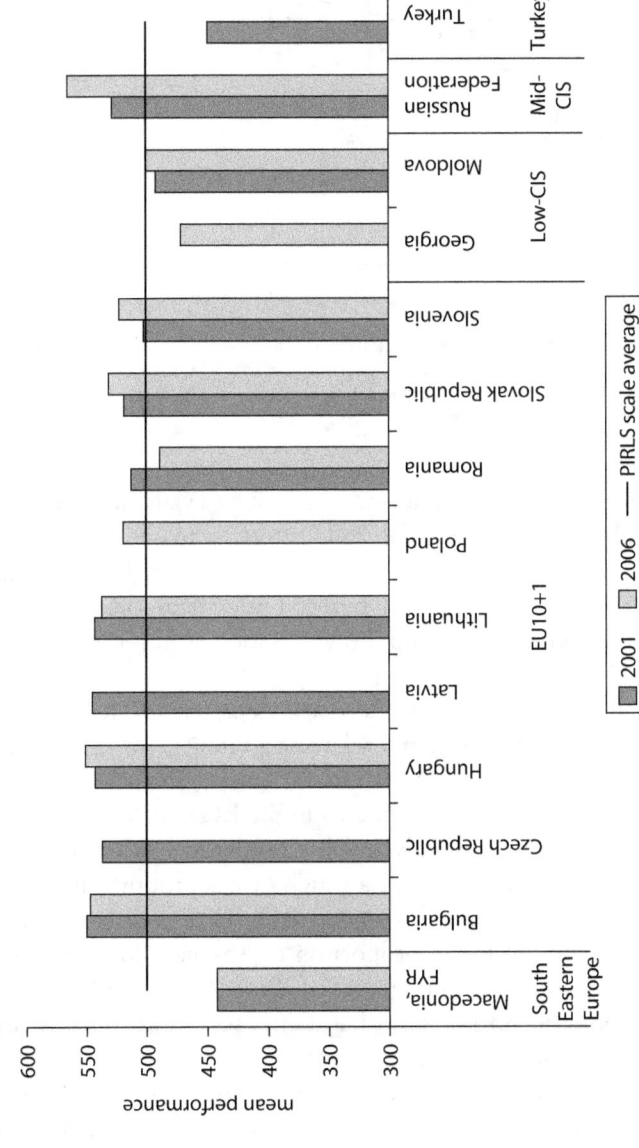

Source: World Bank staff calculations based on PIRLS test score data downloaded from EdStats Database.
Note: Thirty-five countries from around the world (although with limited participation from Latin American countries and no participation from Sub-Saharan Africa) participated in PIRLS 2001. In 2006, 41 countries participated, 15 of which were Western European countries. (A list of participating countries is available at http://nces.ed.gov/surveys/pirls/countries.asp.)

Figure 2.3 Analysis of Reading Competency of 15-Year-Old Students on the PISA 2009

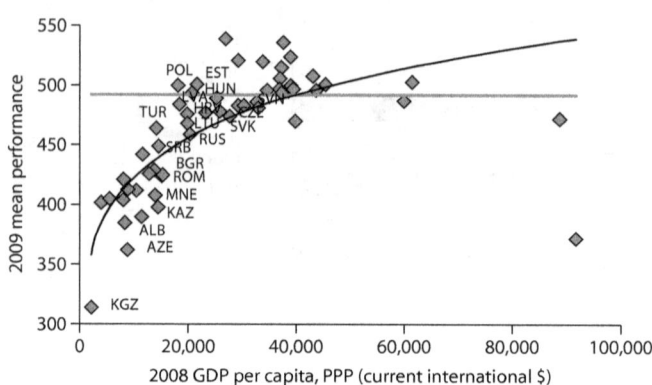

Sources: PISA 2009 Database and World Bank staff calculations based on World Development Indicators Database.
Note: The figure shows a regression line representing countries' predicted PISA scores based solely on GDP per capita, compared to the OECD mean reading score (horizontal line) on the assessment and GDP per capita in 2008. See "Abbreviations" for a key to country abbreviations.

student competencies. The information that is available includes basic cognitive skills but not behavioral skills, referring to such issues as teamwork and attitudes toward the job, which are increasingly sought after by employers. For policy makers to better understand the causes of the emerging skills bottleneck—and how to address it—this information deficit needs to be closed.

In addition to the data gaps, there are clear signs that ECA's education systems are facing problems related to quality, which are likely to be part of the reason why firms are complaining about declining skills. One problem is that too many students in the ECA region are simply not learning what firms increasingly need. Compared to OECD countries, for example, ECA countries have a much larger proportion of students who fail to acquire even the most basic skills. One measure of the magnitude of this problem is the proportion of 15-year-olds who scored at or below Level 1 on the reading part of PISA 2009 (see figure 2.4). In the Kyrgyz Republic, 83 percent of students scored at this low level; in Serbia, the proportion was 32.3 percent.

These students may not be failing according to national guidelines (and tests) for the competencies that a 15-year-old is expected to acquire, but their low scores on this assessment indicate serious deficiencies in their ability to use reading literacy as a tool to acquire knowledge and skills in other areas—an important competency needed to work in the

> **Box 2.2**
>
> **Testing for Reading Competency in the Programme for International Student Assessment (PISA)**
>
> It is important to understand what is meant by competencies in the context of reading. In PISA, "reading literacy" is defined as understanding, using, and reflecting on written texts in order to achieve one's goals, develop one's knowledge and potential, and participate in society (OECD 2007a, 284). This definition goes beyond the traditional notion of decoding information and a literal interpretation of what is written towards more applied tasks. Reading scores in all PISA cycles are reported according to five levels of proficiency, corresponding to tasks of varying difficulty, making it possible not only to rank students' performance but also to describe what students can do. Each successive reading level is associated with tasks of ascending difficulty. Students scoring below 355 points, that is, those who do not reach Level 1, are not able to routinely show the most basic reading skills that PISA seeks to measure.
>
> While such performance should not be interpreted to mean that these students have no literacy skills, performance below Level 1 does signal serious deficiencies in students' ability to use reading literacy as a tool for the acquisition of knowledge and skills in other areas—an important competency. These students may therefore be at risk not only of difficulties in their initial transition from education to work, but may fail to benefit from further education and learning opportunities throughout life.

global economy. Similar weaknesses can be observed when looking at the share of 15-year-olds exhibiting serious problems with numeracy skills (e.g., see box 2.3 on Turkey). Consequently, these students may experience difficulties if they continue past secondary school and, of perhaps greater concern, when they attempt to enter the modern workforce. It is thus likely that when firms complain about workers not having the right skills, they are, in part, complaining about the fact that too many students simply did not learn enough during compulsory education.

Another reason why employers perceive a skills shortage may be that ECA education systems are successful in imparting basic skills, but less successful in imparting problem-solving skills. For example, it can be reasonably interpreted from the discrepancy in students' performance on the PIRLS and the PISA reading assessments (see figures 2.2 and 2.3,

Figure 2.4 Assessing a Competency—Reading Level at Age 15: Share of Students Scoring Level 1 or Below on Reading Section of PISA 2009
(percent)

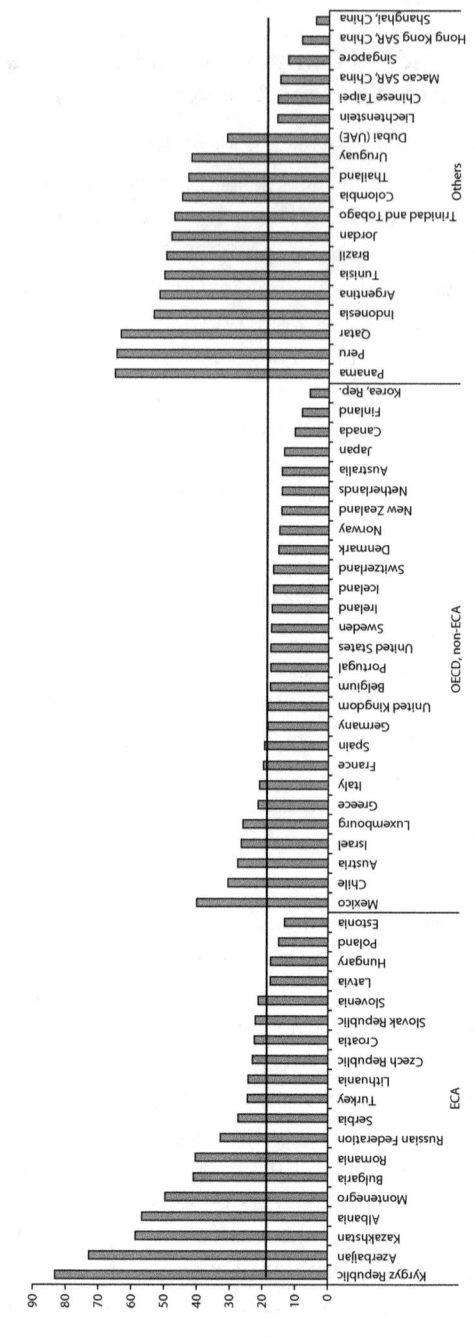

Source: World Bank Staff calculations based on OECD PISA 2009 database.
Note: Horizontal line is the average percentage across OECD countries.

Box 2.3

Turkey: Many Students Fail to Acquire Even the Most Basic Proficiencies

Learning outcomes are vastly uneven across different types of schools in Turkey, resulting in lifelong inequities for students, depending on the location of their schools. While roughly one-third of 15-year-olds in the country had test scores in mathematics on the PISA 2006 that were above the OECD average of 500, nearly 50 percent of students achieved only the most basic proficiency (i.e., they scored below 420). Equivalent disparities were found with respect to reading and science.

Figure B2.3   Distribution of PISA 2006 Math Scores by Type of School in Turkey

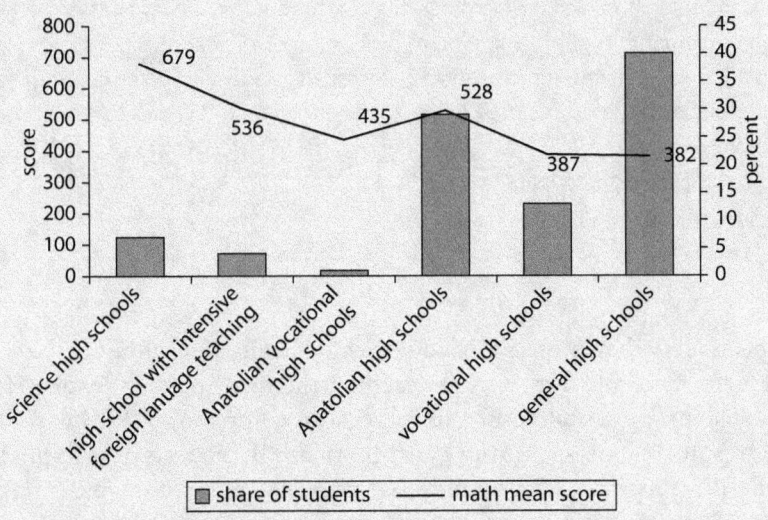

Source: World Bank 2011a.

Well-performing students in Turkey are located in a handful of specialized (elite) schools across the country (science high schools, high schools with intensive foreign language training, and Anatolian high schools). Access to these types of schools, which have better teaching and learning conditions, is controlled by examination and highly correlated with the income and wealth of students' families. One in two students in science high schools and one in three students

(continued next page)

Box 2.3 (*continued*)

in the other two types of high schools belong to the richest 20 percent of households in the country. These asymmetries in access to different types of public schools, and the variable quality of education that these schools provide, constitute a formidable barrier to improving the quality of education for all in Turkey. International evidence shows that very selective systems that track students at an early age, such as the Turkish system, not only significantly increase educational inequality, but also reduce a country's average educational performance (Hanushek and Wößmann 2008).

On a positive note, Turkish students did significantly better on the PISA 2009 test (compared to their performance in 2006) in all tested areas: science, reading, and math. This improvement may be a first indication that recent reforms, most notably the 2004 reform in the primary school curricula—which moved to a student-centered, constructivist approach—may have started to pay off. Despite the improvements, though, a significant proportion of 15-year-olds (25 percent in reading, 30 percent in math, and 42 percent in science) in Turkey continue to perform below even the most basic proficiency levels. It is critical to remember, moreover, that the PISA results represent only the 57 percent of 15-year-olds who are still in the educational system.

Source: PISA 2009 Database; World Bank forthcoming.

respectively) that most ECA countries do well in teaching children to "learn to read" but less well in teaching them to "read to learn." These conclusions are tentative in nature because comparing PIRLS and PISA test results is not straightforward, in that PIRLS tests fourth-graders, while PISA assesses 15-year-olds. Nevertheless, one reasonable interpretation from the discrepancy in their performance on these two tests is that ECA countries do not impart advanced competencies to students as well as they impart basic reading skills.

As a result, 15-year-olds in the ECA region may be able to read proficiently, but not adequately enough to access, store, and utilize information from that reading, which can be described as *functional* literacy. An underlying reason for this underperformance may be that education systems in the region continue to place too much emphasis on conveying facts and knowledge, instead of teaching problem solving and critical thinking (see box 2.4 on Russia). Yet it is exactly these latter skills that more and more firms seem to be seeking.

An additional problem may be that ECA countries are not good at imparting skills that are in demand but not being tested. For instance, behavioral skills (discussed in chapter 1) are consistently being demanded by employers but are apparently not well provided by ECA education systems. The extent to which they are struggling on this front is difficult to quantify, however, since tests such as PISA do not measure these skills (or, for that matter, other skills in high demand, such as knowledge of information technology or a foreign language).

Box 2.4

Russia: Building Higher-Order Skills Is Proving Difficult

Russian students perform relatively well on the knowledge, or factual, dimension of international learning assessments. For example, Russia was the top-ranked country on PIRLS 2006, a test of the reading achievement of grade 4 students. Russian students were also relatively highly ranked on TIMSS 2007, a curriculum-based test of math and science achievement of 4th and 8th graders. By way of contrast, Russian students did relatively poorly on the PISA 2006, which tests a student's ability to use knowledge and thinking skills to solve complex problems in real-world situations. Indeed, detailed analysis of TIMSS results shows that the scores of Russian students on factual knowledge were significantly higher than their scores on reasoning using this knowledge.

These results suggest that the traditional strength of the Russian education system is in conveying facts or knowledge or both, not problem solving or critical thinking skills. A recent detailed analysis (Tumeneva 2006) shows that the Russian curriculum still reflects deep traditions of the Soviet curriculum, focusing more on systematic academic knowledge and less on the application of this knowledge, or critical reasoning. Russian textbooks, for example, typically use texts that are preselected to illustrate specific ideas or themes; Russian pedagogy does not require students to work with real-world situations or original texts. The recent introduction of a school-leaving exam, which also serves as a centralized university entrance examination, has strengthened this orientation. The test places a heavy emphasis on factual knowledge, which encourages teachers and students to memorize answers.

These weaknesses in the Russian curriculum and pedagogy were widely discussed after the results of the PISA 2000 were published, which showed

(continued next page)

> **Box 2.4** *(continued)*
>
> relatively poor performance by Russian students on higher-order skills. The Ministry of Education and Science subsequently led two efforts to develop more "competency-based" standards. Slowly, these efforts have started to show results. Significant improvements in student scores on TIMSS and PIRLS have been observed over time, and for the first time Russian students showed improvements in PISA in 2009. Still, the 2009 score (in reading) was below the score obtained by Russian students in 2000. Even on PIRLS, the biggest improvements in student scores relate to factual content (Kouznetsova 2009).
>
> Many educators in Russia believe that the school-leaving exam needs to be changed to emphasize problem solving and critical thinking skills. This would encourage further changes in standards, teaching, and assessments at the school level. Changes are also needed at the higher education level, which currently promotes narrow specializations over transferrable skills and key competencies.
>
> *Source:* World Bank staff assessment, based on ongoing research by the State University Higher School of Economics, Moscow.

As noted earlier, where it is measured, educational quality in the region has not consistently improved over the past decade in many ECA countries. Only a few countries have managed to improve their test results on all international tests since 1995 (see annex 2A, table 2A.2). The results of four countries (Bulgaria, the former Yugoslav Republic of Macedonia, the Czech Republic, and Croatia) suggest that the quality of education has deteriorated over time, while the majority of ECA countries have mixed results (some of their test results show improvement over time, while others show deteriorating results). Three countries—Turkey, Latvia, and Poland—show steady improvement across all tests and over time. Moreover, three latecomers to international testing—Serbia, Armenia, and the Kyrgyz Republic—show improvement over a shorter time horizon (Serbia and Armenia first participated in international assessments in 2003; the Kyrgyz Republic, in 2006). However, PISA 2009 brought some positive news: several ECA countries (including Bulgaria, Romania, Serbia, the Kyrgyz Republic, and Turkey) showed large improvements from their 2006 results.

Moreover, indirect evidence suggests that the quality of upper secondary and tertiary education also may not be improving. Unfortunately, there is no equivalent of the PISA, TIMSS, or PIRLS for upper secondary or higher education which would enable objective comparisons of the quality of student competencies across countries and across time. Moreover, no ECA country has yet put in place a monitoring system to track the employment and wage outcomes of recent graduates in order to assess their employability and the relevance of their education.[4] This lack of data makes it impossible to draw firm conclusions about the quality of upper secondary and tertiary education. Instead, this book looks at indirect evidence to make inferences.

Limited improvements on international assessments at the end of lower secondary education (PISA and TIMSS) imply only limited improvements in the quality of upper secondary education (a finding that will persist unless upper secondary institutions can make up for the declining competencies of incoming students). One factor, however, may have helped improve upper secondary education: fewer students are enrolled in terminal vocational schools where, in many ECA countries, the quality of schooling has historically varied a great deal. As the experience of Poland shows (see box 4.2), providing students with further general secondary education instead of terminal vocation programs, which can have a big impact on providing them the types of competencies measured by international assessments.

The fact that the quality of compulsory education has not been reliably improving is discussed further in chapter 3. Here, it suffices to note that whatever policy measures have been tried in the past approximately 15 years (the period for which international test results are available) have not worked consistently to improve learning outcomes. Most troubling, the shift to smaller classes and smaller student-teacher ratios (documented in chapter 3) and the consequent increase in per student spending do not seem to be delivering better learning outcomes.

At the tertiary level, the indirect evidence is again not encouraging. It seems probable that the rapid expansion of tertiary education (see figure 2.1) has resulted in poorer-quality education for a number of reasons. To begin with, this expansion took place during a period when few countries had operational quality assurance agencies. When these agencies finally became operational, several acted swiftly to point out the widespread noncompliance of many new institutions of higher learning with even minimum quality standards (see chapter 5). Moreover, the new "mass" nature of tertiary education meant that less qualified students continued to study. As noted earlier, when as many as a third of students at the age of 15 are functionally illiterate in Serbia (according to the 2009 PISA results), such students will unquestionably not graduate with the same level of proficiency from tertiary education as did the smaller, more qualified university cohorts of the past.

In addition, a great deal of the expansion of tertiary education has occurred in new institutions whose short-term motives may be driven more by profits than a need to guard their institutional reputations. Although private, profit-based tertiary education providers can create a more flexible, responsive university system (see chapter 5), there are signs of persistent problems in this sector, including mounting quantitative (as well as anecdotal) evidence of fraud, corruption, and unethical behavior—the scope of which is extensive—raising doubts about its capacity to ensure that students graduate with the requisite skills (and not just diplomas). For example, a recent survey of university students in several ECA countries found that more than 60 percent of respondents knew other students who had purchased either entrance to the university or a specific grade (see figure 2.5).

Finally, a large part of the expansion of tertiary education took place in part-time (or weekend) and long-distance learning programs. The format of these programs was new and their quality unknown. In 2009, for example, half of Poland's undergraduate students were enrolled in weekend programs. In Romania in the same year, 42 percent of students were enrolled in private universities, 66 percent of whom were part-time or long-distance students. It is impossible to determine whether these

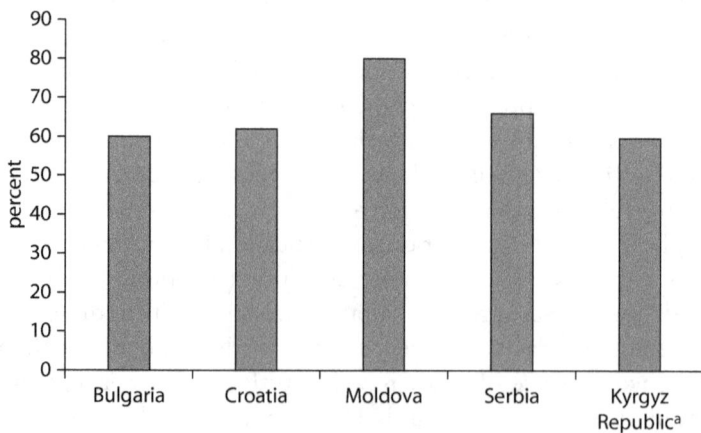

Figure 2.5 Students Aware of Bribery for Grade or Exam in their Faculty

Source: Heyneman, Anderson, and Nuraliyeva 2008.
Note: Data are from a random sample of university students.
a. Data for the Kyrgyz Republic are based on a slightly different question: students were asked if they had "personal experiences with corruption and bribery in their university." The value reported in the figure is the median value of Kyrgyz-owned universities reported in table 3 of Heyneman, Anderson, and Nuraliyeva 2008.

students are receiving the same quality education as their peers in full-time, regular programs.

Students May Not Be Acquiring the Right Skills

It is not only probable that the quality of graduates' problem-solving and behavioral skills are inadequate, but students at both the secondary and tertiary levels may also be graduating with the wrong set of skills. At the secondary level, for example, the collapse of vocational schools may have been too abrupt, stripping students of a viable option to obtain technical skills that are in strong demand. At the tertiary level, too many students may be enrolling in low-cost programs (that is, the only programs available to them), rather than programs that would meet current and future employer needs.

Vocational school systems in the ECA region rapidly declined in the early years of transition for a number of reasons, as students fled from these schools in large numbers (see box 2.5 for a brief history of the vocational school system in the region.) This decline happened in virtually all ECA countries (see figure 2.6), with the noticeable exceptions of Uzbekistan, Serbia, Croatia, the Czech Republic, Moldova, and Turkey. In some countries—Belarus and Armenia, for instance—vocational school systems have become virtually nonexistent.

Students abandoned vocational schools because these schools failed to adjust to new realities. Nevertheless, there is evidence to suggest that firms still seem to want vocational and technical skills. For instance, as mentioned in chapter 1, students who finish school with vocational or technical skills—especially in middle-income CIS countries—are less likely to end up unemployed than students with only a general secondary education (Turkey being an exception). This finding has been corroborated by recent surveys of graduates regarding the school-to-work transition in Serbia and Ukraine (the two only countries where such surveys have been conducted). As table 2.1 shows, it seems easier for students who have technical or vocational training to transition into a job than for those who have only a general education. In Serbia, one-third of graduates of a three-year vocational training course find their first job within six months, compared with only one-fourth of graduates of general secondary schools. In Ukraine, less than 30 percent of graduates of secondary technical schools look for their first job for more than a year, compared to 44 percent of graduates of general secondary schools.[5]

Box 2.5

The History of Vocational Education in the ECA Region

Historically, secondary education has been heavily weighted in favor of vocational training in the ECA region. The former planned economies entered the transition with a very high percentage of upper secondary school students enrolled in vocational programs—averaging 61.3 percent of all such students in 1989 (see figure B2.5 below). Most of these programs were terminal, that is, they did not provide students access to higher education. Most also involved applied training in nearby public enterprises, which typically recruited many program graduates. The most highly vocationalized programs were in Central and Eastern Europe, where the average share of vocational secondary school students was over 70 percent. In Turkey, the single nontransition country in the ECA region, secondary education also has a strong vocational focus, with programs patterned after the German dual-system model.

Figure B2.5 Global Comparison of Average Vocational Enrollment of Upper Secondary Students by Region, 1989, 1999, and 2007
(percent)

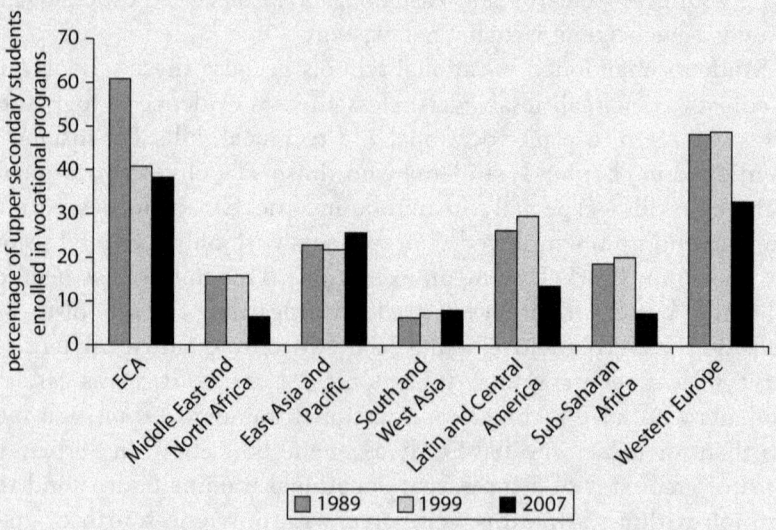

Source: UIS (UNESCO Institute for Statistics).
Note: Percentages represent averages for those countries for which data was available.

(continued next page)

Box 2.5 *(continued)*

The inherited vocational focus of secondary education in ECA countries reflects the incentives of planned economies and the strong linkages that such economies forged between training institutions and state-owned enterprises. Since general secondary education was seen primarily as a preparation for higher education, enrollments in this track were limited to the few students who were expected to progress to university.

Vocational education in the previous system was thus the primary means of training workers for specific jobs in public enterprises. These enterprises typically contributed to the curriculum design of vocational education programs, provided instructors and facilities for practical training, and recruited many graduates, often for lifetime jobs. Labor hoarding proved an effective approach for ensuring that enterprises could meet planned production quotas.

Economic transition has brought new requirements that necessitate widespread changes in vocational education programs, but shrinking budgets have made it hard to carry out these changes, particularly the hiring of instructors and curriculum designers with needed skills. The move to a competitive market economy has also profoundly changed the setting in which firms operate—hard budget constraints and falling sales have put an end to labor hoarding and created widespread unemployment. These conditions have made it impossible for most enterprises to continue to offer training to vocational school students.

Source: Authors.

In sum, the quality and relevance of vocational education in the ECA region appear to be deteriorating at the same time that firms are increasing their demands for higher-level technical skills.

Adult Learning Is Limited in the Region

Demographic trends in the ECA region imply that young people entering the job market directly from the formal schooling sector make up a smaller proportion of the workforce today than just 10 or 20 years ago, a trend that will continue. When firms complain of a skills shortage, they are not referring solely to the quality of new labor market entrants; they are also indicating that the skills they need cannot be found among all workers in the economy. Given the aging of the population in many countries, it

Figure 2.6 Share of Upper Secondary Students Enrolled in Vocational Programs in ECA Countries over Time
(percent)

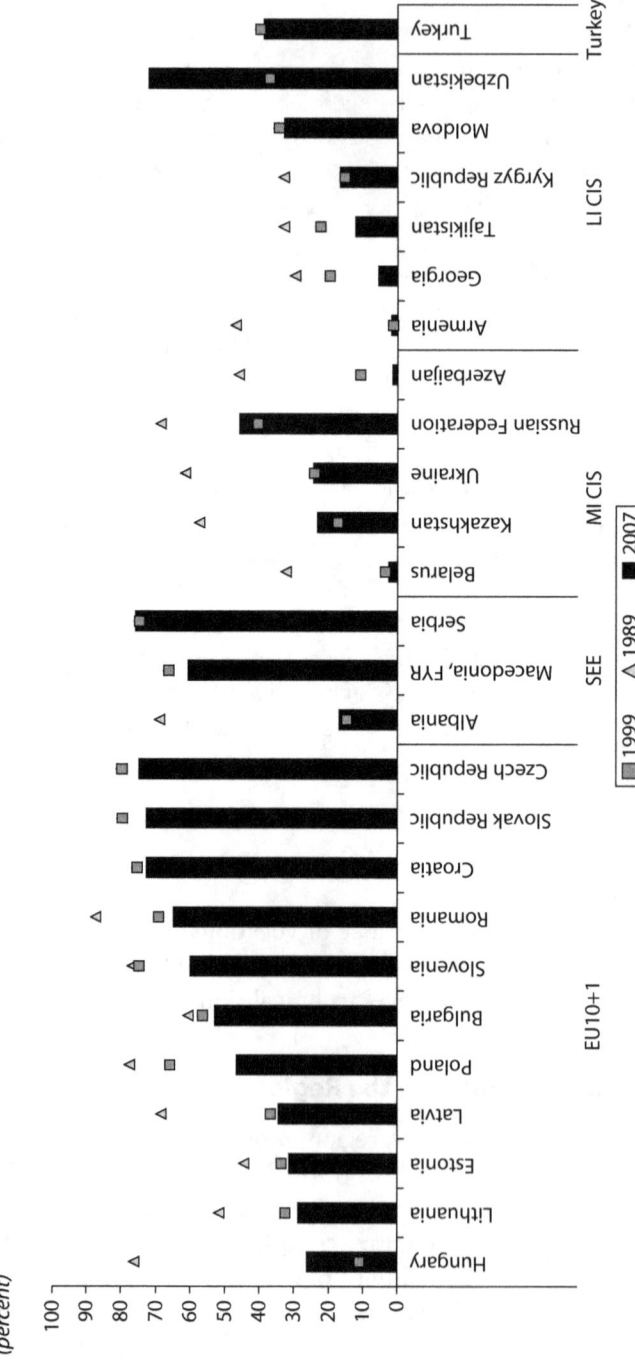

Source: UIS.
Note: LI = low-income, MI = middle-income.

Table 2.1 Time Needed to Find First Job by Level of Educational Attainment in Serbia and Ukraine
(percent)

a. Serbia

	Primary	Secondary trade	Secondary vocational	Secondary general	College	University
No search	7.0	5.7	4.7	9.6	7.7	11.7
1–3 months	22.0	25.7	22.3	19.2	23.1	26.0
4–6 months	8.4	7.5	7.2	6.7	9.1	12.8
7–12 months	10.6	10.8	12.4	8.7	18.0	9.4
1–2 yrs	15.0	15.2	19.5	8.4	13.2	21.6
> 2 yrs	37.0	35.1	33.9	47.3	29.0	18.4
Total	100	100	100	100	100	100

Source: Huitfeldt, Johansen, and Kogan 2008.

b. Ukraine

	Less than secondary	Secondary vocational	Secondary general	Junior specialist	University
No search	0.9	7.3	4.8	9.0	26.6
1–3 months	32.7	49.5	31.4	58.2	44.4
4–6 months	6.7	7.6	10.5	7.4	8.4
7–12 months	7.5	6.9	9.6	6.1	5.2
1–2 yrs	5.2	11.8	9.1	4.5	5.4
> 2 yrs	47.0	16.9	34.7	14.7	10.0
Total	100	100	100	100	100

Source: Huitfeldt, Johansen, and Kogan 2008.

will become increasingly important to ensure that all workers—not just those recently out of school—continue to upgrade their skills.

As much as one-half of the skills and knowledge that an individual accumulates over his or her lifetime is gained during the period after formal schooling (Heckman 1999). A large international literature documented by empirical evidence—largely for OECD countries—shows that adult education and training advances labor market outcomes, including higher wages and employment. This type of training also has a strong positive effect on productivity and a high internal rate of return (see, for example, OECD 2004a and Dearden, Reed, and van Reenen 2000). Significant evidence from countries around the world also documents that market failures tend to lead to underinvestment in adult education and training on the part of both individuals and firms; here, the countries of ECA are no exception (see chapter 6).

In fact, many countries in the ECA region have not yet begun to adequately promote adult learning as a means of addressing the current skills deficit and improving worker productivity in the face of declining demographics. Although a substantial share of workers participate in adult education and training programs in several ECA countries, the percentages vary across the region. Even in countries that have relatively high availability of continuing vocational education and training programs, the people who take part in these programs tend to be already skilled workers, rather than nonskilled and "nonproductive" workers. Finally, it seems that in many ECA countries, programs to help retrain or reskill the unemployed only reach a few of the unemployed.

Adult learning programs (see box 2.6) have remained a blind spot in education and training policy across much of the ECA region. A key component of the socialist production process, worker training has undergone substantial changes as a result of the transition to market economies. Under communism, such training focused exclusively on continuing vocational training of the employed workforce. With the exception of socialist Yugoslavia, unemployment in these countries was nonexistent by definition, hence adult education and training of the unemployed was not a feature of their education and training systems.

Partly, adult education and training remains a blind spot in the region because remarkably few data on the sector are available. While several OECD countries have been conducting national surveys of adult training in firms for many years, such surveys have not been comparative across countries and data for ECA countries is sparse. Even OECD countries focus on the quantity of this learning (i.e., number of participants, hours of learning), not its quality and relevance. For the ECA region as a whole, the 2005 and 2008 Business Environment and Enterprise Performance Surveys (BEEPS 2005, 2008) included some limited questions on adult training by firm size and some degree of worker characteristics; however, problems relating to cross-country comparability make it difficult to reach solid conclusions. In the EU, the firm-based Continuing Vocational Training Surveys (CVTS) of 1999 and 2005, which offer information on worker training, and the Adult Education Survey (AES) of 2007, which offers data on individual participation in formal or nonformal education and training, are the first surveys that permitted cross-country analysis of adult education and training patterns. Both included a number of ECA countries and serve as the basis of much of the analysis in this book. The data used here, therefore, center disproportionately on the EU10+1.

> **Box 2.6**
>
> **Two Forms of Adult Learning**
>
> Two categories of adult education and training are addressed in this report; both categories aim at adults between 25 and 64 years of age (for further discussion, including on the financing of adult education and training, see chapter 6):
>
> *Continuing Vocational Education and Training (CVET).* These programs are aimed at people who are currently employed. First, they offer in-service training designed to aid employees in acquiring new competencies or improving existing ones relevant to their firms' operations. In-service training plays a critical role in increasing the human capital of the existing workforce, addressing skills depletion, and keeping older workers productive for longer, as well as alleviating skills mismatches. Second, these programs offer education and training to individuals who seek to develop skills that will raise their chances of moving to a better job (that is, education and training not related to their current job).
>
> *Retraining and remedial basic skills training ("second-chance" education).* This type of training aims at the nonemployed, that is, the unemployed and people outside the labor force who face skills-related barriers to employment. In many ECA countries, high percentages of the population continue to lack basic skills as a result of leaving school early or poor learning achievement. Most ECA countries provide training as part of active labor market programs and there is reason to believe that well-designed programs can have positive economic returns (Betcherman, Olivas, and Dar 2004). In addition, "second-chance" education programs address (basic) skills shortages, including literacy, in order to help youths and adults access the labor market and further their education and training.

ECA Lags Behind West European Countries in Continuing Education and Training

Today, the provision of continuing vocational education and training (CVET) in firms varies considerably across the ECA region. Figure 2.7 presents data from the 2008 BEEPS survey in ECA countries, showing the share of manufacturing firms that offered formal training programs to full-time employees. The variation is wide between the Czech Republic and Estonia, where about 70 percent of firms provide such training, and Azerbaijan, where only about 10 percent do. With few exceptions, the

Figure 2.7 Share of ECA Firms that Offer Formal Training Programs for Permanent, Full-Time Employees, 2008

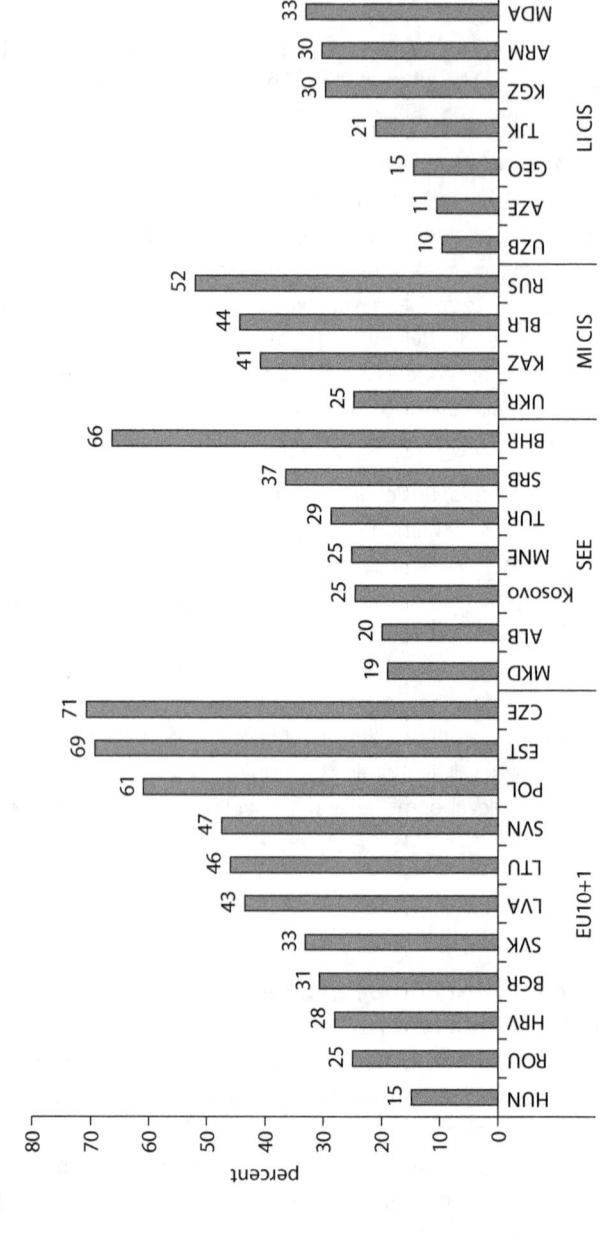

Source: World Bank Staff calculations based on raw dataset for EBRD–World Bank 2009.
Note: LI = low-income, MI = middle-income. See "Acronyms and Abbreviations" for a key to country abbreviations.

distribution broadly follows a GDP per capita pattern, with low-income CIS countries on one side and advanced EU10+1 countries on the other.

Independent of the data source, the Czech Republic, Slovenia, Estonia, and the Slovak Republic appear to lead the ECA region in adult education and training. Many low-income CIS countries occupy the bottom end of the distribution, with the bulk of South Eastern European and middle-income CIS countries in between. However, there are some surprises at both the top and bottom end of the distribution. Bosnia and Herzegovina is in the top half, among EU10+1 countries, while Hungary, Romania, and Bulgaria—despite EU membership—are in the bottom half.

Data from the 2005 CVTS show that more workers in the Czech Republic and Slovenia participate in training proportionately than elsewhere in the EU (see figure 2.8, panel a). Interestingly, results in countries that are thought to be similar, such as the Baltic states, can differ significantly. For example, Estonia shows consistently higher training participation than Lithuania and Latvia. Individual-level data from the 2007 AES confirm this picture (figure 2.8, panel b).

However, several country studies have shown that while the share of firms that offer training may be high in many ECA countries, the share of actual workers who participate in training is relatively low and the hours of training are limited. A recent enterprise survey in Russia, for example, revealed that while 58 percent of firms in a pooled sample of small, medium, and large firms conducted training, only 7.7 percent of skilled and 1.4 percent of unskilled workers actually participated in the training (Tan et al. 2007).[6]

Figure 2.9 (panel a) presents the percentage of EU workers participating in (rather than firms offering) continuing vocational training in those firms that offer training. In the Czech Republic, close to 70 percent of workers in firms that offer continuing vocational training participate in training activities, whereas the equivalent share in Hungary is less than 25 percent. Moreover, panel b shows that with the exception of the Czech Republic, the Slovak Republic, and Slovenia, workers in the EU10 countries of the ECA region participate in such training for fewer hours than their EU peers. This implies that the productivity effects of worker training may be lower in ECA countries than in Western European countries (although obviously the productivity effect also depends on the quality and relevance of the training, which is not captured here).

Compared to other countries around the world, the ECA region fares similarly in terms of uneven participation in CVET, which is concentrated among workers with the best labor market opportunities. According

Figure 2.8 Employee- and Firm-level Data on Worker Participation in CVET Courses, EU10 and other EU Member States
(percent)

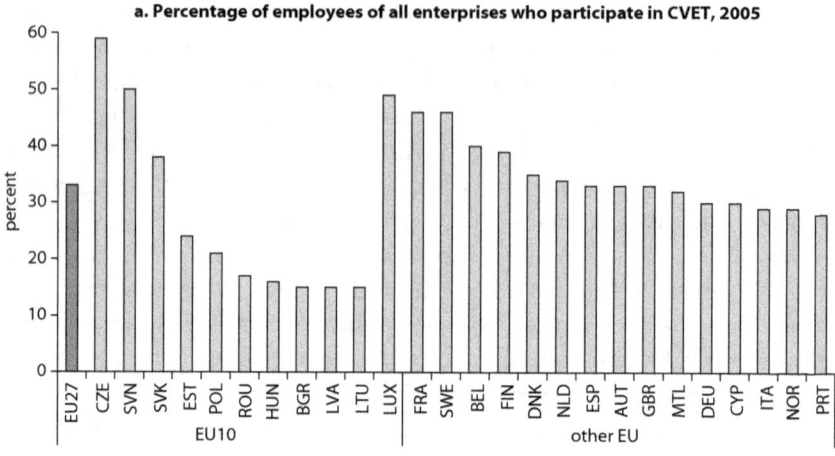

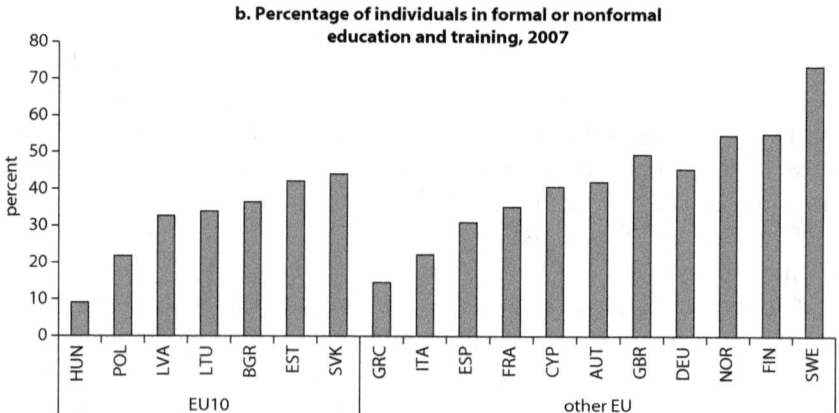

Source: World Bank staff calculations based on CVTS 2005 (a) and AES 2007 (b).
Note: See "Abbreviations" for a key to country abbreviations and groupings.

to BEEPS 2005 data, skilled workers in all ECA countries are more likely to participate in education and training than other workers in the same firm. Figure 2.10 shows that overall, firm-based worker training data mask substantial differences in training rates between skilled labor on one hand and nonskilled and so-called nonproductive workers on the other, with the latter two groups having a lower (sometimes much lower) participation rate than that of skilled workers. This finding is

Figure 2.9 Training Length and Percentage of Employees Participating in CVET Courses, EU10 and EU27
(percent)

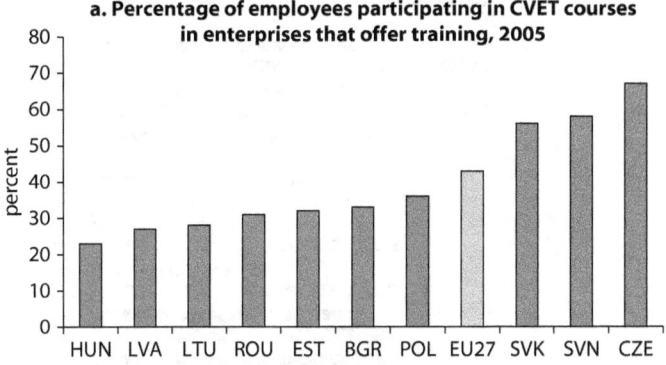

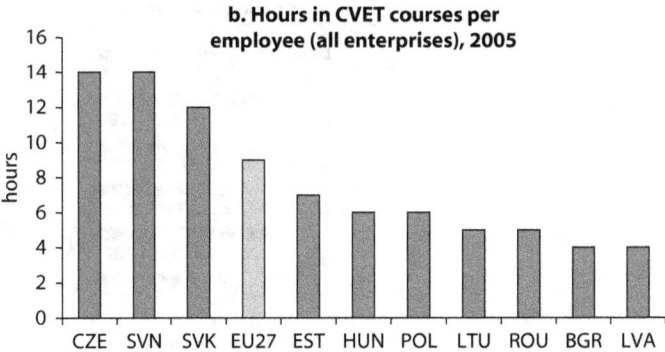

Source: World Bank staff calculations based on CVTS 2005.
Note: See "Abbreviations" for a key to country abbreviations.

consistent with the patterns of adult education and training around the world.

The extent of worker training also varies between large and small firms, with the variation generally larger in ECA countries than in EU countries that have highly developed economies. Large firms worldwide are substantially more likely to invest in worker training than small firms. This tendency may provide one explanation for the relatively lower adult training rates in many ECA countries compared to EU countries with more advanced economies: in the former, the enterprise sector consists primarily of small firms—the very kind that are less likely to make training available.

Figure 2.10 ECA Firms that Offer Formal Training to Employees, by Employee Category, 2005
(percent)

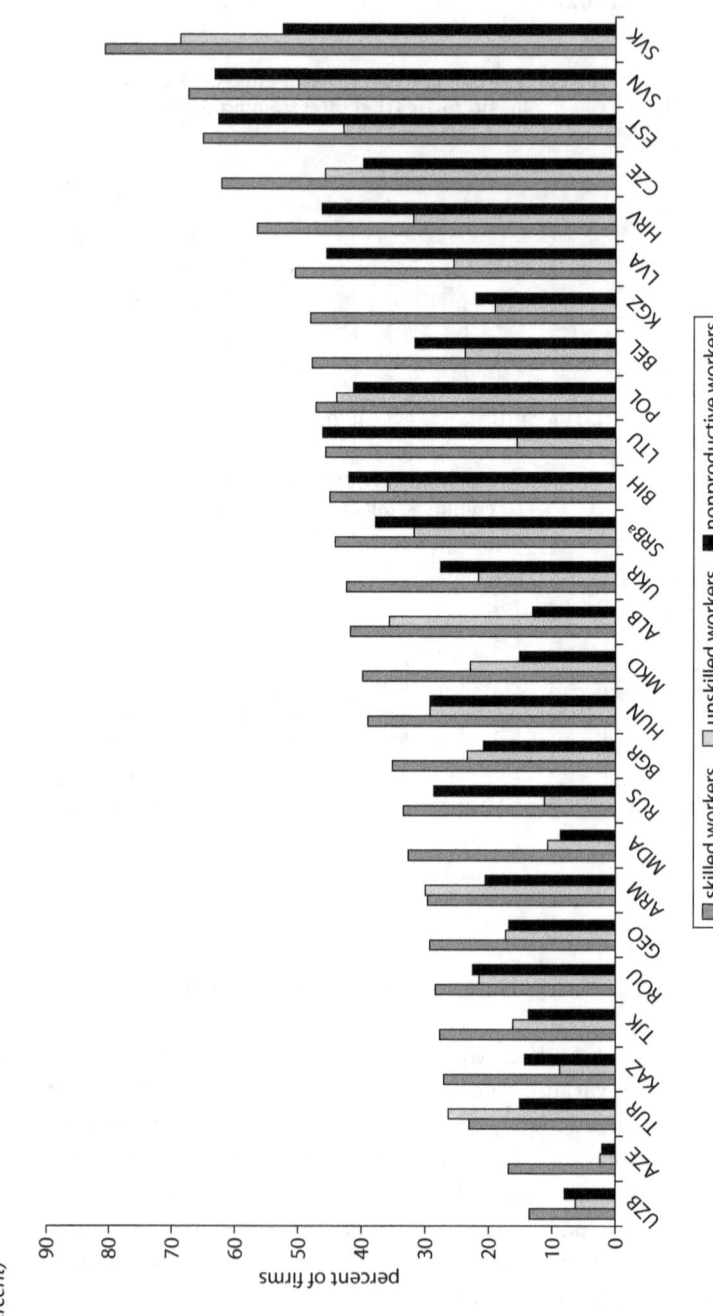

Source: World Bank staff calculations based on EBRD-World Bank 2005.
Note: See "Abbreviations" for a key to country abbreviations.
a. Results for Serbia (SRB) include Montenegro.

Figure 2.11 (panel a) presents 2005 BEEPS data that confirm the internationally well-established fact that large firms provide more training than small firms. The bottom panel presents data from the 2005 CVTS on the best- and worst-performing ECA countries on this measure—the Czech Republic and Bulgaria, respectively—and compares this data with the best-performing EU country in the CVTS sample, the United Kingdom. In Bulgaria and the Czech Republic, there is a wide gap in the share of companies that offer training between small and large enterprises, although at different levels, while the United Kingdom shows little divergence between small and large firms.

Very Limited Training Programs for the Unemployed

Although retraining, if well designed, can be important for promoting employment, the actual use of this intervention for the unemployed in many parts of ECA appears limited. The introduction of passive and active employment policies in ECA at the start of the transition gave priority to interventions that retrained and prequalified workers who had lost their jobs as part of privatization and enterprise restructuring. Today, retraining programs are a well-established component of active labor market policies (ALMPs) throughout the ECA region. While there is no comparative data across the entire region, table 2.2 shows that training participants represent sizable shares of overall ALMP participants in the EU10 countries, in some cases, over 50 percent (similar to the EU27 average). However, not all unemployed participate in ALMPs, and training actually reaches few unemployed overall in EU10 countries compared to the EU27 average, with the exception of Slovenia.

Moreover, it appears that "second-chance" education programs form a relatively small part of the adult education and training system in many ECA countries. These programs are a key tool for helping early dropouts and workers who have lost their jobs in mid-career improve their skills and re-enter the labor market. There is currently no ECA-wide, individual-level data that would allow for a breakdown of participation in second-chance programs by worker characteristics. However, 2007 AES data show that EU10 countries appear to have fewer individuals with lower schooling levels in adult education and training programs than do most older member states (see figure 2.12, panel a). The EU10 also appear to have substantially fewer inactive workers and unemployed workers participating in nonformal education and training programs than most of their EU neighbors (see figure 2.12, panel b).

Figure 2.11 Large and Small Firms that Offer Training to Skilled Employees, ECA, EU, and United Kingdom, 2005
(percent)

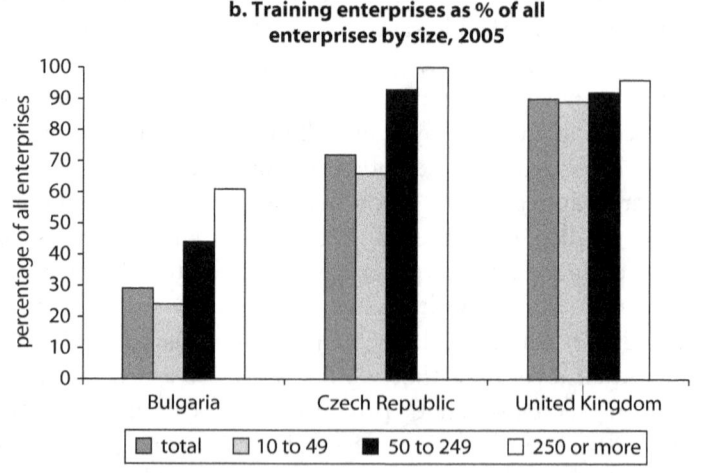

Sources: (a) World Bank staff calculations based on raw dataset of EBRD-World Bank 2005. (b) World Bank staff calculations based on CVTS 2005.
Notes: BEEPS defines small firms as fewer than 50 employees, medium firms as between 50 and 249 employees, and large firms as more than 250 employees. See "Abbreviations" for a key to country abbreviations.
a. Results for Serbia (SRB) include Montenegro.

Table 2.2 Training Participants as Share of Participants in Active Labor Market Policies and of Total Unemployed, EU27 and EU10, 2006

	Training participants as % of ALMP participants	Training participants as % of total unemployed
EU27	33.6	19.8
Bulgaria	10.9	3.8
Czech Republic	12.6	2.0
Estonia	58.4	2.8
Latvia	52.3	6.3
Lithuania	41.0	7.9
Hungary	19.9	4.4
Poland	21.8	4.2
Romania	18.0	2.1
Slovenia	56.8	19.7
Slovak Republic	1.6	0.6

Source: World Bank staff calculations based on LFS database (Eurostat).

Indeed, anecdotal evidence suggests that remedial basic education and training represent a small share of the retraining programs of public employment services in these countries. (Such programs are often coupled with nongovernmental organization [NGO]-provided social inclusion activities). However, several new EU member states have launched second-chance education and training programs, including components on literacy and functional literacy, as part of programs funded by the European Social Fund.

Summary

This chapter has sought to understand why employers in the ECA region increasingly complain of a skills shortage despite high levels of educational attainment, respectable educational quality, and booming tertiary enrollments in ECA countries. Although the arguments presented here can necessarily be based only on the data currently available, the findings nevertheless point to problems with the limited quality and relevance of education as contributing sources of the skills deficit. Graduates of upper secondary and tertiary education appear to either not be learning enough while in school or acquiring skills that are not in demand on the labor market. In addition, the decline of vocational schools at the upper secondary level may have intensified the skills shortage.

Figure 2.12 Adult Education and Training Program Participants in EU, 2007

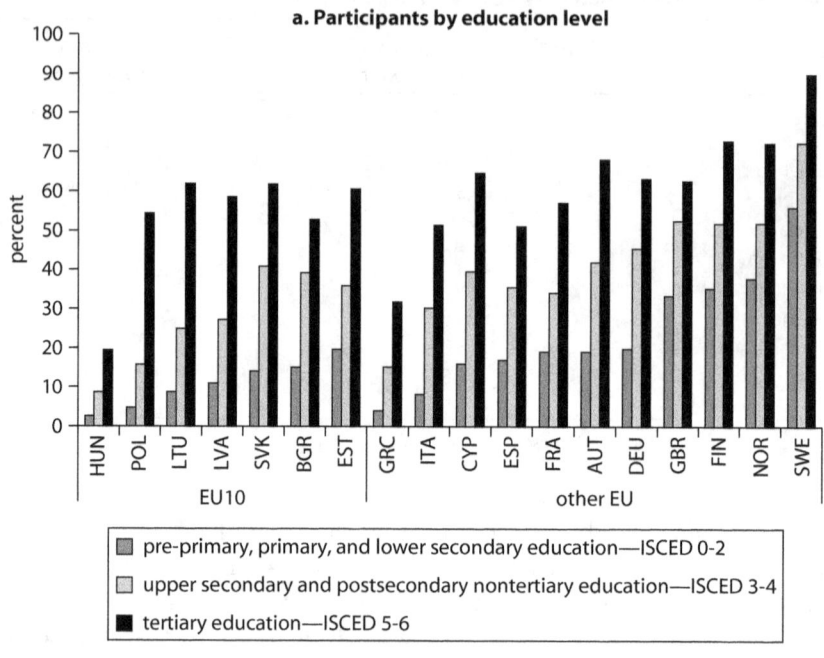

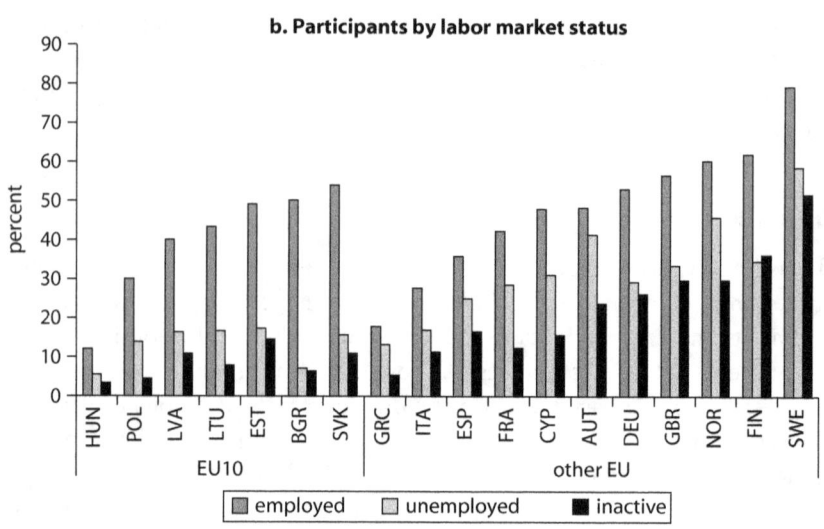

Source: Bank staff calculations based on AES 2007.
Note: ISCED = International Standard Classification of Education. See "Abbreviations" for a key to country abbreviations.

International learning assessments show that education systems in the ECA region are successful in imparting basic skills, but less successful in imparting the higher-order skills sought by employers. These systems continue to place too much emphasis on conveying facts and knowledge, instead of problem solving and critical thinking. The respectable average performance of ECA countries on international assessments, moreover, masks a long tail of underperformers: 15-year-olds who have such poor numeracy and literacy skills that their success in the modern workplace is highly doubtful.

The quality of education in ECA countries, particularly at the lower levels, is good compared to countries at the same income level, but unfortunately, this quality is not improving. In fact, it appears to be worsening at the lower secondary level in many countries, as seen in the stagnant or deteriorating scores of ECA countries on international assessments at this stage. At the upper secondary and tertiary levels, educational quality is less known. Because the tertiary sector expanded significantly without (in many—though not all—countries) strong quality assurance programs and information that parents and students need to make informed choices, the quality of many university degrees is suspect. Qualitative evidence, moreover, highlights significant unethical behavior in university admittance, grading, and graduation policies.

Underdeveloped adult learning systems in the region threatens to cement the skills deficit in the region. Given that the populations of many ECA countries are declining, the need to retrain and reskill adult workers—as well as to train unemployed workers—is becoming imperative. Yet many countries in the region have only begun to lay the groundwork for modern systems of adult learning.

In sum, education systems in the region impart excellent foundational skills, but falter at the secondary level, when students need to acquire the more advanced competencies needed to work in modern, globalized economies. Despite rapid expansion, the tertiary sector does not yet appear to be delivering the skills sought by employers, and adults have very limited educational opportunities to retrain or improve existing skills.

The next chapter takes a detailed look at the sources of the underperformance of ECA education systems and offers a framework for how to reform these systems in order to enhance educational quality and relevance. Subsequent chapters then explore recommendations for improving specific levels of the education system, including continuing adult education and training.

Annex 2A: Education Systems in ECA Today

Table 2A.1 Duration of Education in ECA Countries, Various Years

		1991	2000	2006
Albania	Primary school starting age	6	6	6
	Primary duration	8	4	4
	Lower secondary duration	..	4	4
	Upper secondary duration	..	4	4
	Compulsory years	—	8	8
	Age after compulsory education		14	14
Armenia	Primary school starting age	7	7	7
	Primary duration	3	3	3
	Lower secondary duration	5	5	5
	Upper secondary duration	2	2	2
	Compulsory years	—	8	8
	Age after compulsory education	—	15	15
Azerbaijan	Primary school starting age	7	6	6
	Primary duration	3	4	4
	Lower secondary duration	5	5	5
	Upper secondary duration	2	2	2
	Compulsory years	—	11	11
	Age after compulsory education	—	17	17
Belarus	Primary school starting age	6	6	6
	Primary duration	4	4	4
	Lower secondary duration	5	5	5
	Upper secondary duration	2	2	2
	Compulsory years	—	9	10
	Age after compulsory education	—	15	16
Bosnia and Herzegovina	Primary school starting age	7	6	6
	Primary duration	4	4	4
	Lower secondary duration	4	4	4
	Upper secondary duration	4	4	4
	Compulsory years	—	..	..
	Age after compulsory education	—	—	—
Bulgaria	Primary school starting age	6	7	7
	Primary duration	8	4	4
	Lower secondary duration	..	4	4
	Upper secondary duration	..	3	3
	Compulsory years	—	8	8
	Age after compulsory education	—	15	15
Croatia	Primary school starting age	7	7	7
	Primary duration	8	4	4

(continued next page)

Table 2A.1 (continued)

		1991	2000	2006
	Lower secondary duration	..	4	4
	Upper secondary duration	..	4	4
	Compulsory years	—	8	8
	Age after compulsory education	—	15	15
Czech Republic	Primary school starting age	6	6	6
	Primary duration	4	5	5
	Lower secondary duration	4	4	4
	Upper secondary duration	4	4	4
	Compulsory years	—	10	10
	Age after compulsory education	—	16	16
Estonia	Primary school starting age	7	7	7
	Primary duration	5	6	6
	Lower secondary duration	3	3	3
	Upper secondary duration	3	3	3
	Compulsory years	—	9	9
	Age after compulsory education	—	16	16
Georgia	Primary school starting age	6	6	6
	Primary duration	4	4	6
	Lower secondary duration	5	5	3
	Upper secondary duration	2	2	2
	Compulsory years	—	9	9
	Age after compulsory education	—	15	15
Hungary	Primary school starting age	6	7	7
	Primary duration	8	4	4
	Lower secondary duration	..	4	4
	Upper secondary duration	..	4	4
	Compulsory years	—	10	10
	Age after compulsory education	—	17	17
Kazakhstan	Primary school starting age	7	7	7
	Primary duration	4	4	4
	Lower secondary duration	5	5	5
	Upper secondary duration	2	2	2
	Compulsory years	—	11	11
	Age after compulsory education	—	18	18
Kyrgyz Republic	Primary school starting age	7	7	7
	Primary duration	3	4	4
	Lower secondary duration	5	5	5
	Upper secondary duration	2	2	2
	Compulsory years	—	9	9
	Age after compulsory education	—	16	16

(continued next page)

Table 2A.1 *(continued)*

		1991	2000	2006
Latvia	Primary school starting age	7	7	7
	Primary duration	4	4	4
	Lower secondary duration	5	5	5
	Upper secondary duration	3	3	3
	Compulsory years	—	9	9
	Age after compulsory education	—	16	16
Lithuania	Primary school starting age	7	7	7
	Primary duration	4	4	4
	Lower secondary duration	5	6	6
	Upper secondary duration	3	2	2
	Compulsory years	—	9	9
	Age after compulsory education	—	16	16
Macedonia, FYR	Primary school starting age	7	7	7
	Primary duration	8	4	4
	Lower secondary duration	..	4	4
	Upper secondary duration	..	4	4
	Compulsory years	—	8	8
	Age after compulsory education	—	15	15
Moldova	Primary school starting age	7	7	7
	Primary duration	4	4	4
	Lower secondary duration	5	5	5
	Upper secondary duration	3	2	2
	Compulsory years	—	9	9
	Age after compulsory education	—	16	16
Montenegro	Primary school starting age	—	—	—
	Primary duration	—	—	—
	Lower secondary duration	—	—	—
	Upper secondary duration	—	—	—
	Compulsory years	—	—	—
	Age after compulsory education	—	—	—
Poland	Primary school starting age	7	7	7
	Primary duration	8	6	6
	Lower secondary duration	—	2	3
	Upper secondary duration	—	4	3
	Compulsory years	—	9	9
	Age after compulsory education	—	16	16
Romania	Primary school starting age	6	7	7
	Primary duration	4	4	4
	Lower secondary duration	4	4	4
	Upper secondary duration	4	4	4
	Compulsory years	—	8	8
	Age after compulsory education	—	15	15
Russian Federation	Primary school starting age	7	7	7
	Primary duration	3	3	4

(continued next page)

Table 2A.1 *(continued)*

		1991	2000	2006
	Lower secondary duration	5	5	5
	Upper secondary duration	2	2	2
	Compulsory years	—	10	10
	Age after compulsory education	—	17	17
Serbia	Primary school starting age	—	—	—
	Primary duration	—	—	—
	Lower secondary duration	—	—	—
	Upper secondary duration	—	4	4
	Compulsory years	—	8	8
	Age after compulsory education	—	—	—
Slovak Republic	Primary school starting age	6	6	6
	Primary duration	4	4	4
	Lower secondary duration	4	5	5
	Upper secondary duration	4	4	4
	Compulsory years	—	10	10
	Age after compulsory education	—	16	16
Slovenia	Primary school starting age	7	7	6
	Primary duration	4	4	5
	Lower secondary duration	4	4	4
	Upper secondary duration	4	4	4
	Compulsory years	—	9	9
	Age after compulsory education	—	16	15
Tajikistan	Primary school starting age	7	7	7
	Primary duration	4	4	4
	Lower secondary duration	—	5	5
	Upper secondary duration	—	2	2
	Compulsory years	—	9	9
	Age after compulsory education	—	16	16
Turkey	Primary school starting age	6	6	6
	Primary duration	5	6	6
	Lower secondary duration	3	2	2
	Upper secondary duration	3	3	3
	Compulsory years	—	9	9
	Age after compulsory education	—	15	15
Turkmenistan	Primary school starting age	7	7	7
	Primary duration	4	3	3
	Lower secondary duration	5	5	5
	Upper secondary duration	2	2	2
	Compulsory years	—	9	9
	Age after compulsory education	—	16	16
Ukraine	Primary school starting age	6	7	6
	Primary duration	6	3	4
	Lower secondary duration	3	5	5

(continued next page)

Table 2A.1 *(continued)*

		1991	2000	2006
	Upper secondary duration	2	2	2
	Compulsory years	—	11	12
	Age after compulsory education	—	18	18
Uzbekistan	Primary school starting age	6	7	7
	Primary duration	4	4	4
	Lower secondary duration	5	5	5
	Upper secondary duration	2	2	2
	Compulsory years	—	12	12
	Age after compulsory education	—	19	19

Source: EdStats Database.
Note: .. = negligible; — = not available. For all countries, compulsory education includes primary and lower secondary education, with the exception of the following: Lithuania, where compulsory education includes only part of lower secondary; Azerbaijan, Kazakhstan, and the Russian Federation, where compulsory education also includes upper secondary; Belarus, the Czech Republic, Hungary, the Slovak Republic, Slovenia, Turkey, and Turkmenistan, where compulsory education also includes part of upper secondary in at least some of the years; and Ukraine and Uzbekistan, where the number of compulsory years extends beyond upper secondary education.

Table 2A.2 ECA Country Results on International Assessments since 1995

| | TIMSS | | | | | | | | | | | | PISA | | | | | | | | | | PIRLS | | |
| | Math grade 8 | | | | Math grade 4 | | | Science grade 8 | | | | Science | | | | Math | | | | Reading | | | | Reading | | |
Country Name	1995	1999	2003	2007	2003	2007	1995	1999	2003	2007	2003	2007	2000	2003	2006	2009	2000	2003	2006	2009	2000	2003	2006	2009	2001	2006	*
Bulgaria	511	476	464				518	476	479	470			430		434	439	430		413	428	430		401	429	550	547	Down
Macedonia, FYR		447	435					458	449				381				401				373				442	442	Down
Czech Republic	564	520		504		486	574	539		539		515	498	516	512	500	511	523	509	493	492	489	482	478	537		Down
Croatia															493	486			467	460			477	476			Down
Romania	482	472	475	461			486	472	470	462					418	428			414	427			395	424	512	489	Mixed
Slovak Republic	547	534	508			496	544	535	517			526		495	488	490		498	492	497		469	466	477	518	531	Mixed
Hungary	537	532	529	517	529	510	554	552	543	539	530	536	488	503	503	503	496	490	490	490	480	482	482	494	543	551	Mixed
Lithuania	477	482	502	506	534	530	476	488	519	519	512	514			487	491			486	477			470	468	543	537	Mixed
Slovenia	541	530	493	501	479	502	560	533	520	538	490	518			518	512			504	501			494	483	502	522	Mixed
Moldova		469	460		504		459	472			496														492	500	Mixed
Russian Federation	535	526	508	512	552	544	538	529	514	530	526	546	478	468	475	468	460	468	475	468	462	442	439	459	528	565	Mixed
Albania													381				376			377	349			385			Mixed
Azerbaijan															382	373			475	431			352	362			Mixed
Estonia			531						552						531	528			514	512			500	501			Mixed
Montenegro															411	401			399	403			391	408			Mixed
Serbia			477	486					468	470				436	435	442		437	435	442		412	401	442			Up
Turkey		429		432				433		454				434	423	445		423	423	445		441	447	464	449		Up
Latvia		505	508		536	537	485	503	512		532	542	463	483	489	494	460	483	486	482	458	491	479	484	545		Up
Poland						500							470	490	497	508	483	490	495	495	479	497	507	500		519	Up
Armenia		478	499		456			461	488	437	484				322	330			310	331			284	314			Up
Kyrgyz Republic																											Up

(continued next page)

Table 2A.2 (continued)

Country Name	TIMSS												PISA												PIRLS	
	Math grade 8				Math grade 4		Science grade 8				Science			Math				Science				Reading			Reading	*
	1995	1999	2003	2007	2003	2007	1995	1999	2003	2007	2003	2007	2000	2003	2006	2009	2000	2003	2006	2009	2000	2003	2006	2009	2001	2006
Bosnia and Herzegovina				456						466																
Kazakhstan					549						533				405				400				390			
Ukraine			462		469				485		474															
Georgia			410		438				421		418															471
Tajikistan																										
Turkmenistan																										
Uzbekistan																										
Belarus																										
Kosovo																										

Sources: IEA 1995, 1999, 2003, 2007; PISA Databases 2000, 2003, 2006, 2009; IES 2001, 2006.
Note: * Authors' summary assessment of trends in countries' scores across time and across various tests.

Notes

1. Along lines similar to the OECD DeSeCo project, the European Qualifications Framework for Lifelong Learning identifies eight key competences: (1) communication in the mother tongue; (2) communication in foreign languages; (3) mathematical competence and basic competence in science and technology; (4) digital competence; (5) learning to learn; (6) interpersonal, intercultural, and social competences, together with civic competence (7) entrepreneurship; and (8) cultural expression. In addition, critical thinking, creativity, initiative taking, problem solving, risk assessment, decision making, and managing feelings constructively are seen as playing a role in all eight key competencies (EU 2008). The EU framework identifies the essential knowledge, skills, and attitudes related to each.
2. This is a scale metric established by setting the mean scores of participating countries to 500 and the standard deviation to 100, thus enabling comparisons over time, since all cycles are placed on this metric so that scores are equivalent from cycle to cycle. In contrast, the international average, obtained by averaging across the mean scores for each of the participating countries, needs to be recomputed for each new cycle, based on the set of participating countries and changes from cycle to cycle, depending on the set of countries taking part.
3. Income level is used as a rough measure of the quality of all nonschool factors, including parental inputs, that help students learn.
4. Some ECA countries are making rapid progress in addressing this information gap (see chapter 5).
5. As noted in chapter 1, footnote 6, care should be taken when comparing employment outcomes of vocational vs. general secondary graduates. In particular, it can be argued that better employment outcomes of workers with technical secondary education compared with those of workers with general secondary education reflect the different composition of both groups. One hypothesis is that due to the selection process, graduates of general secondary schools who do not proceed to tertiary education are less able, on average, than the graduates of secondary technical schools.
6. The higher incidence of training among skilled than among nonskilled workers is consistent with evidence from across ECA and the OECD.

CHAPTER 3

Resolving the Skills Shortage in the ECA Region: A Policy Framework

This chapter identifies the major impediments that prevent the education system from delivering the skills that are being demanded by the labor markets as identified in the previous chapters. It then offers a policy framework and policy directions to help overcome these impediments. The impediments and a policy framework for addressing them guide the discussion of education system reform for the remainder of the book.

Here we argue that the three most pressing problems of ECA education systems that get in the way of imparting the needed skills are: (1) the lack of data on the skills and competencies that students actually acquire as a result of the educational process; (2) the legacy of central planning—particularly its effect on the management of education systems in the region—which makes education systems inflexible and resistant to the initiative of front-line actors (who can actually improve education); and (3) the inefficient use of resources, a problem that has become particularly acute in the current economic climate. Certainly these are not the only impediments to making education systems more responsive to skills needs in the region. However, they are common to all ECA countries and lie at the heart of addressing the skills deficiencies discussed in chapter 2.[1]

The lack of data on student performance, the legacy of central planning, and the inefficient use of resources affect all levels of education in the ECA region, but are most apparent at the pre-university level. This level is the foundation of the education system in every country and generally absorbs two-thirds of total education funding in the ECA region. The same three impediments affect tertiary education in a slightly different way, as this sector has already undergone significant reform over the past 20 years, during which time it has doubled or tripled in size in many countries (see chapter 5). Because most ECA countries do not yet have adult education systems in the modern sense, these impediments cannot be fairly characterized as problems of this sector, though the policy recommendations offered in this chapter are applicable to adult education also.

To be fair, ECA countries face these impediments to different degrees, but none have fully escaped the legacy of central planning, which emphasized strict top-down control, compliance with pre-established norms, and intensive management involvement in operational details.[2] In terms of measuring the quality and relevance of education, central planning focused on generating data on inputs—that is, checking whether local actors were in compliance with detailed norms for all inputs. Yet in terms of whether students acquired skills and competencies, these systems operated with the lights off—without the information needed—and as a result, educational spending in the region remains highly inefficient. Today, virtually no ECA country has been able to downsize its school network and staff in the face of falling student numbers. They are accordingly stuck with too many schools and too many teachers, which absorb resources that could otherwise be used to improve the quality of education.

Operating in the Dark: Ministries Know Too Little to Effectively Manage the Education Sector

As mentioned in chapter 2, ministries of education across ECA know far too little about the nature of the skills shortages in their economies or the strengths and weaknesses of their own education systems. As a result, they lack an important precondition for effectively managing the sector. Better data alone does not make better policies. But operating in the darkness makes it impossible to gauge the magnitude of the problems facing policy makers. This section describes the current status of educational data and policy making in the region, identifying the missing data needed and showing how their absence impedes education in the region.

Educational Data Focus on Diplomas, not Skills

It is a problem worldwide that educational data tend to focus on quantity—for example, the number of enrolled and graduating students—and not the quality of education. Where international comparative data are available, they focus on the quality of primary or lower secondary education. Given that the current policy debate in the ECA region focuses on "skills," the lack of data on educational quality is problematic, particularly because very few young people in the region enter the labor market with only a lower secondary education. As figure 3.1 shows, most ECA students complete at least an upper secondary degree. But with no international assessment of the skills and competencies of upper secondary or tertiary graduates, it is impossible to quantify the gap in competencies between recent labor market entrants in, say, Bulgaria and Germany. The data that are available today document how many students graduate in a particular year, not what they offer employers in terms of competencies.

Lack of relevant data on students and their individual performance is particularly acute in the vocational sector because of the large variety of vocational schools in the ECA region and the (likely) heterogeneity of their student populations. The tendency of educational data to focus on quantity, rather than quality and relevance, is also acute in adult education

Figure 3.1 Educational Background of 25–34-year-olds in the ECA Region, 2006
(percent)

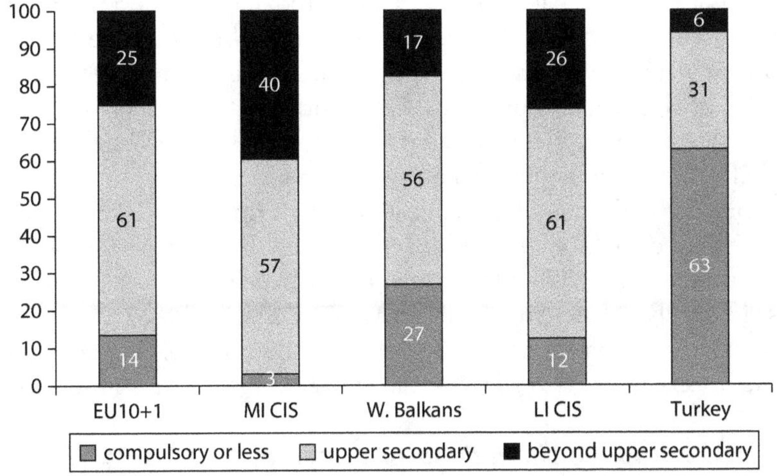

Region	compulsory or less	upper secondary	beyond upper secondary
EU10+1	14	61	25
MI CIS	3	57	40
W. Balkans	27	56	17
LI CIS	12	61	26
Turkey	63	31	6

Source: Author's calculations, based on EBRD-World Bank 2006.
Note: LI = low-income, MI = middle-income.

and training. At best, current surveys in that sector measure the number of training hours and courses in which individuals participate, or whether a firm offers training. But no international comparative data yet exist to compare the quality or relevance of such training.

Narrow focus and understanding of educational quality. Many ECA countries tend to focus on their very best students and equate their performance with "quality education." Indeed, in discussions about the quality of education generally, school principals, local education authorities, and representatives of education ministries often point to particular students' accomplishments at the "Math Olympiads" as examples of how well their schools perform. Similarly, university rectors mention how many of their graduates manage to pursue further education at top universities abroad.

Although it is important to create an environment where excellence can flourish, the few high-achieving students should not be the principal focus of ECA school systems, nor the criteria by which they measure their performance. Whereas the principals of ECA schools know how many of their students compete in and win Math Olympiads, they know very little about the average performance of their students, and much less about the performance of their schools vis-à-vis similar schools elsewhere in the country. As a result, policy makers have little information about the performance of the weakest students in their schools: students with a different mother tongue, a different ethnic origin, or, simply, from economically disadvantaged backgrounds. These students are most in need of support, yet, across the ECA region very little effort is made to understand how far behind they are and whether existing policies—such as small classes, extracurricular activities, or other interventions—are working. Without relevant data, problem areas go unnoticed, and the effectiveness of policy interventions cannot be measured.

A broader understanding of educational performance relies on standardized tests and looks at *all students*, differentiating their performance by external factors (e.g., parental income and socioeconomic background). In this view, truly outstanding schools are not necessarily those with the highest average score on standardized tests, but rather, schools that, compared to their peers, manage to generate the biggest improvements in test scores.

Limited Participation in National and International Assessments

For some countries in the ECA region, information weaknesses are compounded by limited participation in international student learning assessments, such as PISA, PIRLS, and TIMSS. Five ECA countries (Tajikistan, Turkmenistan, Uzbekistan, Belarus, and Kosovo) have never participated in such an assessment. For these countries, it is impossible to assess the quality of even primary and lower secondary education. Moreover, three ECA countries have only just begun to participate in such assessments.

ECA countries have also been slow to use national standardized assessments to measure and analyze student learning outcomes, largely for historical reasons. Prior to 1990, assessing students and granting diplomas were left entirely in the hands of teachers and schools. A recent United Nations Children's Fund (UNICEF) report argues that this approach was rooted in the philosophy "that external checks on outcomes were not needed in a tightly controlled system of educational inputs and processes." As a result, "attempts in the early 1990s to introduce external tests and examinations ran counter to the public mood, which saw them as attempts to re-establish central control and undermine professional trust in teachers' judgment" (UNICEF 2007, 58).

Policy makers in ECA countries are recognizing, however, that objective, standardized measures of learning outcomes are needed for a number of reasons. First, they remain the best indicator available for measuring the performance of an education system (Vegas and Petrow 2008). National and international learning assessments provide policy makers a quantitative indicator of learning outcomes that can be compared across schools and across time. These data in turn shed light on which policies are working and which need tweaking; they also illuminate weaknesses and identify areas where new policies may be needed.

Second, standardized assessments allow students and their parents to compare a student's performance relative to his or her peers, and a school's performance relative to that of other schools. Third, when used alongside other indicators of performance, standardized assessments can be utilized to hold education managers and teachers accountable for results. In a decentralized education system in which local authorities play an important role in day-to-day management, such instruments are especially important for a central government to identify system needs, direct funding where it is most needed, and tailor new policies to support schools and local authorities, as needed (see box 3.1).

Limited experience of using data to drive educational policy. Despite some progress in developing national learning assessments and

> **Box 3.1**
>
> **The Value of Standardized External Student Assessments in ECA Countries**
>
> When small questionnaires on students' socioeconomic backgrounds are administered together with standardized tests (e.g., PIRLS, PISA, TIMSS—see chapter 2), school systems can gauge their performance in imparting knowledge and skills to their weakest students, who are often socioeconomically disadvantaged. These students will never compete in Math Olympiads. They drop out of school earlier than their peers, and, because they are marginal students, never show up in national averages. Yet, an important strength of a school system is measured by how many of these students—those with the weakest parental support—acquire competencies needed for the labor market. Indeed, the most successful school systems in the world, Finland and the Republic of Korea among them, show that the way to raise overall educational quality for all students is to focus on raising the educational quality provided to the lowest-achieving part of the student population.

participating in international assessments, no country in the ECA region has yet moved from regularly gathering data on learning outcomes to using this data to improve policy making. The simple reason is that each step along the path shown in figure 3.2 requires time and capacity building. Specifically, moving from a culture where little or no data are available to a culture where data are gathered, analyzed, disseminated, and actively used to inform educational policies requires new skills.

On a positive note, some countries in the region (primarily the new member states of the EU) now have several years' experience with performance measurement, both in terms of establishing their own national assessment centers and participating in several rounds of international assessments (see figure 3.3). This group of countries is gradually adding the capacity to analyze test scores to design better policies. However, this book finds that no ECA country has, as of 2010, actually reached this stage. Less encouraging, a large number of countries in the region (mostly the low-income CIS countries, but also Turkey and Belarus) have either made no or only small steps in this direction (see far left column in figure 3.3). If this latter group of

Figure 3.2 Learning to Use Data to Drive Education Policy

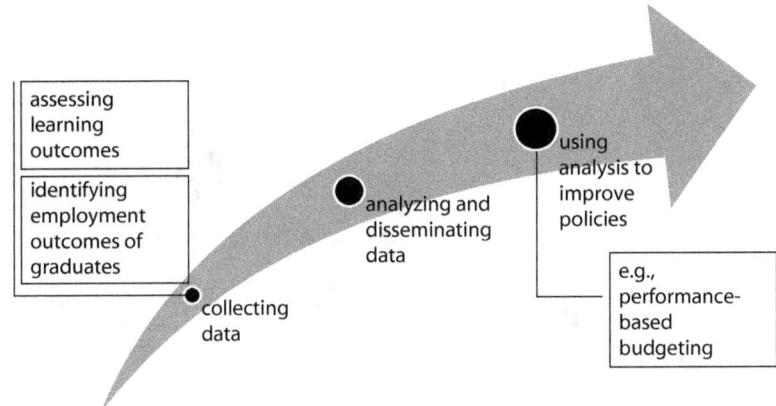

Source: Authors.

countries has begun to participate in international assessments, it has only been quite recently.

No systematic tracking of graduates' employment outcomes. When students graduate, ministries of education in the ECA region do not systematically collect, analyze, and disseminate information on their employment outcomes. Such information is useful for helping policy makers and higher education institutions detect which programs and fields of study are in high demand among employers. Moreover, such information can help students make better choices about which university to attend and which field of study to pursue.

Several OECD countries provide examples of how data on graduation can be collected and disseminated. Norway has tracked such data since 1972; Italy, since 1998; and the Netherlands, since 1989. In the Netherlands, almost all graduates of higher education institutions are surveyed a year and a half after they graduate. The survey collects comprehensive information on a range of different topics, including information on the school-to-work transition (asking such questions as, How long did it take to find a job? Did it involve unemployment spells?); the type and quality of employment, if any (e.g., sector and educational and skills requirements); and students' satisfaction with the education that they have completed (Did it provide a solid basis for entering the labor market? Did it develop the relevant skills? Did it achieve the right mix

Figure 3.3 Status of Measuring and Using Data on Student Learning Outcomes in the ECA Region, 2009

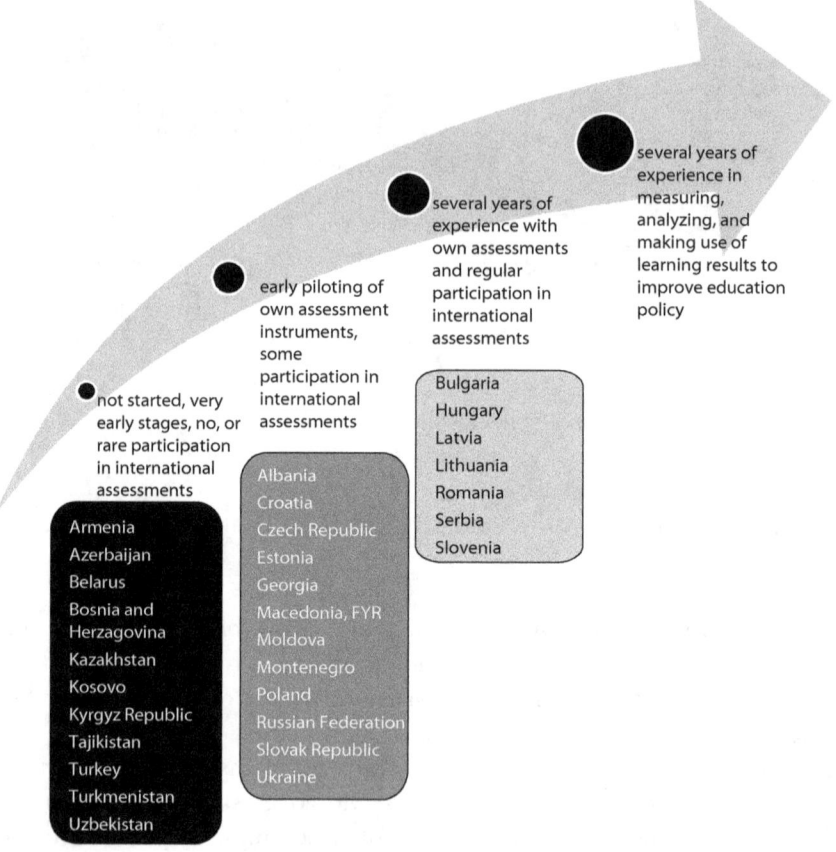

Sources: Authors' assessments based on data from UNICEF (2007, table 2.1); the extent of countries' participation in PISA, PIRLS, and TIMSS since 1995; and inputs from World Bank country experts. The UNICEF data is drawn from "Table 2.1: Status of Reforms of Assessment and Examination Systems, 2006," regarding "Introduction of other school exams or assessments (e.g. basic school)" and "Introduction of sample-based national assessment." In this table, UNICEF scores the progress of countries on a range of 0 to 4, with 0 representing "not planned or started" and 4 representing "operational." In addition, the figure above uses World Bank staff compilations on the number of international assessments in which each country has participated.
Note: As a signal that data-driven policy is a way to build capacity, the year in which countries first participated in an international assessment was one of the indicators used to group countries.

between practical and theoretical knowledge?). Table 3.1 shows the types of information that the survey collects.

Legacy of Central Planning

As noted earlier, many problems in education systems go unnoticed and unaddressed in the ECA region because these systems do not produce

Table 3.1 Information Collected from Tracer Study of Dutch University Graduates, 2007

	Duration of job search (in months)	Full-time employment (%)	Unlimited term contract (%)	Monthly gross income (euros)		Managerial or professional (% ISCO 1 or 2)	High use of skills (%)	High job satisfaction (%)
	Mean	Mean	Mean	Mean	Median	Mean	Mean	Mean
Science and math	0.7	88.4	45.6	2499	2429	83.6	71.0	77.5
Medicine and health	0.7	79.0	41.0	2904	2783	82.6	78.9	81.7
Engineering	1.0	94.4	66.2	2772	2631	87.4	75.2	72.8
Economics	1.0	96.1	71.3	2954	2783	70.3	65.6	70.1
Law	1.2	92.7	57.5	2864	2732	87.8	66.0	70.2
Humanities and arts	1.2	59.1	43.0	2188	2226	66.0	50.4	61.3
Social sciences	1.3	60.6	45.4	2317	2350	72.0	63.9	65.4
Agriculture	1.5	86.7	45.6	2137	2328	84.2	73.2	71.2

Source: Table provided by the Research Centre for Education and the Labour Market (ROA), The Netherlands, 2008, at request of the authors.

sufficient data to gauge their performance. The legacy of highly centralized, Soviet-style management then compounds these problems.[3] Education authorities at most levels of the system have neither the power nor the incentives to make key operating decisions, such as reallocating budgets to meet urgent local needs, that would improve the performance of their respective institutions (see next section). Instead, actors in the sector are held accountable for complying with detailed, centrally determined norms (e.g. on class sizes, or the number of nonteaching staff to be employed).

The implicit assumption appears to be that if norms are followed, a quality education will result. There is little management understanding that there are multiple ways to deliver quality education, some of which must be discovered by the principals and teachers of individual schools. Surveys of the main actors in the sector (undertaken as part of the PISA and Teaching and Learning International Survey [TALIS] studies) verify this general picture of education sector management in the region.[4]

Schools Lack Autonomy and Are Held Accountable for Complying with Norms

ECA countries can be roughly sorted into three groups according to the degree of autonomy granted to schools at the pre-university level. At one end of the spectrum, schools in the new EU member states have been granted significant autonomy over budgets, some aspects of staffing, and—in some cases—instructional content. At the other end, schools in low-income countries, such as the Kyrgyz Republic and Azerbaijan, enjoy very little autonomy and continue to be micromanaged from the center. Schools in the Russian Federation, Serbia, Turkey, and several other countries lie somewhere in between: some autonomy has been granted to schools or to some schools as part of pilot projects.

Rather than provide a "framework" of broad, overall rules for the sector, legislation on education in the region is highly detailed, spelling out minute norms for all operational areas (see box 3.2). Legions of inspectors are employed to visit schools to verify if they are in compliance with these norms, acting more like police officers than pedagogical counselors. The result is a system that focuses on compliance with norms, not quality education.

Complying with norms does not necessarily lead to better results. Detailed data on spending and test scores now exist for some ECA countries, including Poland, and show that complying with input standards

> **Box 3.2**
>
> ## Detailed Regulations Set Norms Even for Education Facilities in the ECA Region
>
> In Ukraine, the following school norms are set at the ministerial level. They offer an example of the top-down management style that focuses on getting local actors to comply with detailed norms, irrespective of whether or not they make sense in local circumstances:
>
> - 1 deputy school director for 11–24 class groups; 2 if more than 38 class groups
> - 1 managing deputy director if an urban school has more than 600 students or if a rural school has more than 400 students
> - 1 pedagogue if a school has more than 8 class groups (regardless of the total number of students in the school)
> - 1 extracurricular activities group leader per each 16 class groups (regardless of the total number of students in the school)
> - 1 cleaner per 500 square meters (0.5 per each 250 square meters)
> - 1 coat room attendant per 200 coat spots in school
> - 1 yardkeeper per 1.5 hectares of school property
>
> The examples above are commonplace across the region—remnants of the types of detailed norms that governed all aspects of society during pre-transition days. It is common for such norms to leave no room for a school or local authority to consider, for example, alternative ways of achieving a clean school (e.g., by outsourcing the task to a private company) or whether or not staff specified in the norms are actually needed. Norms may even exist for which there is no need, such as a norm that determines how many heat inspectors should be hired per classroom, with no provision for whether or not classrooms are actually in use.
>
> *Sources:* World Bank 2008d; authors' observations.

does not necessarily produce good-quality education. In fact, two very similar localities can be in compliance with norms, but spend drastically different amounts of resources per student and end up with the same results. An analysis of educational expenditures and student test scores in more than 3,000 municipalities of Poland that was undertaken for this chapter shows that high-spending municipalities often end up with students who perform worse on standardized tests than their peers in municipalities that spend less.

An example of this analysis compares the two municipalities of Tarłów (in the south-central region of Poland) and Rutka-Tartak (in the northeast), both in compliance with norms for class sizes in Poland. The two localities are also very similar in a number of ways: both are rural, have a similar proportion of adults with secondary or higher education, and roughly similar income levels. While they are similar in a number of ways, the educational spending and results of the two towns vary widely—suggesting large inefficiencies. Sixth-graders in Tarłów scored an average of 18 out of 40 on a national achievement test in 2009, while sixth-graders in Rutka-Tartak scored, on average, 26—a full eight points higher. Oddly, the high-performing municipality, Rutka-Tartak, spent the least per student: an average of only Zl 3,710 per pupil, compared to an average of Zl 8,330 per student in Tarłów (see figure 3.4). That is, Rutka-Tartak achieved much better results at half the cost.

Further analysis revealed that the differences mostly boiled down to differences in class sizes. Tarłów's higher per student costs were a result of relatively smaller classes (an average class size of 15), compared to an average class size of 24 in Rutka-Tartak (see figure 3.5). Smaller classes imply higher per student costs, yet test score results suggest that these smaller classes are not resulting in better learning outcomes.

Figure 3.4 Relationship between Primary School Test Scores, Adult Education Levels, and Per Student Spending in Two Municipalities of Poland

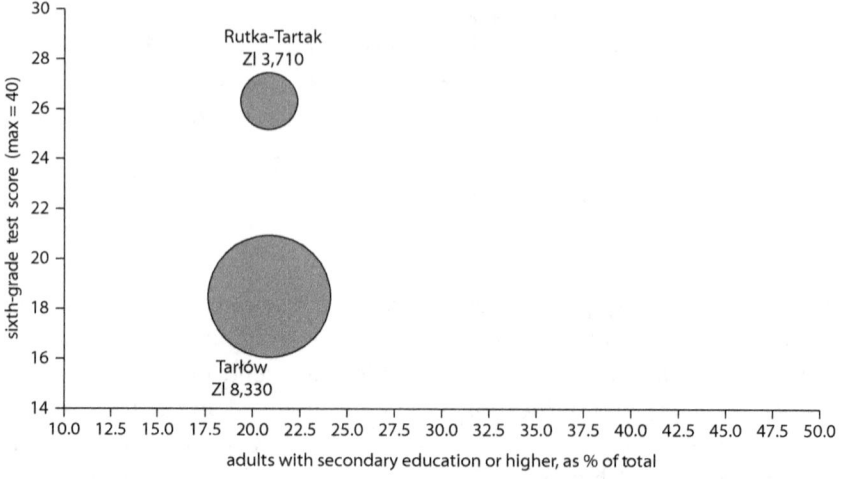

Source: Authors' analysis of data from the Ministry of Finance, Central Statistical Office, Ministry of National Education, and Central Examination Board, Poland, and the World Bank's BOOST database; Kheyfets and others 2011.
Note: Size of bubble indicates relative size of per student spending.

Figure 3.5 Relationship between Primary School Test Scores, Average Class Size, and Per Student Spending in Two Municipalities of Poland

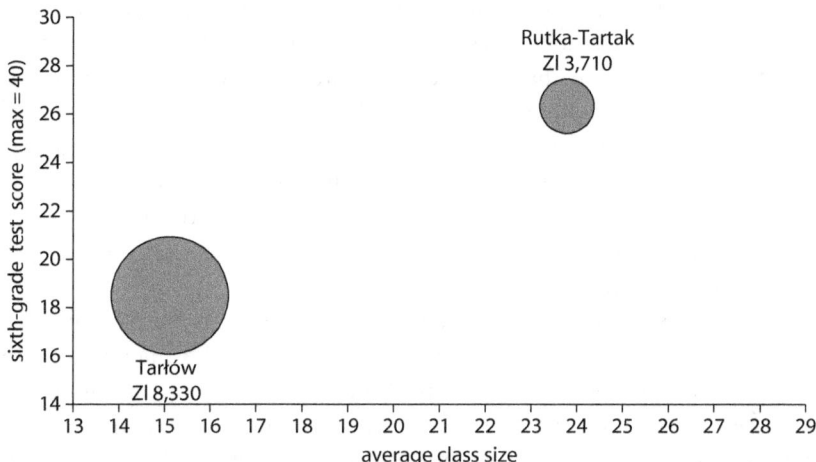

Source: Authors' analysis of data from the Ministry of Finance, Central Statistical Office, Ministry of National Education, and Central Examination Board, Poland, and the World Bank's BOOST database; Kheyfets and others 2011.
Note: Size of bubble indicates relative size of per student spending. See end note for data sources used for this analysis.

The story of Rutka-Tartak and Tarłów illustrates what is a widespread phenomenon across the region: educational spending varies widely and has little connection to learning outcomes. Furthermore, there are no management mechanisms built into the education systems of these countries to take corrective action in such cases. In fact, there are no mechanisms to collect per student spending and test scores in different localities. Not surprisingly, actors in these education systems care about complying with norms, not about what it costs to deliver education services or what results are achieved.

Inflexible Management Inhibits Reform

The strong focus on meeting detailed norms, together with the lack of student performance data, has created rigid education systems that are unable to respond to changing conditions. One area in which this inability to reform is highly apparent is vocational education and training (VET). ECA education systems inherited large numbers of vocational schools from the communist system, which in pre-transition days supplied workers to state-owned enterprises. Despite large drops in student numbers, these schools still enroll almost 40 percent of all upper secondary graduates (the largest proportion of any region in the world, see figure B2.1). The most highly vocationalized programs were in Central and Eastern Europe, where the average share of vocational secondary school students was over 70 percent in 1989. Turkey, not a transition country, also has a strong vocational focus in secondary education, with programs patterned after the German dual-system model. As economic conditions and employer requirements have changed, however, education systems in these countries have been unable to reform the sector to deliver the skills in demand on the labor market. In addition, the majority of these programs were terminal, that is, they did not provide access to higher education.

Given that secondary education was overwhelmingly focused on vocational and technical training in planned economies, the management of vocational secondary education was often separated from that of general secondary education programs. (The latter was the gateway to university study, an opportunity that was limited to the select few in these economies.) In many ECA countries today, management of secondary education is thus divided across two or more ministries. Even in Turkey, the one nontransition country in the ECA region, there is a distinct fragmentation of responsibility and oversight of secondary education within the same ministry.

A further complication is that local governments in the ECA region are typically responsible for the management and, to some degree, the financing, of general secondary education in most ECA countries, whereas the central government remains responsible for managing and funding vocational secondary education. Specifically, in many countries it is the national Ministry of Education that retained management control over vocational schools (as did other national-level ministries that ran such schools, for example, a Ministry of Agriculture that sponsored a forestry school). The fragmentation is thus not only across ministries, but across authority levels (national and local) also.

This double management fragmentation makes it more difficult to adjust the supply of education programs to changes in demand (i.e., changes in skills requirements and labor market opportunities, which are then translated into changing student demand). This reluctance or incapacity to reform these education programs to meet skill needs is exacerbated by the fact that core ministries, including ministries of finance and economy, are often more concerned than ministries of education—where management control is actually located—about the efficiency of education programs and their responsiveness to changing skill needs.

Due to the fractionalized authority structures, the lack of autonomy, and a management focus on norms, principals of vocational schools or local education planners have been virtually incapable of modernizing these dinosaurs into attractive secondary education alternatives for students. Economic transition necessitates widespread changes in education at this level and in vocational education programs in particular, but rigid and divided management systems and shrinking budgets have made it hard to implement these changes. Many vocational schools remain unreformed, with outdated equipment, an outdated curriculum that offers too many narrow specializations, and an aging (and possibly increasingly unqualified) teacher workforce. Paradoxically, firms in the region are seeking more graduates with technical skills and have raised salaries in areas with skills shortages to attract workers with these abilities. Nevertheless, vocational programs in the region are still largely failing to provide the needed skills.

Inefficient Use of Funds

Education funding in the ECA region is also dictated by norms rather than a common-sense response to conditions on the ground. With money tied to norms, schools and local authorities have no flexibility or incentive to improve the efficiency of spending. In particular, schools in most countries in the region continue to be financed based on the number of classes and teachers employed (i.e., inputs), not the number of students that they serve. Centrally determined norms dictate the subjects that must be taught, and how many classes must be created at each grade level. Norms on class numbers determine the required number of teaching hours, which establish the required number of teachers. Funding flows are then rigidly earmarked for either personnel costs or nonpersonnel costs, leaving local managers no ability to reallocate funds where they are most needed. As a result, the system finds it difficult to correct course in the face of change.

The most glaring example of this problem has been the inability of the sector to downsize in response to falling student numbers over the past two decades. The ensuing crisis has strained the resources of education systems throughout the region and brought the teaching profession to the brink—compromising both its quality and attractiveness to future teachers. Although the problems associated with smaller student numbers are presently most urgent at the pre-university level of education, they will soon impact the university sector as well.

All but five ECA countries—Turkey and a few low-income CIS countries—have experienced a dramatic decline in student enrollments as a result of demographic trends in the past 20 years, differing only in terms of the severity of the decline and its onset. As figure 3.6 shows, in some countries student numbers have declined by as much as 40 percent since the beginning of the transition.

Despite highly centralized management, the responsibility for identifying which schools to close was placed on the shoulders of regional or local authorities or both in most ECA countries. Yet these actors had no incentive to undertake the politically sensitive and administratively difficult task of closing schools, particularly if their schools remained in compliance with generous norms on class sizes. With norms for class sizes allowing for variations as large as 25 percent (e.g., a minimum of 20 and a maximum of 25 students) or with no minimum class size at all (e.g., Serbia and Belarus), years could pass before a school was not in compliance with class size norms. Even then, local authorities usually had ways to postpone closing schools by asking education ministries for exceptions, adding additional financing from their own sources to keep schools in operation, or inflating student numbers to keep schools in compliance.

Figure 3.6 Dynamics of the 6- to 12-year-old Population in the ECA Region, 1990–2006
(1990 = 100)

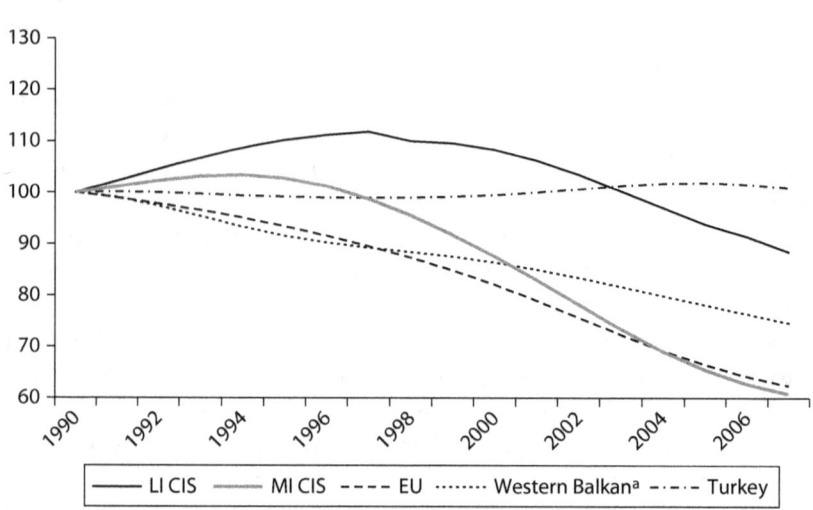

Source: EdStats Database.
Note: LI = low-income, MI = Middle-income.
a. Western Balkan population estimates are based on Albania, Bosnia and Herzegovina, and FYR Macedonia only.

Plummeting Student-Teacher Ratios Reflect the Failure to Adjust to New Realities

Declining student-teacher ratios across the region provide clear evidence that policy adjustments to date have not successfully addressed inefficient spending in the sector. Take the example of Moldova. The average school in Moldova was built in 1971, when pre-university students totaled 1.2 million and demographics looked favorable. After the Soviet Union collapsed, student numbers soon started to plummet. By 2010, there were less than 700,000 students in the country's schools (a 44 percent drop from the peak student population of 1995). Yet the number of teachers in these schools has not declined since 2003. In fact, there were as many schools in Moldova in 2009 as there were in 1994; on average, each school has only 56 percent of the students for which it was built. Student-teacher ratios are one way to look at the inability to adjust to falling student numbers. Before the transition, average student-teacher ratios in the ECA region were roughly similar to those observed in other regions in the world, but have since dropped significantly (see figure 3.7).

Figure 3.7 Primary School Student-Teacher Ratios in ECA Compared to Other Regions of the World, 1990–2008

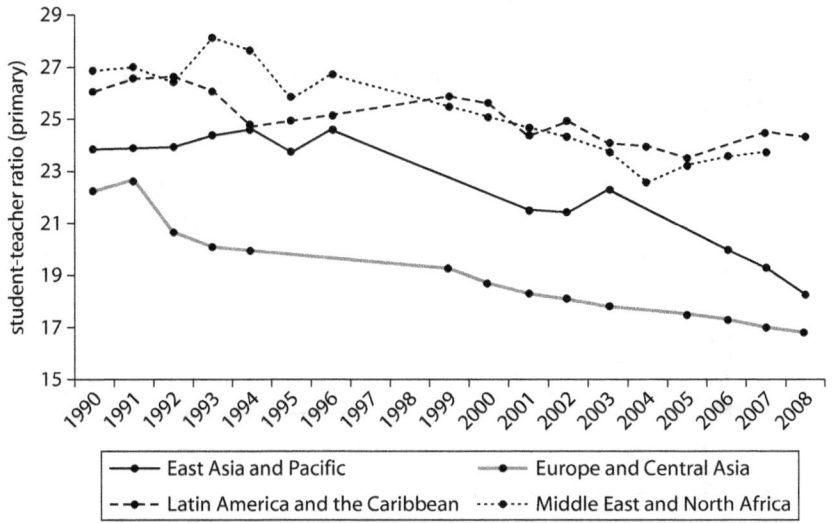

Source: EdStats database, plus author's linear interpolations for missing years.
Note: Actual data are marked with dots. One of the problems with international data on student-teacher ratios (in both the World Bank's EdStats database and other international education databases) is that it is unclear whether or not data for a particular country is reported on a full-time equivalent basis.

These low ratios are problematic for two reasons. First, other things being equal, lower student-teacher ratios imply that it is more costly to finance education per student. There is no evidence, however, that these rising costs have resulted in better-quality education (for instance, see figure 3.8 for the case of Romania, where TIMSS scores have remained roughly flat for a decade). Second, lower student-teacher ratios mean that more of the education sector's scarce resources are tied up in employee costs, leaving very few resources available for either innovations or much-needed classroom learning materials (e.g., new textbooks, computers, Internet access).

Teaching Profession Increasingly Devalued

The largest casualty of inefficient resource use has been the teaching profession, with evidence pointing to its significant devaluation—and a resultant deterioration in its quality at the pre-university level. Given limited resources, a teaching work force that is oversized relative to the number of students is poorly paid; indeed, teachers in most ECA countries earn salaries below the national median.[5] Over time, low wages and uncertainty about the future have diminished the attractiveness of teaching in the ECA region.

The current teaching workforce has become overwhelmingly female and is aging rapidly (see figure 3.9). The percentage of female primary

Figure 3.8 Real Per Student Expenditure Compared to TIMSS Math Scores in Romania, 1999–2008

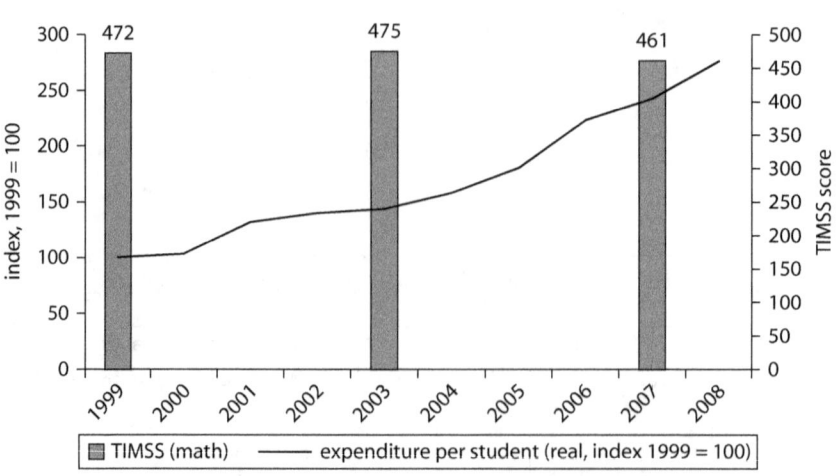

Sources: Authors' calculations based on TIMSS (various years) and expenditure data obtained from Romania's Ministry of Public Finance.

Figure 3.9 Percentage of Students with a Teacher Over 50 Years Old in ECA Countries, Selected Years

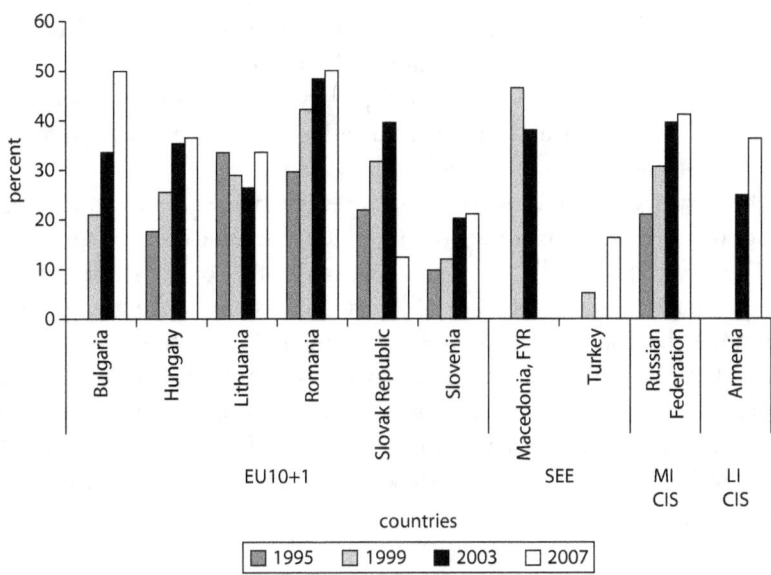

Sources: IEA (1995, 1999, 2003, and 2007): Mathematics and Science Teacher Background Data Almanacs.
Note: LI = low-income, MI = middle-income.

school teachers in non-EU members of the region is, in fact, considerably higher than in the EU15 countries (EdStats Database). And education systems throughout the region are finding it difficult to hire qualified teachers in key subjects, such as English and information technology.

Finally, the quality of students now applying to pedagogical schools is inferior to that of students applying to other programs of study, with few of the brightest university graduates entering the profession. A recent study (Silova 2009) looked at the situation of teacher training institutions in two countries in the ECA region (Azerbaijan and the Kyrgyz Republic) where detailed data on centralized university admission tests—ideal for such analysis—were available. Consistent with the other indicators reviewed in this section, Silova's analysis supports the thesis that the prestige and attractiveness of the teaching profession is low and declining in both countries.

Considered separately, these facts might not be alarming. Taken together, however, they make a compelling case that ECA countries are failing to attract the professionals who are urgently needed to improve the quality of education in the region.

Addressing the Skills Challenge

Education systems in the ECA region are facing daunting challenges with limited resources. Resolution of the most urgent challenges of these systems—overstaffing at the pre-university level, delivering the skills and competencies needed on the contemporary job market, and revamping vocational education and giving it an appropriate weight in secondary education—can no longer be delayed.

The very urgency of these problems presents policy makers in the region an opportunity to reform the way in which the education sector is managed overall. Specifically, they can systematically collect student performance data in order make better-informed decisions, make greater efforts to reduce the role of the central government in day-to-day operational issues at the school level, and link educational spending to agreed performance goals. As will be discussed in more detail in chapter 5, some of these principles have already been employed in many ECA countries at the tertiary level. The challenge is to disseminate these same principles at all levels of education.

Turn on the Lights

In order to provide quality learning for all, countries in the ECA region first need to understand how much their students are actually learning. As noted earlier in this chapter, all ECA countries need to begin systematically collecting data on how their education systems are performing, principally via standardized student assessments and graduate tracer studies (both of which need to be linked to student background information). Central ministries can then use this data to design policy improvements. To accommodate such a shift, education ministry staff will need training in both analyzing trends in education performance data and developing education policy options based on such data.

Participation in international assessments such as PISA and TIMSS is a valuable step in this direction, as it gives countries access to significant practical advice on how to design and administer student achievement tests, analyze results, draw policy conclusions, and, equally important, manage the dissemination and communication of these results to system stakeholders and the media. This subject is discussed in more detail in the following chapter.

Introduce Autonomy and Accountability at Lower Levels of the Education System

Overcoming the legacy of central planning involves changing the focus of education management away from detailed norms and instead holding actors accountable for *performance* (or results). School principals and local authorities need more decision-making authority to pursue new opportunities, and the flexibility to experiment. At the central level, this implies that policy makers in the ECA region would relinquish certain duties and assume others so that education systems may innovate and improve student learning outcomes. The opportunity before central governments in these countries is to move away from micromanaging schools and classrooms and focus instead on "steering" the system.

Extending autonomy throughout education systems means placing authority and responsibility in the hands of the people most able to innovate and improve the quality of education: local managers and education authorities (see Osborne and Gaebler 1992). The solution is not simply to scrap norms altogether and replace them with expanded autonomy at lower levels—a change in accountability relationships is also needed. The art of reform will thus challenge central governments in ECA countries to build new and more sophisticated relationships with local authorities, principals, teachers, and other stakeholders—relationships based on incentives and accountability relationships that make these actors partners in achieving agreed performance goals. Not surprisingly, most systemic education reforms that have taken place in OECD countries since the 1980s have focused on devolving responsibility for day-to-day decisions to the front lines, that is, to individual schools (OECD 2004b).

Aligning the incentives of stakeholders in the education sector with the student learning outcomes desired by policy makers will require education ministries to set overall performance goals; articulate who is responsible and accountable to whom and for what; and ensure that these responsibilities are agreed, accepted, and understood. Ministries will also need to provide lower-level actors the support they need to meet agreed education goals, whether in the form of financing, advice, or knowledge sharing of best practices. Collaborative structures, shared leadership, and the spirit of public service will be invaluable for supporting efforts to improve learning outcomes in the region. Teachers, students, and local education authorities need both resources and the organizational and human capacity to perform. Teachers in the region, whose salaries are rarely competitive with private sector wages, also need to feel valued, respected, and recognized for their service.

Introduce Performance-based Financing

Education financing in the ECA region can be more than just a flow of monetary resources, it can signal a desired policy direction to local education managers. More flexible, smarter financing in the form of block grants (i.e., contract- or performance-based) offers funding to learning institutions in return for meeting agreed learning outcomes. Not only does such financing give local education managers much-needed flexibility that line-item, input-based budgets do not permit, it keeps them focused on student results.

The majority of ECA countries have recognized the limitations of input-based financing schemes and have come to appreciate that financing can be used as a policy instrument. At the pre-university level, a typical first step away from input-based financing is to introduce a funding formula in which the number of students enrolled in a school is the main component. In fact, 11 ECA countries have introduced such formulae and fully abandoned input-based financing (see figure 3.10).[6] In essence, this means that public money is being allowed to "follow the

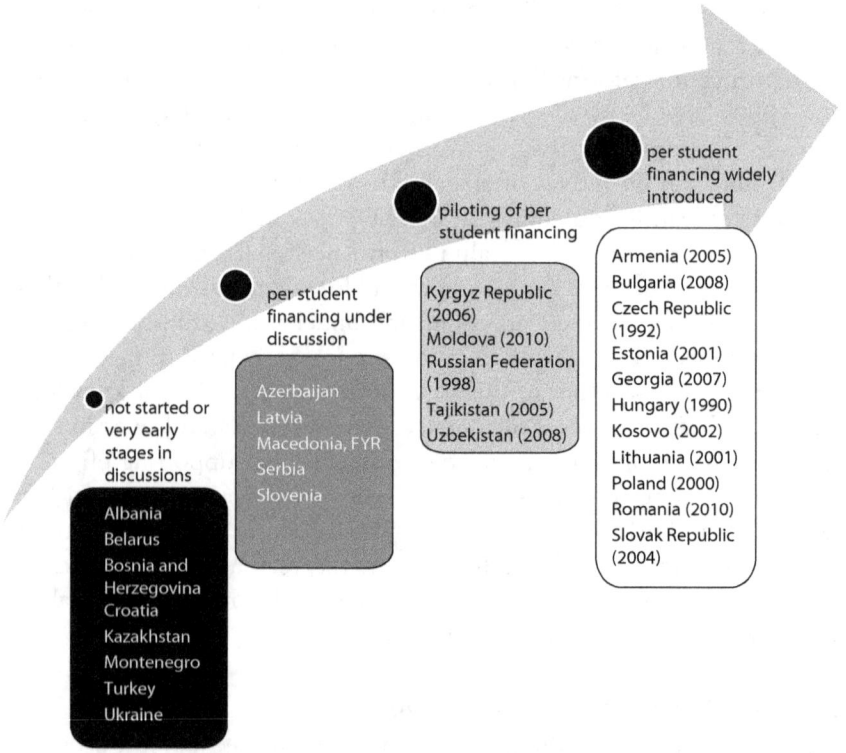

Figure 3.10 Progress Towards Results-based Education Financing in the ECA Region, 2010

Source: Authors' assessment.

student" rather than inputs (e.g., staff). Money can follow the student in many forms, such as student vouchers and block grants tied to student numbers. Countries that introduce per student financing typically design formulae that make it explicit and transparent how much a school will receive (see chapter 4).

Summary

There are three major impediments preventing education systems in ECA countries from helping to reduce the skills shortage in their region. First, ECA education systems have been operating without crucial information—in the dark. By focusing on top-achieving students, they neither seek to deliver quality education to all students, nor do they systematically collect data on the learning and employment outcomes of all students. Second, the legacy of central planning keeps the governance and management of school systems highly centralized, with central policy makers intensely involved in operational details. A focus on compliance with norms, together with financing schemes based on inputs and not outputs, means that most local education authorities and school principals in the ECA region lack the autonomy and authority to make crucial management decisions for their own institutions.

Third, education systems in the ECA region use financial resources highly inefficiently. Nowhere is this more apparent than in the preuniversity sector, where few countries have adjusted teacher staffing levels in response to falling student numbers over the past 20 years. As a result, student-teacher ratios have fallen sharply as per student costs have risen—more so than in any other region in the world.

Policy makers in the region can overcome these impediments by committing to quality education for all students, supported by systematic data collection on student outcomes; expanding autonomy at lower levels of the education system in return for accountability for student performance; and introducing performance-based financing. ECA countries are specifically encouraged to develop national learning assessments, systematically participate in international assessments, conduct regular tracer studies of graduates to determine their employment outcomes, and then use this data to inform education policy.

Overcoming the legacy of central planning will require central policy makers to reduce the role of the central government in day-to-day operations of their education systems. By concentrating on setting system standards and overall goals, the central government can then manage education systems for performance instead of compliance with norms. Greater autonomy can be granted to local education authorities and school principals in return for their accountability for improved student (and school) performance. Finally, policy makers can introduce performance-based financing (through such mechanisms as block grants or vouchers) and grant greater flexibility and decision-making power over school budgets to local education managers in return for meeting agreed learning outcomes.

The remainder of this report focuses on how governments can use the conceptual framework presented in this chapter—the three key problems impeding the education systems' ability to address the skills shortage and their corresponding policy solutions—to improve educational outcomes in pre-university, tertiary, and adult education, respectively, with an emphasis on practical options.

Notes

1. As a nontransition country, Turkey sometimes represents a different case. Although much of the discussion in this chapter is relevant to Turkey, it will be noted in those cases where it is not.
2. Although Turkey was not a command economy, it too has a very centralized system, evident, for example, in the lack of autonomy and accountability in the education system.
3. Again, though Turkey was not a command economy, it has a very centralized education system.
4. The PISA assessment conducted by the OECD provides evidence of these large differences in school autonomy, based on a questionnaire administered to school principals (in which three questions relate to budgeting). Data from the 2006 PISA show that schools in Estonia enjoy the most autonomy of all ECA countries, irrespective of how the question on budgeting is asked, while schools in Azerbaijan enjoy the least. It should be noted that PISA data must be interpreted with some caution, as it is unclear what is meant by "having more autonomy on budgeting." Does it mean more autonomy to formulate budgets, to re-allocate resources within budgets, to determine salaries and annual increases, or something else? Still, certain ECA countries have unambiguously granted substantially more flexibility to schools, principals, and governing boards than have others. A much better source of information on differences in school autonomy is provided by the Teaching and Learning International Survey (TALIS) study, also conducted by the OECD. In this survey, teachers and principals are asked more specific questions related to the degree of autonomy in their schools. Unfortunately, only six ECA countries

(Turkey, plus all new EU member states at the time) participated in the 2008 study, which confirmed that schools in Estonia enjoy substantial autonomy.

5. Comparing teacher salaries to those of other professions is not an easy task, both because salary differentials can derive from differences in educational background, experience, and other factors, and because different professions enjoy different noncash benefits. However, available data show that teacher salaries in the ECA region are low and that the gap between their salaries and the median economy-wide salary has widened in many countries. See the following data sources on teacher salaries: for OECD countries, OECD 2008 (accessible online at www.oecd.org/edu/eag2010); for CIS countries, CISSTAT, online database of the Interstate Commerce Committee of the Commonwealth of Independent States (Statistics of the Countries of the CIS, Annual Data from 1991 to 2010, http://www.cisstat.com/2base/frame00.htm); for economy-wide annual salaries for all countries, OECD StatExtracts, http://stats.oecd.org/Index.aspx. (All URLs accessed December 2010.)

6. The "result" referred to in this figure is a student enrolled. As discussed in chapter 4, a more desirable per student financing scheme would be to finance a student who is graduating, or better yet, a student who is graduating with a desired level of competencies. However, even the most advanced ECA countries (in terms of moving to school financing based on results) still base financing on the number of students enrolled (an intermediate result, at best). This report therefore intentionally distinguishes between the inputs of teachers, classes, and finances, and among students "enrolled," "graduating," "graduating with a desired level of competencies," or "graduating and finding a job" as results (or outputs).

CHAPTER 4

Managing for Results at the Pre-University Level of Education

The policy framework elaborated in chapter 3 can be applied to primary and secondary education in the ECA region to help create education systems more capable of meeting the skills gap outlined in chapter 1. First, policy makers in the region can overcome the debilitating lack of data on the performance of their education systems. Second, a more sophisticated relationship can be put in place between the central government and lower-level actors in the school system based on this data: greater autonomy at lower levels of the school system in return for holding local educational authorities and school directors accountable for improved student performance.

Freed from the day-to-day management of schools, policy makers will be able to devote more of their attention to elaborating strategic educational policy, including research and analysis of system and fiscal performance, and setting overall system goals, standards, regulations, and guidelines. One area of immediate concern will be designing long-term teacher policies to renew the teaching force and re-establish the prestige of the teaching profession in the ECA region.

Finally, current sector resources could likely achieve superior educational outcomes if schools were larger and if fewer but better paid teachers taught slightly larger classes. Linking financing directly to student performance will help to increase the efficiency of fiscal resources and hold local-level actors accountable for achieving the education goals of the central government. Special care must, however, be taken to prevent performance goals and financing mechanisms from punishing schools that have larger numbers of lesser-achieving students and instead reward them for improving these students' academic achievement. In the end, financing modalities that give schools the flexibility to allocate resources to the areas of greatest need will help schools improve the performance of *all* students, not just the highest achievers.

Track Student Learning and Employment Outcomes

Better data alone do not lead to better-quality education. Partly due to difficult demographic trends and partly due to history, ECA education systems have wound themselves in a knot that will be very difficult to untie without devoting greater attention to data on results. The legacy of central planning has created a system where bureaucrats manage the sector by writing detailed norms into legislation and then managing principals so that they comply with these norms. Generations of managers have lived with this system for their entire lives. When asked to improve education system performance, they therefore reach for the tools that they have always used, either by revising norms or ramping up inspections. This chapter argues that the solution is not to rewrite norms or expand the inspectorate but rather, to reach for different tools. However, none of the new tools will work without better data on performance: what competencies are students mastering and are graduates finding jobs?

As described in chapter 3, management of the education sector needs to shift from managing inputs to managing for results. This type of management requires a more sophisticated partnership between the central government and actors at the school (and local government) level, based on a shared and measurable understanding of what is to be achieved. That is, data on performance are what *enables* the central government to start managing for results, rather than for inputs. The chief source of this performance data is national and international student learning assessments, together with surveys of graduates that determine their employment outcomes.

Implement Yearly National Assessments

As noted earlier in this report, many ECA countries have begun to develop and, in some cases, implement national assessment exams. However, few (if any) countries in ECA are yet using the results of these exams to help design educational policies. To do so effectively, several key actions are needed. Most importantly, some background information about the students who take national assessment exams needs to be collected. The importance of this information should not be underemphasized: in its absence, the usefulness of test scores is severely constrained.

In Bulgaria, for example, a national assessment center can generate average national and regional scores on student achievement tests, but this data cannot be disaggregated to identify the performance of either different groups of students or individual students. The problem is that the assessment system (which gathers data on student test scores) is not linked to either socioeconomic information about students (e.g., data collected via survey when students take the test) or to the individual student identification numbers assigned by the Ministry's education information system. This oversight means that education policy makers in Bulgaria are unable to answer crucial questions related to the large wave of school closures that took place during the summers of 2007–2009, such as whether students who were moved to new schools are doing better or worse academically.

Further recommendations to improve assessment systems include the need to administer such tests on an annual basis, not only to collect standardized longitudinal data, but also to enable countries to have a baseline of student achievement results before and after educational reforms are introduced. Moreover, countries need to move beyond using national assessments solely for examination purposes (that is, to certify that a student has mastered a curriculum at the end of compulsory and upper secondary education) and begin using such tests to *assess* the quality of education at different stages in the cycle. For instance, policy makers may want to use a standardized test administered each year in order to evaluate how well fourth-graders are reading.

Continue (or Initiate) Regular Participation in International Assessments

International assessments give countries outside benchmarks with which they can gauge how well their education systems are performing. In addition to being able to track their performance against countries worldwide, participation in such tests as PIRLS, TIMSS, and PISA, will give ECA countries access to substantial technical assistance in how to analyze, understand, and use test results to design better education policies. Finally, systematic participation in international assessments enable countries to

Box 4.1

Using Data to Measure Gaps and Design Better Policies: Three Examples

In Serbia, researchers used PISA test scores for 2006 and 2009, together with student socioeconomic and ethnic information, to shed more light on what is widely known in the region: Roma students significantly lag their non-Roma peers (see table B4.1). Through careful analysis of this data, the researchers were also able to show that part of this performance gap was due to socioeconomic factors. That is, students with a Roma background were, on average, from more disadvantaged backgrounds (such students tend to do worse than their peers from better-off families). However, even when controlling for the fact that Roma students tend to come from more disadvantaged backgrounds, the gap is large, especially in math, suggesting that Roma students will need additional support to catch up, over and above that needed by children from other socioeconomically weak backgrounds. Such information on its own does not provide policy recommendations, but it sheds light on where problems exist, quantifies them, and provides a baseline against which policy initiatives can be measured.

Table B4.1 Learning Gaps between Roma and Non-Roma Students in Serbia, as Measured by PISA 2006 and 2009 Results

	PISA 2006		PISA 2009	
	Gap without controlling for socioeconomic differences	Gap when controlling for socioeconomic differences	Gap without controlling for socioeconomic differences	Gap when controlling for socioeconomic differences
Math[a]	107	77	86	43
Reading	77	44	91	52
Science	81	45	81	38

Source: Baucal and Pavlović-Babić 2010. These findings are corroborated by Baucal's 2006 study of the performance of Roma children on Serbia's national school assessment exam.
Note: Gaps shown above are calculated as the score of non-Roma students minus the score of Roma students.
[a] Statistically significant.

In Romania, researchers used PIRLS 2001 and 2006 data to quantify the extent to which students from rural schools lagged behind their peers from urban schools (Romania 2009). Equally important, they pointed out that the gap had widened, not narrowed, between the two tests. The magnitude of the gap played an important role in triggering the design of a project (financed by the World Bank) to address the quality of education in rural areas (see World Bank 2003b).

(continued next page)

> **Box 4.1** *(continued)*
>
> Finally, to gauge the risk that tertiary students were withdrawing from school as a result of the ongoing financial crisis, researchers in Romania administered a survey of students to identify those most at risk of dropping out (Pricopie et al. 2010). These results can be used by policy makers to design policies to mitigate this risk.

examine their educational progress over time because the tests are compatible and administered at pre-determined time intervals (e.g., PISA is administered every three years; PIRLS, every five years).

Monitor Student Labor Market Outcomes

The labor market outcomes of secondary graduates is another critical part of the performance data needed to manage education systems for results. This information is particularly important for transforming secondary education in the ECA region. This level of education can only respond to student and employers' demand if policy makers have accurate and timely information about the career implications of students' educational choices. In principle, this type of data should be gathered through regular labor market surveys (which exist in most ECA countries), periodic employer surveys (which are implemented in most countries on an ad-hoc basis), and graduate tracer studies (which exist nowhere in the region, save Romania and Hungary as of 2011). Tellingly, most countries have statistical agencies that conduct regular labor force surveys, but ministries of education tend not to analyze and use such results to design a more responsive education sector. Moreover, the results of these surveys are rarely made available to students or parents in a readily digestible and user-friendly form.

Create demand for more data and analysis. In order to mobilize and sustain resources to collect and analyze data, demand for this data and analysis must be stimulated. If such data are not used in the policy process, moreover, policy makers are quick to axe resources allocated for these purposes. Given the weak internal capacity of most ministries of education in the region, central governments might consider relying on outside researchers—such as university and policy institute experts—for help. This could be done in a number of different ways, including the following:

- Set aside competitive grants for researchers to write policy notes and research papers using assessment data.
- Make entire datasets more readily available. For instance, the OECD makes the entire PISA dataset publicly available for researchers to download online (http://pisa2009.acer.edu.au/; accessed December 2010).
- Change policies to make data matter, such as making improved student learning outcomes a component of teacher and school evaluations. (If the results of assessments have no impact, whether directly or indirectly, on policies or people's careers, it is very difficult to mobilize and sustain resources to maintain assessment centers and train people to analyze results.)

Expand Autonomy in Exchange for Accountability for Results

The OECD (2004b) has recognized that high-performing education systems tend to have local schools and education authorities with a high degree of autonomy. Not surprisingly, most systemic education reforms that have taken place in OECD countries since the 1980s have focused on devolving responsibility for day-to-day decisions to the front lines, that is, to individual schools. The underlying logic behind such devolution is to empower school principals. These principals, who are familiar with their respective staff, students' needs, and local conditions, are better suited to make operational decisions than bureaucrats in capital cities. School-based management, moreover, allows for stronger accountability relationships than micromanagement from the center (see, for instance, Barrera-Osorio, Fasih, and Patrinos 2009).

Policy makers can employ a range of different options for strengthening accountability, some of which are more rudimentary—and can be put in place faster—than others. All of these options entail risks and trade-offs that must be considered to prevent unwanted effects. With respect to school performance, ministries of education can do the following:

- Create and empower school councils and create incentives for their active participation in school decision-making processes, and provide them with adequate capacity and training, to increase the participation of parents and the community (see Patrinos et al. 2010).
- Administer national student assessments at key stages of the education cycle (e.g., after the 4th, 7th, and 12th grades) and make this data read-

ily available to parents and school councils to help hold schools accountable for results. Making assessment results more readily available has helped improve state-level accountability and student achievement in the United States (Hanushek and Raymond 2005; Carnoy and Loeb 2002) and Mexico (Alvarez et al. 2007).

- Require schools to prepare school development plans that outline each school's strengths and weaknesses, together with a vision and action plan for making improvements. Ideally this exercise should take as its starting point student scores on a national assessment exam, together with an institutional self-evaluation.

- Prepare "school scorecards" for all schools that include basic indicators (whichever are available), giving parents and students a sense of a school's performance. Such scorecards should be made available on the ministry's website and disseminated to local authorities and schools. Such score cards should publish the "value-added" of a school (e.g., an increase in test scores that takes into consideration students' socioeconomic background).[1]

- (Ideally) disaggregate school score cards—where regulations permit—by the performance of
  ○ Minority students
  ○ Low-income students
  ○ Students with limited proficiency in the language of instruction
  ○ Students with special education needs or disabilities or both

- Agree on criteria that objectively identify "a school in need of improvement" and decide what actions will be taken to support such schools. More specifically, they can agree on the ultimate sanctions for continued failure to improve performance, such as
  ○ Re-constituting the school (i.e., formally closing it down but reopening it immediately with new management and the possibility of staff re-applying for their jobs).
  ○ Turning the school over to private management

- Provide rewards to high-performing or improving schools or both. Here policy makers should avoid characterizing a "high-performing school" simply as one that has high average student scores on a standardized test or a large number of graduates who go on to university, as these indicators may merely reflect the fact that the school attracts high-caliber students (possibly from well-off families). Rather, a school should be judged as high- (low-) performing based on whether it delivers (does not deliver) learning to all types of students, including those from low-income and minority households. This is why it is so important that the performance of a school, in terms of student learning outcomes, be disaggregated to show the achievement of different types of students (e.g., low-income and minority students).

At the level of the school, education ministries can do as follows:

- Require that principals provide explanations for a schools' failure to improve student learning outcomes.
- Revisit the issue of who can hire and fire a school principal and to whom he or she is accountable. Given enhanced autonomy and more flexible financing, the most important question to ask is: Who is best positioned to ensure that a principal performs? The education ministry? A regional inspector? The local mayor? A school council (perhaps with representatives of all of the above)?
- Require that school principals undertake training and be licensed and institute programs to make this possible.

There are numerous risks related to holding schools accountable for results that policy makers must acknowledge and manage. For example, if an accountability system is based on tests that measure basic skills—and if these "high-stakes" tests carry great weight in school evaluations—the system risks focusing the education system solely on the measurement of basic skills, ignoring the overall goal of creating well-rounded, creative, active citizens and productive workers capable of engaging in lifetime learning.

A well-functioning accountability system requires credible consequences for success and poor performance, recognizing that outside factors also play a role in determining student learning outcomes. In the case of success, schools need to be recognized and rewarded. In the case of poor performance, schools need to be sanctioned in some way. At the very least, if learning outcomes deteriorate at a given school, the principal should provide an explanation for why this has happened (e.g., the composition of the student body changed in such a way that the school now has more students from challenging socioeconomic backgrounds). In the United States, the ultimate sanction is to "reconstitute" a school, which means replacing the principal and asking all teachers to re-apply for their jobs. In most U.S. states that have the power to reconstitute schools, however, schools are first placed on probation for two to four years, during which time they receive support and guidance to improve student achievement.[2]

Relax Class Size Norms

In the ECA region, moving toward greater school autonomy implies relaxing or abandoning the detailed norms or both that govern virtually all operational decisions. The most crippling norm that constrains school principals from managing for results is the class size norm. As noted in chapter 3, this norm—together with a centrally imposed curriculum—determines how many teachers can be hired. This number in turn determines 65 percent or more of most schools' annual budgets. Thus, this norm, more than any other, restricts principals from making the best decisions for their schools in terms of student learning and financial efficiency. The regulation is, moreover, fiercely protected by teacher's labor unions because it protects jobs. In this respect, Denmark provides an example of how to gradually eliminate class size norms (see box 4.2).

Abandon the Policing Mindset

Moving toward greater autonomy also implies changing a "policing" mindset that treats all schools more or less the same to an "auditing" mindset that differentiates management based on local capacity. Today, many schools in ECA countries are "policed" by inspectors, Ministry of Education staff members and financial managers: every school is visited at the beginning and end of a school year to check if norms and regulations are being complied with. Few schools have their own bank accounts and those that do sometimes need multiple approvals to make mid-year corrections to their initial budgets. The entire system seems designed based on the implicit assumption that wrong-doing can only be prevented by wrapping lower-level actors in as many layers of control as possible.

This "policing" culture will need to be abandoned to make local or school-based autonomy effective. Ministry of Education staff members and inspectors may very well need to continue to vigilantly manage certain schools (e.g., small schools with poor capacity), but others (e.g., large, well-established, and well-run schools) can be managed with a much lighter hand. For instance, rather than making every transaction subject to approval (still the case in many countries), well-run schools should be evaluated on the basis of performance criteria (i.e., specific learning outcomes) and year-end auditing of their financial statements.

> **Box 4.2**
>
> ### Eliminating Class Size Norms in Denmark
>
> Upper secondary schools in Denmark used to be governed by class size norms similar to those that exist across the ECA region today. Today, however, school principals have the discretion to determine the appropriate class size, while ensuring that their schools remain attractive in the eyes of prospective students.
>
> The Ministry of Education in Denmark long mandated that class sizes in upper secondary schools could not exceed 24 students. This norm was removed by the late 1960s, after which labor contracts with teacher unions specified that teachers teaching classes of more than 28 students would receive (substantial) additional compensation. Since 1999, an agreement was reached between the unions and the central ministry to abandon an upper limit, allowing school principals to determine this limit.[a]
>
> In determining the appropriate class size, principals must weigh economic, pedagogical, and "marketing" factors. Since schools in Denmark are considered self-owned institutions, economic factors are an important consideration. Collapsing two classes into one allows for considerable savings. On the other hand, principals must take into account pedagogical considerations so as to ensure high-quality education. Finally, principals know that students and parents—who are free to choose the school that their children will attend—value both smaller classes and a large selection of free electives.
>
> *Source:* Meeting with school administrator in Denmark, summer 2008.
> *Note:* a. Certain broad guidelines and requirements exist regarding class sizes. For instance, if 10 students at a particular school choose a particular "free elective," the school must offer it. Moreover, the ministry can mandate that a particular school offer a particular course in the interest of making sure that a specific geographic area of Denmark has sufficiently broad course offerings.

The ultimate goal of greater autonomy is to make an education system more flexible and responsive to student and employer demands. This is particularly needed in vocational education and training in the ECA region (see box 4.3), enabling it to expand or contract course offerings in response to student and employer demand, not on rigid governmental norms.

Introduce Autonomy Gradually to Offset Corruption

Education and finance officials in the region are rightly concerned about expanding institutional autonomy in an environment characterized by weak managerial capacity and widespread corruption. Such concerns are justified: as chapter 5 points out, the experience of expanding institutional

Box 4.3

Rethinking Secondary Education

One area where more local flexibility is needed is in the area of vocational education, where ministries of education in the ECA region continue to play too dominant a role. In many countries, these ministries continue to directly manage the profile, course offerings, and budgets of vocational schools. This has left the sector largely underfunded and unreformed. It has also maintained a strong dichotomy between vocational and general education schools. This chapter recommends expanding autonomy in this field by allowing either principals or local authorities (whether at the municipal or regional level) a greater say in determining the future of their schools, irrespective of their profile. In exchange for more autonomy, school principals should be held accountable for improvements in learning outcomes or improvements in the rate at which graduates progress to further study or find jobs.

The still strong dichotomy between vocational and general education in the ECA region stands in contrast to the trend worldwide, which is away from separating secondary education into general and vocational tracks and toward a common secondary curriculum. This curriculum offers students course options and defers job-specific education and training until after secondary school (Rutkowski and Scarpetta 2005). Moreover, many of the skills for which worldwide demand is growing most rapidly—such as foreign-languages and scientific problem-solving proficiencies—are normally provided by general secondary and higher education programs. To that extent, general secondary education is becoming, in effect, relevant vocational education. Given the need for lifelong learning and skills upgrading in a global knowledge economy, all secondary education programs should thus aim to provide the foundation for further educational development, including the deepening and refinement of skills.

Recent reforms in Poland, which led to consistent improvement in student learning outcomes, provide a powerful example of how educational quality at the secondary level can be enhanced by postponing the early sorting and streaming of students into academic and vocational tracks. Research suggests that the improvement in Polish students' test scores can be traced to the increased exposure of all students, especially low-performing students, to academic instruction (Jakubowski et al. 2010). This goal was achieved by delaying the start of vocational education, with its traditionally greater emphasis on narrow job-related skills, by one year for all students. The result was much stronger grounding of students in reading and mathematics, especially among weaker students who had previously been tracked into vocational schools, and consequently, better performance in assessments of student learning such as the PISA.

Sources: Rutkowski and Scarpetta 2005; Jakubowksi et al. 2010; authors' analysis.

autonomy at the tertiary level in the ECA region has not been without problems. Unfortunately, unethical behavior is flourishing at the tertiary level, which undermines the sector's ability to deliver quality education for all.

There are, however, ways of moving forward at the pre-university level while addressing these concerns. For instance, institutional autonomy does not have to be granted to all schools at the same time. Since central authorities might reasonably have concerns about granting autonomy for management when capacity at lower levels is very limited, one practical approach would be to start with larger schools (and larger local educational authorities), which usually have more managerial experience. From an implementation perspective, the benefits of focusing on large schools are obvious. In the case of Romania, for example, focusing initially only on large schools would involve training, say, 1,000 school principals and accountants, rather than the principals and accountants of more than 7,000 small schools.

The degree of autonomy granted to schools can also be expanded gradually, with country circumstances influencing the ultimate degree of autonomy eventually granted. It is important to note that autonomy—like accountability—is complicated. For instance, granting schools more autonomy in budgetary matters is unlikely to have much impact unless this autonomy includes the ability to make staffing decisions (since staff costs are the single largest budget item). Similarly, autonomy over staffing decisions will, inevitably, involve providing schools the autonomy to determine class sizes. Policy makers are thus urged to simultaneously make changes to a number of rules and regulations as part of a change in class sizes.

Improve the Efficiency of Resource Use

An essential step toward more results-oriented management of basic education is linking funding to results, which will advance several objectives. First, performance-based funding signals the desired result. Because information on results enters budget discussions, education systems are forced to collect data and measure results more systematically, creating "demand" for student achievement data and its analysis. Second, such funding embeds incentives into financing flows: actors in the system are rewarded by delivering results and will therefore seek to do so. As a result, performance-based financing can help address the large inefficiencies characteristic of education sectors in the ECA region. With money linked to results—as opposed to inputs—principals will, for example, hire the number of teachers and janitors needed (and that can be afforded), not the number mandated by norms.

In addition to instituting performance-based financing, education ministries can do the following:

- Require local authorities and schools to present their expenditures in a specific format that allows them to be compared nationwide, as well as have them audited by an outside party.
- Require schools to run surpluses or deficits no greater than a specified percentage of their total budget for a specified time period, say, one year.
- Require that school budgets and actual expenditures be made publicly available on school bulletin boards or websites or both.

Per Student Financing

In pre-university education, the most basic way to introduce performance-based financing—the path that several ECA countries have begun to pursue (see figure 3.10)—is to tie school funding to the number of students enrolled. Hence this type of financing is referred to as "per capita financing" or "per student financing." Theoretically, defining a "performance" measure as a student "enrolled" is somewhat unappealing. A theoretically more appealing measure would be "a graduate" or even "a graduate who has obtained a certain level of proficiency" (or even "a graduate who finds a job within a fixed time frame").

It is important to note that per student financing does not imply that the number of students enrolled is the only factor that determines the amount of money transferred from the central government to a local school. In fact, most countries allow the per student amount to vary according to a formula. Allowing for different per student amounts makes sense because the cost of providing education is not uniform in a given country. For example, it is more costly to enroll and graduate a socioeconomically disadvantaged or minority student because this student will require more attention and support. Similarly, areas of the country with few inhabitants will naturally have smaller schools that, in turn, imply larger costs. Good formulae take these differences into account to avoid punishing schools and local authorities that serve challenging student populations or locations or both. Box 4.4 provides an example of a

Box 4.4

Per Student Funding Formula: Recognizing the Varied Costs of Providing Education

The new financing system that became effective in Bulgaria on January 1, 2007, establishes individual per student financing standards for four different types of municipalities. Figure B4.4 presents these per student standards and the criteria that were used to differentiate between municipalities. The first type consists of municipalities that have 70,000 or more people living in the municipal center. The remaining municipalities (all of which have less than 70,000 inhabitants living in the municipal center) are divided into three groups: (1) municipalities with a population density greater than (or equal to) 65 people per square kilometer; (2) municipalities with a population density less than 65 people per square kilometer; and (3) small mountainous municipalities (a subgroup of 1 and 2) with more than three settlements and less than 10,000 inhabitants living in their municipal centers.

Whenever the financing scheme for education is changed, there are winners and losers. Identifying the losers and providing them with an adjustment path is thus part of a good implementation program. In Bulgaria's case, the Ministry of Education and Science (MES) recognized that 88 out of 264 municipalities would

Figure B4.4 Groupings of Bulgarian Municipalities, Together with Baseline Per Student Financing Amounts and Adjustment Coefficients, 2007

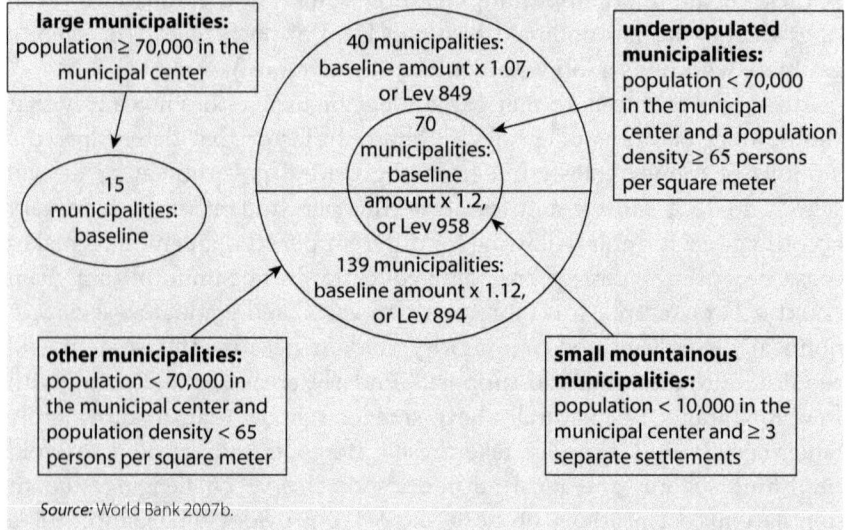

Source: World Bank 2007b.

(continued next page)

Box 4.4 *(continued)*

receive less funding (in nominal terms) under the per capita scheme than they had received the year before the new scheme was introduced (i.e., in 2006). To allow these municipalities time to adjust their class sizes (and, if needed, reduce the number of schools), they were entitled to receive compensation equivalent to the difference between the allocation based on the new per student amount and their allocation in 2006 during the initial year of implementation.[a]

However, to ensure that these "losing" municipalities would eventually be able to operate in a fiscally sustainably manner under the new regime, they were required to present a school consolidation plan to MES and the Ministry of Finance in order to qualify for the compensation. In addition, the MES clearly communicated that the compensation would only be available during the first year of implementation. Thus, losing municipalities had strong incentives to initiate school consolidation; with wages increasing by about 5–10 percent per year (at the time) in nominal terms, the only way for them to become financially viable under the per capita scheme was to consolidate their school networks. As expected, the reforms led to a large number of school closures, as municipalities moved to create more viable schools.

Source: Authors based on World Bank 2007b.
a. On the other hand, implementation plans did not specify any ceilings on funding for municipalities that would be "winners" under the new scheme. Thus, municipalities that had well-optimized school systems would experience increases in their education budgets.

formula used in Bulgaria that differentiates between the underlying costs of providing education in different circumstances.

Create incentives for larger class sizes. As mentioned in chapters 2 and 3, student-teacher ratios, class sizes, and school sizes have fallen precipitously in most ECA countries over the past 20 to 30 years. As a result, education systems in most of these countries are wasting scarce resources (from an educational perspective): they are heating and maintaining half-empty buildings; employing, training, and paying salaries to a larger staff than needed; and maintaining class sizes that could, in all likelihood, be increased (e.g., to their levels of just 20 years ago) without affecting the quality of education.

Small class sizes and a large number of teachers relative to students are observed in all countries of the region for which data are available, except Turkey. For instance, class sizes at the primary level (i.e., grades 1–4) in Poland, Serbia, and Azerbaijan are 20, 14, and 12, respectively, compared to 23 in France, 26 in the United Kingdom, and 31 in Chile and the Republic of Korea (see figure 4.1). School-level data show that the small class problem in the ECA region is not only a problem of small schools—even the largest schools in these countries have relatively small classes (see figure 4.2). The fact that even large schools have small class sizes suggests that significant savings can be generated merely by *within-school* optimization, that is, forcing existing (large) schools to create larger classes.

As noted in chapter 3, there is no "magic" size that fits all students and learning circumstances. What works, on average, in a Korean school in 2010 may not work in a Ukranian school in 2010, and what works for some students may not work for others. A class size of 35 may be appropriate in an urban classroom taught by the country's best teachers, whereas a class size of 5 may be suitable for a tiny, rural school where every student is from an ethnic minority. Rather than focus on determining a general "appropriate" class, ministries of education would thus be better off trying to change the rules of the game for principals and local authorities. Specifically, as discussed in the previous section, they should expand local autonomy to let principals determine the appropriate class size for their respective schools (taking into consideration local circumstances and needs) and use a per student financing formula to ensure that financial performance is also part of a principal's management considerations.

Encourage school optimization. The experience of ECA countries that have implemented per student formulae suggests that these formulae alone do not lead to school closures; their introduction needs to be complemented by other policy initiatives (e.g., a program to finance the transportation of children to their new schools). However, putting such a formula in place can signal to school principals and local communities that certain schools are no longer financially viable.

Until its recent push to close underutilized schools, Bulgaria had many villages with large school buildings capable of accommodating hundreds of students (see box 4.5). These schools were standing virtually empty, with only 50 to 100 students enrolled. Addressing the inefficiencies that result from such an oversized school network—underutilized space, small class sizes, and scarce maintenance resources stretched across many buildings—is a necessity throughout the ECA region. Closing and merging schools will, however, be substantially more difficult than increasing class sizes in large schools. In addition, school closures may produce certain associated costs, including

Figure 4.1 Comparison of Average Size of Primary School Classes Worldwide, Various Years

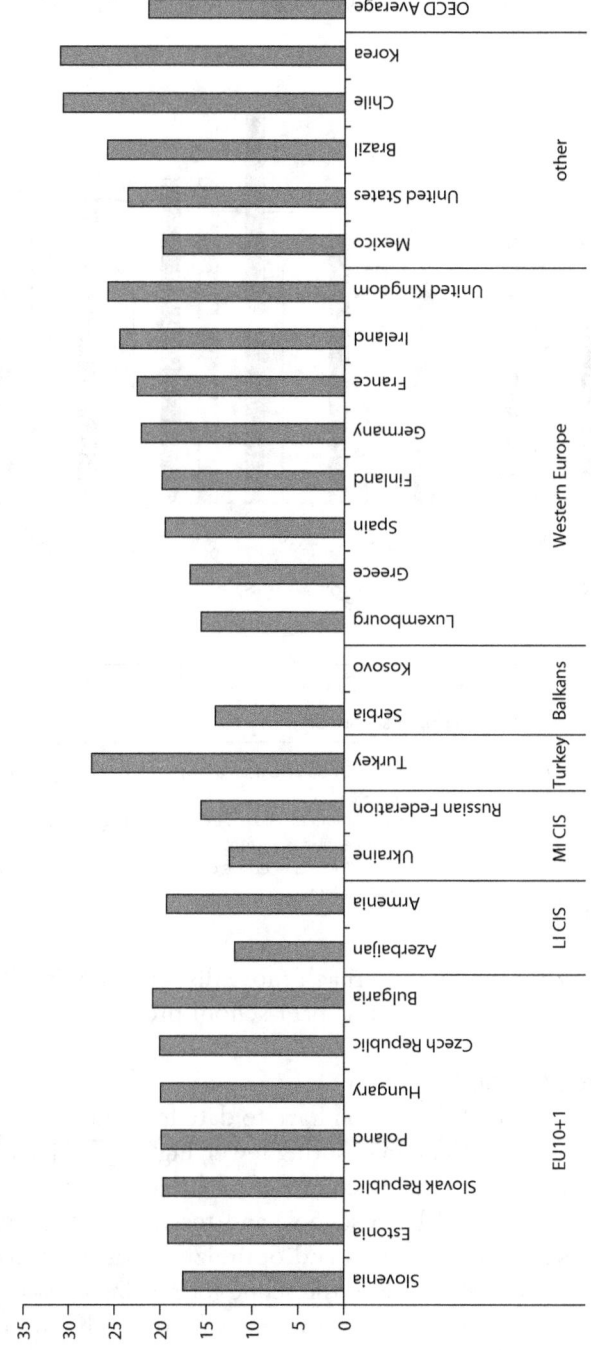

Sources: OECD Education At a Glance Database for OECD and partner countries; authors' calculations based on Ministry of Education data (from education management information systems) for Azerbaijan, Serbia, and Romania, and on National Statistical Institute school-level data for Bulgaria.
Note: Most recent data for each country (2005, 2006, 2007, or 2008).

Figure 4.2 Average Class Size in Large Primary and Secondary Schools in Nine ECA Countries, Various Years

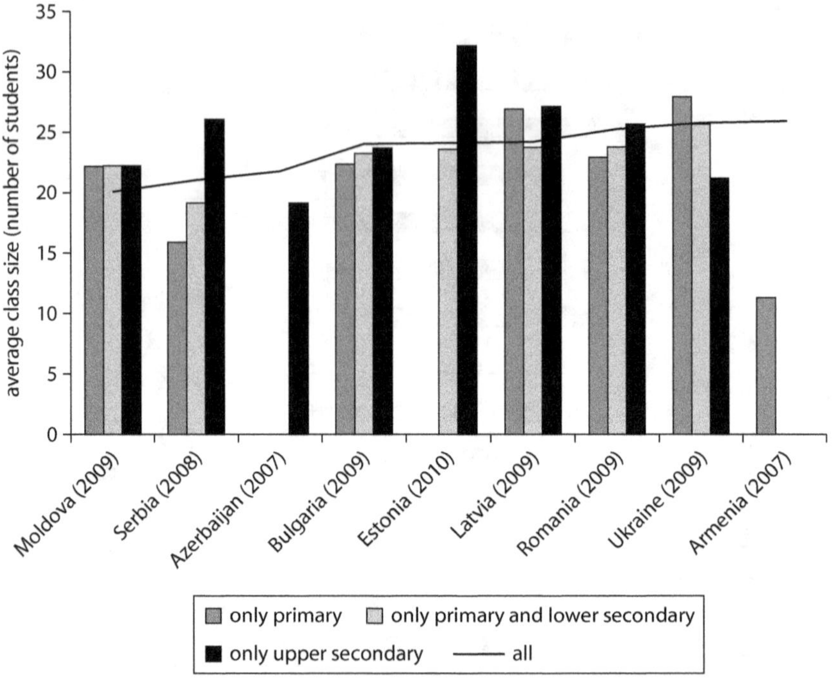

only primary   only primary and lower secondary   only upper secondary   ——— all

Source: Authors' analysis based on school-level data obtained from the ministries of education or national statistical agencies of nine ECA countries for various years.
Note: The definition of a "large" school is flexible in order to recognize different types of schools in ECA countries. A primary school that teaches only grades 1–4 is defined as a large school if it has more than 50 students per grade and thus a total of more than 200 students. A comprehensive general school that teaches grades 1–12 is defined as a large school if it has more than 600 students.

transportation for students to reach more distant schools, refurbishing receiving schools, and providing after-school programs.

Address Overstaffing

School systems in the ECA region have to date focused more on protecting teaching positions than on ensuring fewer, higher paid jobs. In light of mounting cost pressures, many countries in the region are now trying to downsize the number of both schools and teachers in their systems. In addition to increasing class sizes and optimizing existing schools, countries in the region might explore the scope for retiring over-age teachers. Specifically, they could use the impending wave of teacher retirements to implement an orderly reduction in the number of teaching positions,

Box 4.5

Rationalizing Class Sizes in Bulgaria

Recent efforts in the ECA region indicate that significant cost savings can be gained from rationalizing class sizes. Bulgaria's recent experience provides the clearest piece of evidence. Starting January 1, 2007, the Bulgarian government shifted the financing system for primary education from one based on inputs (i.e., teachers) to one based on student enrollment. The bulk of financing for education to municipalities is now provided in the form of a large earmarked grant based on the number of students in the municipality. Municipalities can then decide themselves how many schools they want to maintain. Not surprisingly, many municipalities quickly decided they could do with one, two, or three fewer schools than they had previously maintained, together with larger class sizes. As a result, they started approaching the Ministry of Education with requests for school closures.

The Ministry of Education in Bulgaria still plays an important role in the school closure process. It has the final say in school closings and monitors compliance with a fairly elaborate set of procedures that municipalities must undertake before closing a school. For instance, a school closure proposal has to include a discussion of how the transportation needs of affected students will be addressed and demonstrate that nearby schools have sufficient capacity to accommodate the additional students. The government has also introduced a program to monitor dropout rates at receiving schools. And it has established a number of additional national programs to support municipalities in the process. For instance, municipalities with school closures can apply for school buses, additional payments for laid-off teachers, and resources to refurbish "central" (or newly "merged") schools. Finally, the ministry has put together a list of "protected schools": schools that cannot be closed because no nearby schools exist, thus ensuring access to education for all. Additional resources to finance such small schools (usually located in mountainous areas) are also provided by the ministry.

The results of this process in Bulgaria are shown in figures B4.5A and B4.5B below. After many years of unsuccessful attempts to close schools (interrupted by brief spikes in school closures in 1997 and 2000), Bulgaria has seen a sharp increase in school closures since per student financing was put in place in 2007. Prior to these closures, average class sizes had been gradually decreasing even in large schools. However, with better incentives and greater freedom to take action, the principals of these schools turned around this trend: the average class size rose for the first time (albeit only marginally) in 2008–09 (see figure B4.5A).

(continued next page)

Box 4.5 *(continued)*

Figure B4.5A Estimated Number of Public School Closures in Bulgaria from 1991–92 through 2008–09

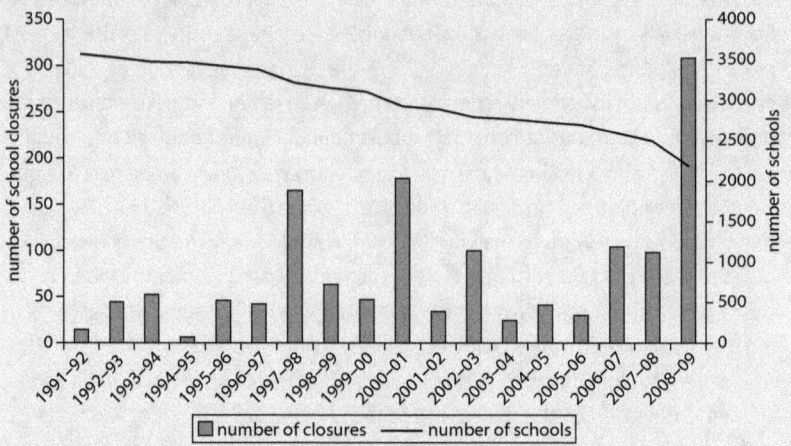

Source: World Bank staff calculations based on Bulgaria National Statistical Institute Web site (www.nsi.bg/index_en.htm) and estimates for the 2008–09 school year.
Note: The number of "school closures" has been estimated somewhat crudely, as has the difference in the number of public general education schools (i.e., the "net change" in the number of schools). Thus, in principle, there could have been more school closures in a given year if new schools were opened that same year.

Figure B4.5B Average Class Size and Student-Teacher Ratios in Bulgaria, 2000–08

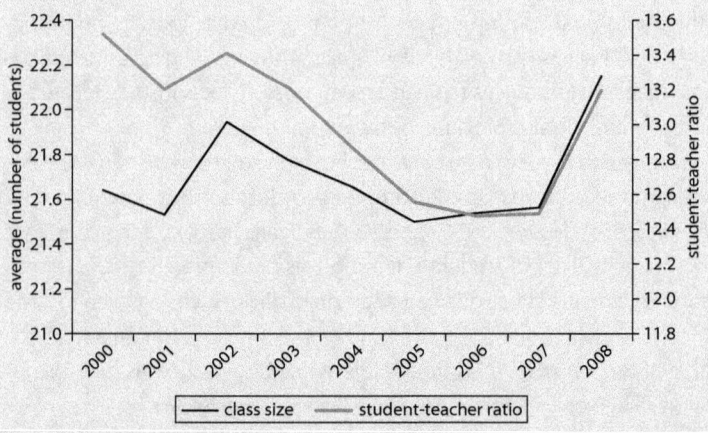

Source: Authors' calculations based on school-level data obtained from Bulgaria's National Statistics Institute Web site, www.nsi.bg/index_en.htm.

while slotting new hires for subjects in greatest demand, such as information technology. The use of stronger redundancy or retraining packages or both for departing teachers might make departures more acceptable. The experience of countries now in the process of reducing teacher numbers in response to the ongoing economic crisis (e.g., Latvia and Romania) may provide valuable lessons in this area.

At the same time, governments in the region will need to develop strategic policies to reinvigorate the teaching profession (see box 4.6).

Box 4.6

Developing New Teacher Policies

When policy makers in the ECA region are freed from the daily operational work of managing schools, they can devote more time to managing the most important asset in the education sector: teachers. Specifically, they have the opportunity to design long-term policies to restore the prestige of the teaching profession, attract higher-caliber teachers, and motivate them to remain in the profession. The importance of good teachers is well understood as a central feature of top-performing education systems worldwide, which all share one important feature: the ability to attract high-performing individuals into a teaching career and turn them into effective instructors.[a]

One innovation that ECA countries could consider would be to introduce performance as a more formal criterion for teacher remuneration. In Chile, the Ministry of Education introduced a productivity bonus called the "National Subsidized School Performance Evaluation System" in 1996. The aim of the program was to improve academic performance via the bonus, which was given to teachers working in institutions that showed the best test score results over the course of two years. To ensure that test score results were compared between similar schools (i.e., schools with students from similar socioeconomic groups), "homogenous school groups" were created and the competition between teachers and schools were created within these groups. The scheme in Chile is thought to have been associated with generating better learning outcomes (Contreras, Flores, and Lobato 2003).

Another innovation that ECA countries could consider is to more carefully monitor teaching practices (as opposed to monitoring student test score results alone). Having standardized information on classroom teaching practices in addition to test score results would provide policy makers with intermediate information on strengths and weaknesses in the learning process.

(continued next page)

Box 4.6 (*continued*)

In the United States, a recent large-scale evaluation of teacher policies relied on a prominent tool—the Vermont Classroom Observation Tool (VCOT)—that may offer a suitable starting point for ECA countries. The VCOT reportedly measures those teacher practices that current research suggests are essential to good teaching or that have been linked to student achievement. According to the researchers involved in the evaluation, who reviewed all available tools for this purpose, VCOT has a number of desirable features, including the following:

- An appropriate level of detail on teaching practices that are deemed to be good instruction, including the ability to capture complex teacher behaviors, such as whether a teacher makes connections between reading and writing
- Relatively simple implementation in the field (see Glazerman et al. 2009).

Needless to say, more conventional tools to heighten the quality of future teachers are also important, such as accrediting teacher training programs and requiring that teachers be certified before entering the classroom. Best practices mandate that accreditation be performed by an independent agency and focus on evaluating the learning outcomes of teacher training programs, rather than prescribing fixed ways to accomplish prescribed learning objectives (OECD 2005a). Teacher certification, moreover, can be an effective way to assess whether teaching candidates possess the qualities essential to the profession.

Sources: McKinsey & Company 2007, 2008; Glazerman et al. 2009; OECD 2005a; authors' analysis.
a. Although perhaps unsuitable for a national strategy, the Teach for America Program in the United States and the Teach First Initiative in the United Kingdom provide invaluable lessons for policy makers seeking to develop aggressive teacher recruitment strategies. Both programs employ the same tools used by top private firms to attract high-caliber candidates (see McKinsey & Company 2008).

Summary

To manage for results at the pre-university level, education ministries should implement national student assessment exams on an annual basis, as well as participate regularly in student assessments such as PISA, TIMSS, and PIRLS. For assessment data to produce the kind of information needed to improve student outcomes, however, background information on the students who take these assessments must be collected at the time of the tests. Without such information, the usefulness of test scores is severely constrained because the data cannot be disaggregated by different types of students, such as those from different socioeconomic backgrounds or ethnic minorities. Policy makers can create greater demand for this data in part by making student learning outcomes a component of teacher and school evaluations.

Perhaps most important, countries in the ECA region need to move beyond using national assessments solely for examination purposes and begin using such tests to *assess* the quality of education at each level and thus inform policy making in the sector. In addition to performance data, ECA countries need to regularly collect data on the labor market outcomes of secondary graduates, primarily through labor market surveys and periodic tracer surveys of graduates.

Central education ministries should also abandon a "policing" mindset that manages schools for compliance with norms and instead grant schools greater autonomy in return for accountability. This means giving lower-level actors greater decision-making power over school operations and budgets, as well as relaxing central norms on class sizes. Greater autonomy is particularly needed in vocational education and training, where programs need the ability to response to demand. Among the potential accountability mechanisms that policy makers can implement are the creation of school councils; school development plans that outline each school's strengths and weaknesses; "school scorecards" that include basic indicators on a school's performance; and the sanctioning of low-performing schools and rewarding of high-performing schools, defined—in both cases—as schools that improve (or not) the learning outcomes of all types of students, including those from low-income and minority households.

Significant improvements in the direction of greater autonomy and accountability will, however, be difficult to achieve in the school system unless policy makers in the region address the neglect of the teaching force, an effort that will involve resolution of serious overstaffing problems and improving the pay, professional development, and work conditions of teachers. Specifically, policy makers should take advantage of the impending wave of teacher retirements to implement an orderly reduction in the number of teaching positions, while slotting new hires for subjects in greatest demand, such as information technology. The use of stronger redundancy or retraining packages or both for departing teachers may make departures more acceptable.

Finally, per student financing should be introduced in the school system using a formula that allows the per student amount to vary according to the cost of providing education in a given region or school. Such funding also embeds incentives into financing flows: actors in the system are rewarded by delivering results and will therefore seek to do so.

Notes

1. For an example of school scorecards, see the Ministry of Education of Chile website at www.simce.cl. For an example of school report cards with value-added results, see U.K. school results on the U.K. Department for Education website at www.education.gov.uk/performancetables./ (both URLs accessed January 2011).
2. U.S. Department of Education. 1998. "Turning Around Low-Performing Schools: A Guide for State and Local Leaders." U.S. Department of Education, Washington, DC. http://www.ed.gov/pubs/turning/intervene.html. Accessed September 2010.

CHAPTER 5

Managing for Results in the Tertiary Education Sector

Despite certain areas of excellence and growing numbers of students, the quality of tertiary education[1] among countries in the ECA region continues to be of concern. The sector has expanded, but the growth has occurred without sufficient quality assurance mechanisms and without the necessary information enabling users to make informed choices. As a result, it is unclear if tertiary students are graduating with the advanced competencies needed by future employers.

A number of countries in the region have already granted tertiary providers considerable autonomy.[2] These countries, while continuing to promote local management of this sector, now face the additional hurdle of improving academic and fiscal integrity by introducing accountability mechanisms that focus on improving learning outcomes. Other countries in the region have yet to change their centralized management practices. These countries face the simultaneous challenges of enhancing university autonomy and developing stronger accountability mechanisms. All of the ECA countries, however, need to make greater efforts to collect data on student learning and employment outcomes, and introduce performance-based financing.

Even though fundamental integrity problems remain widespread in the university sector, it is important that ECA policy makers refrain from attempting to resolve these problems *before* they devolve authority to universities and introduce flexible financing. The great temptation in the region—given its tradition of strong centralized control—is to fix integrity problems with even stronger centralized control and management, which history suggests is unlikely to improve the situation. Even if it could, more control is unsuited for improving either relevance or financial efficiency in the tertiary sector. Instead, greater autonomy is needed if local decision makers are to discover and adopt local, innovative solutions that equip their graduates with the competencies needed on local labor markets.

In addition to strengthening accountability, all ECA countries need to focus on collecting more student outcome data. Here, the region shares the problem of advanced industrial nations: an inability to evaluate sector performance based on student learning outcomes. Performance in tertiary education continues to be primarily evaluated based on the data that are easy to generate, namely, the number of academic publications by faculty, which says very little about the quality of teaching and even less about how much students have learned. The only way to shift the discussion of performance towards student learning outcomes is to start using standardized tests to measure what students learn.

Greater use of performance-based financing in the sector is also critical for improving the accountability and efficiency of higher education institutions. In addition, more private resources will be needed to help the tertiary sector meet rising student demand, with fee-based mechanisms offering an additional way to strengthen the focus on results.

Introduce Learning Assessments and Track Employment Outcomes

As in the pre-university sector, the need for better outcome data in the tertiary sector is the first priority of central governments in the ECA region because without such data, they cannot address the legacy of central planning. That is, they cannot move from micromanaging inputs to steering the system through policy guidance and standards. Specifically, policy makers need to know whether scarce public resources (and existing rules and regulations) in the university sector are working or need adjustment. For such an assessment, a range of different data is required, with data on student learning and employment outcomes the most important. Only this type of data can answer the question: What is the sector achieving in terms of results?

Governments are not the only actors that would benefit from better information on outcomes. Employers, students, and parents also need objective, standardized data to make informed decisions. The market for tertiary education is a classic example of the seller (i.e., universities) being vastly better informed than their consumers (i.e., students, parents, and future employers), or even their financiers and donors (i.e., governments, for the most part) (Carey 2010). When students make choices about future universities and degrees, they usually do so without having met the professors who will teach them and with little to no understanding of the skills that they will acquire. This asymmetry places a great deal of power in the hands of the seller, which can contribute to worsening quality and higher costs for the consumer. In other parts of an economy characterized by similar informational asymmetries, policy makers usually play a strong regulatory role or mandate that providers provide better information to consumers or both.

Currently, data on tertiary outcomes in the ECA region as elsewhere focus on research outcomes, such as how many publications the faculty of a university is producing. Unfortunately, when this is the only performance indicator available, it inadvertently receives more attention than it should. Indeed, rankings of universities in the region place significant weight on the number of publications that they produce. However, from a skills perspective, the outcome that matters most is whether students are graduating with the competencies in demand on the job market and finding jobs. Currently, these outcomes are not being measured. Governments in the ECA region can change this situation by granting tertiary institutions public resources in return for them providing useful information about student learning and employment outcomes. There are several complementary ways of gathering this information, some of which are more direct than others. These include rankings or league tables, tracer studies, and direct measurement of student competencies via standardized tests.

As noted in earlier chapters, standardized tests are the best available indicator for measuring student performance, especially when socioeconomic characteristics are collected for each student (allowing the results of different socioeconomic groups to be compared). Such data are especially useful if organized to track the progress of individual students over time. Together with other indicators, these tests provide data on differences in learning outcomes between weaker and stronger students and institutions. Without this information, policy makers have no way of identifying—and thereby rewarding—institutions that do the best job of giving the largest number of students a quality education. Unfortunately,

> **Box 5.1**
>
> ## The Difficulty of Measuring Competencies at the Tertiary Level
>
> It is perhaps understandable that higher education institutions around the world have been reluctant to let governments interfere in designing tests and measuring competencies of their students, arguing that such attempts would interfere with academic freedom. Any attempt to introduce such tests should accordingly be carried out in cooperation with higher education institutions.
>
> Several countries around the world have introduced standardized tests to measure what competencies their tertiary students acquire during the course of their studies. For instance, in the United States, the Collegiate Learning Assessment (CLA) was developed in the 2000s by a subsidiary of the RAND Corporation, and is currently used only by roughly 400 institutions. Recognizing that students choose very different academic specialties in college, "the CLA tests the higher-order thinking skills that all college graduates should possess: critical thinking, analytic reasoning, and communication. The exam is given to a sample of freshmen and seniors to estimate how much students learn in college" (Carey 2010, 16–17).
>
> Similarly, since 1949, the Graduate Record Examination (GRE) has been used as an admission requirement by numerous graduate programs in the United States. It is a standardized test that seeks to measure verbal and quantitative reasoning, analytical writing, and critical thinking skills.
>
> The OECD is currently preparing an assessment of tertiary students called the Assessment of Higher Education Learning Outcomes (AHELO), a tool that will "assess learning outcomes on an international scale by creating measures that would be valid for all cultures and languages."[a] However, the OECD does not expect a full-scale AHELO to be launched before 2016.
>
> *Sources:* Carey 2010; author's analysis.
> *Note:* a. See the AHELO website for more details: www.oecd.org/edu/ahelo (accessed September 2010).

a standardized international learning assessment for tertiary students is not expected to be launched until 2016 (see box 5.1). Thus, to gather the necessary data now—when it is needed—ECA countries will need to begin with their own, domestically developed approaches. Several countries around the world have already started introducing standardized tests to measure student learning outcomes (see Salmi 2011 for a review). Such efforts would provide complementary information to the international comparisons that Assessment of Higher Education Learning Outcomes (AHELO) will generate in the coming years.

Experiment with Measuring Learning Outcomes

All countries in the ECA region save Tajikistan, the Kyrgyz Republic, Uzbekistan, Turkmenistan, and Kosovo, have become signatories to the Bologna Process and the push to create a European Higher Education Area (EHEA) by 2010.[3] As participants in the Bologna Process, most ECA countries have taken important steps towards establishing and strengthening quality assurance institutions, and, most important, moving towards an environment where university degrees are described based on learning outcomes, competencies, and student workloads (Adelman 2003). "Learning outcomes" in the Bologna process are generic statements of what a learner knows and is able to do at the end of a period of study. This initiative has established learning outcomes for the three levels, or cycles, of tertiary education (bachelor, master, and doctorate), as well as for so-called "short degree" or "short higher education" programs.[4] Important preparatory work in this area has been done by the Tuning Project,[5] which brought together academics from all over Europe to develop subject-specific learning outcomes for a range of professions, including, for example, history and nursing.

The establishment of a European Qualifications Framework for Lifelong Learning, followed by the national qualifications frameworks (NQFs) of individual countries, are other important milestones toward the measurement of learning outcomes. Within EHEA today, qualifications frameworks and the European Credit Transfer and Accumulation System (ECTS) allow teachers and students to establish how many "credits"—the quantitative indicator for units of learning—a student obtains from finishing a course, program, or other unit of learning. However, countries in the EHEA have not yet moved toward introducing standardized assessments to measure what students acquiring these credits can do in terms of skills.

One way that ECA countries might begin to measure the learning outcomes of tertiary students would be to introduce standardized testing within fields of study where these outcomes have been clearly defined. Alternatively, ECA ministries of education might develop tests of the broader competencies that all tertiary graduates can be expected to have (e.g. verbal reasoning, quantitative abilities, analytical writing, and critical thinking skills). The OECD's DeSeCo project (OECD 2005b), discussed in chapter 2, could provide a starting point for the definition of such broad competencies.

Start with rankings, tracer studies, and student surveys. Although it is likely to take years before the competencies of tertiary students can be measured using standardized tests, policy makers in the ECA region can take immediate steps to provide more information about the quality of the tertiary sector. First, they can mandate that all tertiary institutions survey their students after graduation, using graduate tracer studies. Such studies can be implemented relatively quickly and would provide initial insight into a system's current strengths and weaknesses. Second, regular surveys on the practice of purchasing admission and cheating may also be worth considering, given the magnitude of reported fraud in the tertiary sector (see the next section), even though such surveys would not be a measure of quality per se. Third, regular (standardized) surveys of students regarding their satisfaction with their university choice and the teaching at that institution could also be implemented relatively quickly and provide additional information for the compilation of rankings.

With respect to tracer studies, two countries in the region—Hungary and Romania—are making rapid progress. In fact, these studies are becoming a core element of tertiary management in these countries. In Hungary, 2010 marked the first year that results from the new "Graduate Career Tracking System" were produced (spanning graduates from 25–30 institutions). This project is the culmination of work that began in 2008 and involved 30 ongoing EU-financed projects. In Romania, data from a graduate survey will be available in 2011. By that time, policy makers will have results from surveys of students who graduated in 2008–09 (i.e., 12 months after they graduated), as well of students who graduated in 2004–05 (i.e., five years after they graduated). As is the case with Hungary, the development of the tracer study in Romania is being financed by EU Social Funds.

Hungary is moving ahead rapidly on tracer surveys for several reasons. In the first place, central policy makers in the country are pressuring tertiary institutions to start collecting such data. The 2005 Higher Education Act of Hungary, for example, makes it mandatory for every university and college to carry out surveys of graduates. The central government has also made tracer studies a part of quality assurance discussions, with the availability of such surveys now (or soon to be) tied to institutions' accreditation agreements. In addition, the government is using the power of the purse, tying tracer survey data (or their availability) to three-year financing agreements. In the second place, institutions of higher education in Hungary themselves consider tracer data useful for a number of reasons: (1) they want labor market feedback to help them design better programs; (2) the data can be used in marketing; (3) the data is valuable for internal quality assurance; and (4) tracer surveys are one of many engagement tools for strengthening an alumni network.

Rankings have also played an important role in helping broaden what performance in the higher education sector means, moving the definition well beyond a simple measure of the total number of publications a university faculty produces. For instance, the British newspaper *The Guardian* provides "University League Tables" on 46 different fields of study (from programs focusing on "agriculture, forestry, and food" to "veterinary science") that includes measures of student satisfaction with courses and teaching.[6]

Conceptually, rankings are fundamentally a less valid performance indicator than student assessments or surveys of employment outcomes because they focus primarily on inputs and processes, rather than student outcomes. Nevertheless, rankings play a powerful role by providing certain key information on institutions, strengthening competition among them, and highlighting the idea that "performance" matters.[7] For example, the multidimensional ranking of the Center for Higher Education Development (CHE) (see Usher and Medow 2009), has gained a strong international reputation. The risk, however, is these efforts promote competition along the dimensions—that is, inputs and processes—that may not necessarily be relevant to outcomes, thereby possibly diverting attention and resources away from the outcomes that really do matter.

Introduce greater autonomy and encourage private sector participation. As noted at the outset of this chapter, authority for operational management of tertiary institutions has been most fully devolved in the new EU member states and to a lesser degree, in the countries of South Eastern Europe and in Ukraine and the Russian Federation (see box 5.2 for a description of this process in Romania). By contrast, the reform process has barely begun in Belarus and many other CIS countries. In countries where more freedoms have been granted, institutions of higher education have begun to act in a more entrepreneurial fashion, align their programs to a greater degree with the demands of students and the labor market, and respond efficiently to government incentives.

University autonomy is not, however, generally expanded through a straightforward transfer of authority between two static entities: the national government and tertiary institutions. Rather, tertiary institutions themselves have changed as governments have developed new methods of providing guidelines—a trend that has occurred more to date in Europe and North America than in the ECA region. In his recent study, Usher (2009) notes that governments have not simply handed authority over to traditional self-governing universities, but rather, transferred

Box 5.2

Decentralization of the University Sector in Romania

The degree of autonomy granted to tertiary institutions in Romania rapidly expanded between 1995 and 2005, a period that saw less state regulation, more academic self-governance, and greater managerial governance at the university level. Stensaker, de Boer, and Enders (2006) have recorded the changes in these three criteria for a number of ECA and non-ECA countries. When judged against these standards, Romania's tertiary institutions (along with those of many other ECA countries) have experienced a large increase in autonomy. The financing of higher education in Romania also underwent major reform, shifting from input-based funding (i.e., linked to the number of professors employed) to student-based funding (i.e., linked to the number of students enrolled).[a]

Increases in autonomy and flexibility in financing happened very quickly—before nascent measures aimed at holding institutions accountable could take hold. For instance, the rapid expansion in enrollment that began in 1990 occurred when the newly established Romanian Council for Accreditation (CNEAA, established in 1993), was still discovering its mandate and trying to establish its institutional credibility. Many new (mostly private) institutions were established during the boom years, but CNEAA simply did not have the capacity to review and accredit every new program or institution; that task was, in some instances, outsourced to public universities, which—in exchange for a fee—were charged with taking a private, growing institution under their wings. By 2005, the shortcomings of CNEAA had become apparent and it was replaced with a new quality assurance agency—the Romanian Agency for Quality Assurance in Higher Education (ARACIS)—modeled on the European Standards and Guidelines (ESG) for quality assurance (see Korka 2008).[b]

There is visible evidence that the accountability framework in Romania today remains insufficient. For example, a long-lasting tug-of-war continues between the Ministry of Education, Research, and Innovation (MERI) and the largest private university (Spiru Haret University)—where as many as one-eighth of all university students are enrolled—over the right to enroll students without a license. Although MERI has refused to accredit certain long-distance learning programs because of a lack of adequate professors, the private university continues to enroll and graduate students from these programs. There are also widespread integrity problems in the sector, as revealed by the Coalition for Clean Universities in a 2009 report, "University Integrity Contest." As discussed in more detail in box 5.4, the Coalition identified three concrete problems that undermine universities' ability

(continued next page)

> **Box 5.2** *(continued)*
>
> to deliver quality education: increased tolerance of plagiarism, extended nepotism, and a lack of transparency in decision making and the academic process.
>
> In response to these weaknesses, the government introduced a new law on education in 2011. The new law imposes many restrictions on the administrative, financial, and staffing autonomy of universities. At the same time, the new law includes key measures to strengthen accountability for performance. For instance, the law requires extensive reporting by the universities and much transparency in their operations. Importantly, the law also introduces new ways to sanction public universities (including by withholding public funds).
>
> *Sources:* Stensaker, de Boer, and Enders 2006; Korka 2008; Nastasescu 2006; Coalition for Clean Universities 2009.
> *Notes:* a. As noted earlier, this book refers to a student enrolled as an "output" (not an "input") and teachers, textbooks, books, financing, and so forth, as "inputs."
> b. One of the differences between CNEEA and ARACIS was that CNEEA was a consultative body of the Ministry of Education, while ARACIS was established as an independent body. Another difference between the two bodies is that CNEEA did not involve international peers, whereas ARACIS does (see Nastasescu 2006).

authority to an entirely new managerial level that largely superseded former governing entities. At the same time, these governments have put greater emphasis on quality assurance and accountability structures at the university level. According to some authors (see Santiago and Tremblay 2008), this shift in emphasis enhances, rather than reduces, their ability to direct higher education systems. Thus, while they have increasingly devolved day-to-day decision-making powers to a new level of university manager, governments have intensified their oversight of higher education. This is now the central task before the group of ECA countries that have already largely decentralized their university systems.

Low-income CIS Countries Need to Initiate Reform

In ECA countries that have maintained tight centralized control over the tertiary sector, the task ahead will be to start devolving authority to institutions of higher education. In some of these countries, however, the very opposite has occurred, with governments now forcing private institutions to comply with a host of new curricular and budgeting regulations. Ministries would instead benefit from delegating detailed operational responsibilities (e.g., controlling the number of student seats in various programs, managing budgets) and focusing on monitoring educational quality, mobilizing resources, and designing policy to improve strengths and reduce weaknesses in the tertiary education.

Azerbaijan is a good example of a country in which the tertiary sector remains highly centralized (see Salmi 2009). Very little autonomy has been granted to public universities in the country and there has been virtually no growth in the number of private universities. The Ministry of Education continues to centrally control student intake at every university in the country, even in the few private ones that exist. The ministry also decides which programs a university may open and enforces the closing of programs in areas perceived to be either saturated or of little relevance. For example, in 2006, a number of universities had to terminate their programs in law, medicine, and international relations.

The financing of higher education in Azerbaijan has also not been reformed and continues to be based on historical norms, with funding tied to the number of professors. In terms of strengthening quality assurance (an important component of strengthening accountability for results), the Bologna scorecard ranks Azerbaijan's progress as very limited, with a score at the very bottom of the list of 22 ECA countries that participate in the Bologna Process.[8] Within this restrictive framework, it is very difficult for more dynamic tertiary education institutions to emerge and expand.

It is important that this group of ECA countries not take the path of the group that provided autonomy first without accountability, but instead introduce the two as mutually reinforcing policy instruments. This is not only considerably more effective, it is also politically more feasible to implement, as it is easier to grant the two together than to try to impose accountability later on already autonomous institutions. In carrying out this reform, policy makers in these countries need not simply transfer autonomy to static, traditional universities but can instead mandate that increased autonomy be accompanied by more "businesslike" and accountable leadership and management. Such change should aim, among other things, at professionalizing institutional governance and management (Stensaker, Enders, and de Boer 2006). A number of countries (or autonomous regions within countries) provide examples of how this can be done. For example, in Denmark and Norway and in Quebec (Canada), the wider tertiary education community is held accountable by university boards that have a majority of outside members and the power to hire and fire the leaders of individual institutions (Fielden 2008, as cited in Salmi 2009). Recent reforms in Lithuania are moving the governance of higher education in this direction (see box 5.3).

Box 5.3

Introducing Businesslike Leadership and Management in Lithuanian Universities

Policy makers and university managers in Lithuania know that it is not easy to get the right balance between institutional autonomy and accountability. Lithuania's Law on Higher Education of 2000 was amended six times during the period 2000–09. On April 30, 2009, additional sweeping reforms were introduced when an entirely new law on science and higher education was adopted.

The 2009 reforms aim to tackle a common problem of countries that have granted more institutional autonomy to universities: How do you get more businesslike leadership and management from university leaders and make them more accountable to outsiders? Prior to the 2009 reforms, the crux of the problem in Lithuania—as in many other countries of the ECA region—was the position of rectors. Rectors were usually elected from within the university; consequently, they felt accountable only to other faculty members (whose ranks they expected to rejoin after having served their term). They also usually had limited managerial experience. Reformers in Lithuania recognized that changing the way rectors were elected (and to whom they were accountable) was not a "magic bullet" for getting better university management, but without this change, major reform of university governance was unlikely.

The essence of the 2009 reforms was twofold. First, it narrowed the mandate of the Senate by clarifying that its main task was to safeguard and promote the academic integrity and prestige of the university (i.e., approving study programs and ensuring admittance follows academic standards), not to manage it. Second, it made explicit that rectors were accountable to a broader set of stakeholders than just faculty members, one that included taxpayers. This was achieved by changing the way rectors are nominated and selected. In the future, the Governing Council—two-thirds of whose members are from outside of the university—will establish an election committee and hold open competitions to search for suitable candidates. (See table B5.3 for a summary of the reforms.)

In exchange for these reforms, university leaders have sought even greater institutional autonomy from the central government. In particular, they pointed to inherent inconsistencies in the major pieces of legislation governing higher education. For instance, although Article 5 of the Law on Higher Education states that the activity of higher education establishments is based on academic freedom and autonomy, the same article also says that this activity is determined

(continued next page)

Box 5.3 *(continued)*

Table B5.3   Summary of Changes

Governing body	Before 2009 reforms	After 2009 reforms
Governing Council	Role: Supervisory; confirms that Senate and Rector conform to the Statute and whether the activity and administration of the university are transparent Composition of Council: 2/3 appointed by Ministry of Education 1/3 University representatives (including Rector and student leaders)	Role: Highest governing body responsible for strategic decisions Composition of Council: Same composition, but with greater efforts to select more business leaders as Council members New mandate: Establish an election committee and have open competition for selecting Rector
Rector	Role: Highest administrative office responsible for the management of the university	Role: Unchanged
Senate	Role: Highest self-governance institution in the university, responsible for its general affairs (including selection of Rector) Elect Rector	Role: Highest body dealing with academic matters; approves study programs and ensures admittance follows academic standards

Source: E-mail correspondence of authors with Ministry of Education of Lithuania, 2009.

not only by this law and the statute of the institution, but also by other laws. In practice, this meant that universities could not own their buildings or borrow funds, and were only able to spend budgets as they saw fit to a limited extent. As part of the 2009 reforms, these inconsistencies are being addressed by changing the legal status of universities from a budgetary to a public entity. This will provide them more freedom and the right to own property, as well as expand their rights to manage the property entrusted to them by the state.

Create an Accommodating Environment for Private Providers

Another possible way to create a more flexible university sector is to provide an accommodating environment for private providers to establish universities and flourish. Although clearly not a panacea—and not without some attendant integrity problems (see below)—private resources are nevertheless critical because the cost pressures facing higher education in the region are simply too great. Private providers can be advantageous because they are usually (although not always) nimble and responsive, being less constrained by a top-heavy bureaucracy and political factors. They are also often run by especially motivated and entrepreneurial individuals who, in many instances, establish an institution because they see unmet demand. This type of creativity can prove very valuable to an education and training system that is seeking to become more responsive to rapidly changing labor markets—provided, of course, that adequate quality standards are enforced. (For more on the subject of private providers and private funding for tertiary education, see the section on financing below.)

Private providers in many ECA countries already play a crucial role in absorbing the increased demand for tertiary education that public providers have been unable to meet. Indeed, the rapidly growing and vigorous role of private providers in the ECA tertiary sector is one of the more notable features of the region's educational systems. While the private sector at the tertiary level is not equally strong across the entire region (in a number of countries, particularly Croatia and the Czech Republic, private education is notable by its almost complete absence), it generally has a much stronger presence than in Western Europe, accounting for as much as one-third of total enrollment in some countries. For example, in Romania, private universities have played a crucial role in accommodating a tripling of the number of tertiary students since 1998. By 2007–08, private enrollment there accounted for approximately 40 percent of all students enrolled at this educational level (World Bank 2008b).

In fact, the boom in private tertiary education in the ECA region is a characteristic example of governments using the nongovernmental sector to absorb demand (Slantcheva and Levy 2007). Most countries that embraced this solution have created a large number of small institutions that specialize in subjects that are inexpensive to teach (primarily law, social sciences, economics, and business administration) and whose teaching staff consists primarily of academics from the public sector who teach part-time to supplement their incomes (see, for instance, Linden, Arnhold, and Vasiliev 2008). This has been an efficient way to meet the niche demands of specific employers, satisfy demand in smaller and more remote areas of countries where public institutions are not available, and introduce new (usually foreign) teaching techniques and curricula to a local market (for example, New York University in Tirana).

These private institutions have, to a certain degree, even taken part in attempts to change the prevailing culture with respect to transparency, markets, and democracy (for example, Khazar University in Azerbaijan and the European Humanities University in Belarus). However, private sector providers have not yet been able to offer education in the sciences or engineering or to provide education in a research setting. Throughout the ECA region, these specializations have remained the preserve of the public sector, with the notable exception of the British-Kazakh University in Almaty.

Strengthen Accountability

Accountability at the most basic level refers to fundamental academic and fiscal integrity, which touches on such issues as admissions and financial fraud, plagiarism, and professorial nepotism. Here, almost all ECA countries continue to have serious problems. Strengthening accountability in tertiary education also entails ensuring that public resources are spent effectively, the education provided is of high quality, and that study programs are relevant to students' future in the workforce. Although it might seem necessary to address basic integrity issues before dealing with higher-order accountability issues, all of these problems can be addressed concurrently, a task made easier by the fact that most basic accountability instruments also address higher-level concerns.

Improve Fiscal and Academic Integrity

At the lowest level, strengthening accountability in higher education means safeguarding the system's basic integrity. With regard to finances, this implies preventing embezzlement, fraud in public tenders, collusion, and so forth. With regard to academics, it means avoiding examination fraud, unethical behavior among faculty, noncompliance with admission standards, research fraud and other forms of plagiarism, and deception in the quality assurance process (Salmi 2009).

With the exception of a few new EU member states, evidence suggests that higher education across the region is still struggling with basic integrity issues, both academic and financial. As discussed in chapter 2, this evidence comes in different forms. For example, when randomly selected university students in a number of ECA countries were asked a range of different questions related to purchasing grades, admission, and diplomas, more than 60 percent of respondents reported knowing of other students who had purchased either entrance to the university or a specific grade (see figure 2.6). Newspapers and other media regularly report on fraud and corruption in the sector. For instance, a scandal erupted in the Czech Republic in 2009 following revelations that a number of students had been awarded law degrees by the University of West Bohemia in Pilsen after only a few months of study. The scandal led the Minister of Education to order a national audit of all university degrees awarded since 2000, covering some 315,000 graduates (see Holdsworth 2009).

The fact that such problems persist is also evident in the work of national quality assurance and accreditation agencies. For instance, in Georgia, when a National Education Accreditation Center was finally established in October 2004—13 years after the first private provider was allowed to operate—its first assessment of the 178 existing institutions of higher education (both public and private) brought sobering news: only 78 passed the minimum quality requirement established by the center. While both private and public institutions were barred from admitting students in 2005, the vast majority of barred institutions were private. During the years when there was little or no regulation of quality, an estimated 20–30 percent of all tertiary students graduated from unregulated—and largely unmonitored—private institutions (Pachuashvili 2007).

As a recent report (Salmi 2009) documents, countries around the world utilize a range of different instruments to address basic integrity problems *and* strengthen accountability for educational quality and fiscal efficiency. The good news is that more sophisticated instruments generally help with accountability problems across the board, that is, with both basic integrity and higher-order accountability concerns. The various instruments available and their uses are summarized in table 5.1.

Many new members of the EU in the ECA region are already familiar with the instruments used to strengthen accountability for better learning outcomes. Yet these tools also strengthen basic integrity. One such instrument is licensing, which is critical for strengthening academic integrity in tertiary institutions. Other tools that promote both academic integrity and the quality of education include regular institutional evaluations, such as accreditation procedures, academic audits, and other forms of evaluation. Public disclosure laws are also useful. In addition, it is possible to foster programs in which outsiders—or anyone with no vested interest in the university system—review an institution's academic integrity (this

Table 5.1 Tools for Strengthening Basic Academic and Fiscal Integrity in University-Level Institutions

Tools that strengthen academic integrity	Tools that strengthen fiscal integrity
• Licensing …and educational quality	• Financial audits …and fiscal efficiency
• Accreditation, academic audits, and evaluations	• Public disclosure laws
• Public disclosure laws	• Strategic budget plans
• Fostering of outsiders to review academic integrity (e.g., Romania)	• Performance contracts based on performance indicators
• Performance contracts based on performance indicators	• Student loans, scholarships, and vouchers
• Creation and dissemination of rankings, benchmarks	• Embedding of incentives into allocated resources (e.g., tying funding to the number of students enrolled or graduated, rewarding good performers, etc.)

Sources: Authors' review of available instruments, as presented in Salmi 2009.

tool been used in Romania, see box 5.4). Performance contracts based on performance indicators can also help ensure integrity and educational quality. Finally, it can be valuable to facilitate the creation of rankings or benchmarks or both and then disseminate these data in an appropriate manner.

Instruments that address basic fiscal integrity also have an impact on the efficient use of resources. One obvious tool for improving basic financial integrity is the financial audit. Tools that accomplish both fiscal integrity and the efficient use of resources include public disclosure laws, strategic budget plans, performance contracts, external watchdogs (see box 5.4), and student loans, scholarships, and vouchers. In addition, it can be useful to embed incentives into the resources allocated to higher education institutions, for example, by linking funding to the number of students enrolled or graduating or using it to reward good performers. These suggestions are discussed in greater detail in the section on financing below.

Implement Immediate and Long-term Quality Assurance Mechanisms

Strengthening accountability for educational quality is an especially long and difficult process. At the outset, setting up effective accreditation or quality assurance mechanisms requires building a country's capacity for these tasks. In view of the relatively weak institutional capacity for

Box 5.4

Using External Watchdogs to Shed Light on Integrity Problems

In 2007 in Romania, a group of 14 nongovernmental organizations (NGOs) combined forces to form the Coalition for Clean Universities (CUC) to monitor Romanian public universities and establish norms for good governance. The CUC piloted a methodology to assess the academic integrity of these universities. A questionnaire was designed and teams of external evaluators—composed equally of experts and students—set about requesting information from the universities (see Mungiu-Pippidi 2009 for a detailed description of the methodology). In its widely disseminated report, the CUC emphasized three findings:

Evidence of increased tolerance for plagiarism. Despite numerous scandals regarding plagiarism, universities have no tools to control this phenomenon. With the exception of a single university, evaluators could not identify procedures for combating plagiarism, either at the diploma level or the level of papers elaborated by research staff.

Evidence of extended nepotism. In a number of universities, evaluators identified the existence of so-called "academic families," raising serious questions about the objectivity of promotions and evaluations among colleagues. In one university evaluated by the CUC, eight pairs of academic families existed: three husband-wife pairs and five father-son pairs. Taking into account the total number of teachers (45), the incidence of "academic families" was very high.

Lack of transparency in decision making and the academic process. CUC found that the competition for certain teaching or academic positions is kept quasi-secret; in the most common cases, there was, in fact, a single candidate. Similarly, the procedure for approving a university budget (revenues and expenditures) is often carried out without any real consultation with the university's senate. Promotions and pay increases are also governed by nontransparent procedures, without clear benchmarks. Evaluators have also witnessed problems in the publishing of asset and interest declarations, as well as the absence of declarations on cooperation with the former secret police. Restrictions in accessing public records of public acquisitions are also a major problem.

(continued next page)

> **Box 5.4** *(continued)*
>
> The lack of transparency regarding internal procedures and administrative or academic results or both can be discovered simply by trying to access university websites, as they frequently do not include such information on such topics as employment opportunities, teaching jobs, teacher performance, program content, or decisions of internal governing bodies.
>
> *Source:* Coalition for Clean Universities 2009.

monitoring educational quality and relevance among universities and ministries of education in the ECA region—including newly established or nonexistent quality assurance agencies—policy makers need to employ many different, complementary tools to strengthen accountability for results (see box 5.5). These tools include rankings and tracer studies (which also provide useful data on institutional performance in the absence of standardized assessments), together with an enabling environment for private sector participation. Counting on a quality assurance agency to quickly establish the capacity needed to externally monitor a rapidly growing sector is risky—this kind of agency needs to be part of the solution, but not the only response.

In 2003, the ministers responsible for the Bologna Process began a consultation designed to lead to a common, but not unified, system of quality assurance in the tertiary education sector. Two years of consultations between quality assurance agencies, higher education institutions, and student representatives followed, resulting in the adoption in 2005 of the European Standards and Guidelines for Quality Assurance (ESG) in the European EHEA.[9] The main features of this consensus are the following:

- Tertiary institutions have primary responsibility for quality and are required to have processes of internal quality assurance.
- Tertiary institutions are subject to external oversight by an agency charged by the government with assuring the competency of quality assurance mechanisms.
- Quality review agencies themselves submit (on a voluntary basis) to quality assessment procedures through the European Quality Assurance Register, which is a joint project of the European Network of Quality Assurance Agencies (ENQA), together with the European

> **Box 5.5**
>
> **Two Approaches to Strengthening Accountability**
>
> As noted by Alex Usher (2009), two approaches have been used throughout the world in the past 20 years to improve tertiary educational quality by strengthening accountability. The first approach is generally referred to as "quality assurance" or "accreditation," and has traditionally focused on ensuring that certain minimum levels of resources (i.e., inputs) and standards are present to ensure a "quality" education. In addition, the approach seeks to put requirements in place so that tertiary institutions themselves monitor the quality of their education.
>
> The second approach focuses on learning conditions and learning outcomes. This method includes rankings systems and systems of performance indicators. It also relies to a much larger extent on using students and parents to exert outside pressure on tertiary institutions to deliver results. Thus, parents and students, rather than a state agency, become the driving force behind better accountability.[a]
>
> These two approaches to enhancing accountability are complementary to, and not substitutes for, one another. As Jongbloed (2008) has noted, quality assurance is the equivalent of a restaurant health inspector, while university rankings are the equivalent of a Michelin guide. Both have their place and neither can replace the other.
>
> *Sources:* Usher 2009; Jongbloed 2008.
> a. In the terminology of the *World Development Report 2004*, the first approach is the "long" route to accountability, while the second is the "short" route (World Bank 2003c).

University Association (EUA), the European Association of Institutions in Higher Education (EURASHE), and the European Students Union (ESU).

In principle, this structure means that national quality assurance bodies now coordinate to determine mutually acceptable evaluation frameworks, and thus, visions of institutional quality. At the same time, institutions are empowered to assess themselves within the framework of wider agreements on institutional quality and evaluations that their representative organizations have worked to develop. This situation is indicative of a broader governance trend (and changing government role): increased institutional operational autonomy coupled with strengthened webs of external coordination.

158 Skills, Not Just Diplomas

Regular stock-taking exercises are carried out to assess whether Bologna participants are meeting concrete measurable goals towards the bigger goal of creating an EHEA. That is, whether they are making academic degree standards and quality assurance standards more comparable and compatible throughout Europe (see Rauhvargers, Deane, and Pauwels 2009). The last such stock-taking exercise took place in 2009 and revealed that many ECA countries have a considerable way to go in terms of strengthening quality assurance mechanisms. In particular, the exercise showed that many countries in the region have not yet incorporated international peer reviews—one of the three key benchmarks in the stock-taking exercise—into their quality assurance processes. Figure 5.1 groups ECA countries into three categories, according to their Bologna scorecard for implementing quality assurance mechanisms.

Figure 5.1   Progress on Implementing Quality-Assurance Mechanisms: The Bologna Scorecard

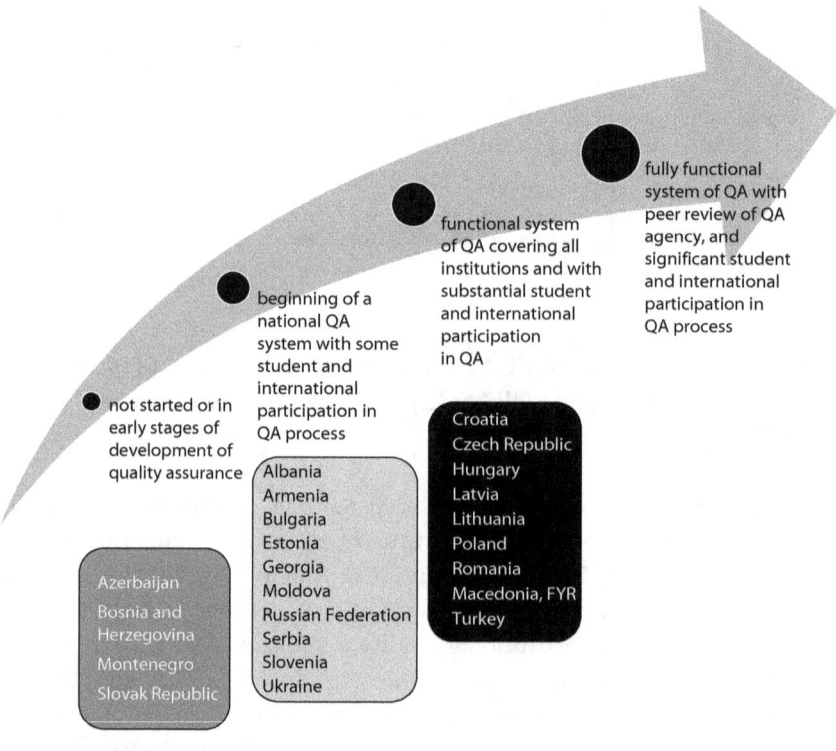

Source: Authors' assessment.
Note: QA = quality assurance.

The 2009 stock-taking exercise also revealed significant weaknesses in establishing internal quality assurance mechanisms.[10] For example, some countries (both ECA and non-ECA) treat internal quality assurance within institutions of higher learning only nominally (i.e., having institutions prepare a "self-assessment report"), thereby ignoring an essential part of the ESG that focuses on "learning outcomes-based and improvement-oriented internal quality assurance systems" (Rauhvargers, Deane, and Pauwels 2009, 51). A key failing of many countries is that they have still not managed to induce higher education institutions to describe programs in terms of learning outcomes. Even fewer countries have moved to introduce "student assessment procedures designed to measure achievement of the intended learning outcomes" (Rauhvargers, Deane, and Pauwels 2009, 55).

Introduce Performance-Based Financing and Encourage Private Funding Resources

Financing can be a central government's most potent policy instrument for steering education providers. First, budget discussions—whether annual or pluri-annual—are recurrent events that give policy makers a regular opportunity to reward or discourage managerial behavior. Granting more autonomy or strengthening accountability instruments, on the other hand, are more protracted and lengthy processes. Second, in most ECA countries, public resources continue to provide a large share of tertiary education funding, giving the central government an important seat at the table. Finally, public resources can be used to influence the behavior of private institutions that may not otherwise have formal reporting arrangements with the government. In turn, private resources can strengthen a results-oriented outcome by encouraging greater competition in the sector and increasing students' stake in the end result of their educations.

Per Student Financing

Per student financing is the simplest and most effective instrument for moving toward output- and outcome-based financing in ECA countries. Per student financing, combined with autonomous management of both public and private education institutions, creates a competitive environment in which students select the best institutions that most closely meet their educational goals. Creating built-in incentives for individual institutions to compete for students transforms an input-oriented, supply-driven education delivery system into an output-oriented, demand-driven system. Several ECA countries (for example, Poland and Romania) have already adopted per student financing as a core element of managing public tertiary education institutions, shifting their focus away from inputs and toward results.

Although most countries start the move towards per student financing by linking financing to students enrolled, conceptually, this is not ideal. Policy makers should encourage high student graduation rates, as well as high rates of subsequent employment—not simply enrollment. Systems in Denmark and the Netherlands provide an excellent model, one in which the funding formula is based on the number of graduates produced. Other output-based funding measures are also possible, for example, linking funds to survey results showing alumni success in the labor market, giving institutions clear incentives to ensure that programs are relevant to labor market needs, and aiding students in their transition to the labor market. These steps also motivate institutions to focus on the true outcome desired by policy makers: more qualified workers. Financing reforms also need to be accompanied by accountability measures in order to prevent reduced program rigor.

Performance Contracts

The introduction of performance-based budgeting can be a powerful instrument that ministries of education (and finance) can use to guide the sector, as it causes governments to shift from line-item to outcome-based funding (OECD 2007c). At the same time, universities are given greater autonomy in how they spend their budgets and are held accountable for delivering results. Three models of performance-based funding are currently being used in higher education (Ziegele 2009): (1) formula funding, (2) target agreements, and (3) competitive funding (see table 5.2).

A recent report (OECD 2007c) reviewed the experiences of OECD countries with performance-based budgeting and highlighted five potential benefits. First, this type of budgeting generates a sharper focus on results within the public sector. Second, it provides more and better information on government goals and priorities, as well as how different programs contribute to these goals. Third, it encourages greater emphasis on planning and signals what is working and what is not. Fourth, it improves transparency by providing greater and more useful information to the central government and the public. Finally, it has the potential to improve both the efficiency and the management of individual programs.

Table 5.2 Three Models of Performance-Based Funding

Formula funding	Target agreements	Competitive funding
Quantitative indicators representing goals	Negotiation on objectives	Central funds with defined purposes (e.g., research excellence, national priorities)
Technical issues: weights, cost differences, formula construction	Written and signed performance contract	
	Performance criteria tailor-made to different organizations	Application procedure, often including peer review
Usual indicators: students, graduates, Ph.D.s, external income, international students, etc.	"Contract" definition of rewards *and* sanctions	Institutional and individual funding, project funding
Ex post measurement of performance	Ex ante definition and ex post measurement of performance	Ex ante discussion on performance

Source: Ziegele 2009.

Encourage more private financial resources in tertiary education. Mobilizing private resources can also help strengthen results-oriented outcomes in tertiary education in the ECA region in two fundamental ways: (1) by increasing competition, as more nimble and innovative private providers help bring innovations to public providers; and (2) by increasing students' connection to the education process. When students and parents pay tuition fees—whether to a public or a private provider—they are generally more demanding about the quality and relevance of the education provided.

As noted earlier in this chapter, one of the most prominent features of the tertiary sector in many ECA countries is the presence of a vibrant network of private educational institutions. It is thus necessary to look at structures and levels of fees in both sectors to get a full picture of private financing of higher education.[11] Private higher education institutes in the region for the most part do not receive government funding for core operating purposes (Turkey is the prime exception here). In many countries, they can apply for and receive funding for scientific research, but because their research facilities tend to be poorer than those in public institutions, their success rate is often quite low. As a result, private institutions are for the most part entirely self-funded via tuition fees.

Public institutions in many countries have also been given considerable latitude to raise funds through tuition fees. The introduction of fees has occurred despite deep political resistance (and even, on occasion, constitutional prohibitions on the practice), which is a legacy of the region's communist past. Generally speaking, the introduction of tuition fees has come via a "dual-track" method in which a certain portion of students—usually those deemed especially meritorious—are not required to pay. On top of these students, institutions are permitted to enroll a number of fee-paying students, although the institutional freedom to determine both fees and the number of additional students varies widely across the region. Thus, higher education in ECA countries has managed a delicate political balance by both introducing the principle of fees while retaining the principle of free tuition.

Given the significant private returns to people who graduate from tertiary schools, however, there is an argument that the main beneficiary of this education—the graduate—should contribute a larger share of the costs relative to his or her peers who chose not to attend, or are not able to attend, university. There is no single ideal level of funding for higher education and no single ideal mix of public and private funding sources. Different countries will make different kinds of trade-offs. Yet if ECA countries want to simultaneously raise participation rates and increase the quality of tertiary education, more private resources will be needed—the cost pressures facing higher education are simply too great.

Governments could, for example, permit public institutions to collect more revenue in return for commitments to enroll more students, or they could facilitate the development of more private tertiary education institutions. In either case, it is critical that all institutions be given the right to fully use their fees. It is also important that the expansion of private institutions take place within an overall system of quality assurance, and that appropriate financial assistance measures be put in place to assist students in need.

Summary

In terms of the relationship between the central government and tertiary institutions, ECA countries today can, broadly speaking, be divided into two groups. The first group consists of most new EU member countries, which have already expanded the autonomy of their tertiary institutions. Their main challenge today is to strengthen a still weak accountability structure, evident in persistent allegations of corruption in the sector and doubts as to whether existing accountability mechanisms (such as sanctions, accreditation agencies, and so forth) are sufficiently strong to induce providers to focus on improving learning and employment outcomes (as opposed to other goals of tertiary institutions). The second group of countries—mostly low-income CIS countries—have maintained tight centralized control over tertiary institutions. In order to create a more flexible and responsive tertiary sector, these countries need to impart more autonomy to universities, make financing a more active policy instrument (i.e., introduce performance-based financing), and, as with the first group of countries, introduce a range of mechanisms to strengthen the accountability of tertiary providers.

Because strengthening accountability for educational quality is an especially long and difficult process, ECA policy makers will need to employ many different, complementary tools to strengthen education providers' accountability for results. In addition to quality assurance agencies, introducing rankings, tracer studies, and standardized tests to measure student learning outcomes, together with more effective private sector participation, will enable countries in the region to launch both immediate and long-term quality assurance mechanisms. Counting on a quality assurance agency to quickly establish the capacity needed to externally monitor a rapidly growing sector is risky—this kind of agency needs to be part of the solution, not the only response.

An essential part of strengthening accountability will be to collect more student outcome data at the tertiary level. Without standardized tests to measure what competencies graduates acquire and tracer studies to establish the kinds of jobs they find on the labor market, institutions of higher education are severely hampered in their ability to measure their own performance or respond to the changing demand for skills.

Finally, in addition to introducing or improving performance-based financing in the sector, countries in the region need to find ways to encourage more private financial resources in tertiary education. Not only will fee-based mechanisms enable the sector to meet rising student demand and introduce needed competition among providers, they offer an additional way to strengthen these providers' accountability for results.

Notes

1. Given the complexity of the tertiary sector, some clarifications are needed. First, the "providers" discussed in this chapter, both public and private, are all institutions that offer tertiary education programs. Second, it is readily acknowledged that tertiary education institutions serve important societal goals that stretch far beyond that of providing graduates with employable competencies. For instance, through their research, these institutions help expand a society's collective knowledge and can contribute to innovations in the economy, giving students employable competencies in the process. And through their political independence, universities help society hold public

officials accountable. Yet, the focus of this book—the need to create education systems that are more responsive to labor market needs—implies that these broader goals of tertiary institutions (and the policies related to enhancing their performance in those dimensions) are beyond its scope.

2. See a recent report on university autonomy by the European University Association (Estermann and Nokkala 2009). The EUA report does a careful job of discussing the complexities and all dimensions of university autonomy.
3. The Bologna Process was kicked off by the signing of the Bologna Declaration in 1999.
4. See Bologna Working Group 2005 for further details.
5. For additional information on the Tuning Project, or Tuning Educational Structures in Europe, visit its official website at http://tuning.unideusto.org/tuningeu/ (accessed September 2010).
6. See the online guide at www.guardian.co.uk/education/universityguide/ (accessed January 2011).
7. For a discussion of rankings, Kehm and Stensaker 2009.
8. The scorecard is the result of a regular stock-taking exercise undergone by countries that participate in the Bologna Process. The last such stock taking was carried out in 2009.
9. The "European Standards and Guidelines for Quality Assurance in the European Higher Education Area" is available on the website of the European Quality Assurance Register for Higher Education at http://www.eqar.eu (accessed January 2011).
10. In addition to scoring countries on three indicators related to quality assurance ("external quality assurance," "student participation in quality assurance," and "international participation in quality assurance," the 2009 stock-taking exercise included a "qualitative analysis" of various aspects of internal quality assurance.
11. Private expenditures on higher education are somewhat difficult to capture. Data from the UNESCO Institute for Statistics on this subject is quite inconsistent, in part because it includes income from many different sources (see the UIS website, http://www.uis.unesco.org/; accessed September 2010). However, it is possible to look at fee income in a relatively straightforward way, based on accessible published sources. In most of the OECD region (with the exception of Japan, the United States, and Mexico), for example, fee income accrues almost entirely to public educational institutions.

CHAPTER 6

Advancing Adult Learning in ECA

Lifelong learning and adult education and training are fast becoming an important element of education systems across the ECA region. Although demand for labor in the ECA countries has already shifted toward higher-order, multifaceted competencies, it has also become more unpredictable, indicating the need for a market-responsive sector that can easily facilitate the reskilling of the adult labor force. The reskilling of the work force is needed not only to compete in the global economy, but also to address the lag effects of the transition to market economies. Significant segments of the labor force—often comprised of less-skilled and more disadvantaged workers—remain inactive in many areas. Given the rapid demographic decline expected in many ECA countries, maintaining high rates of growth will require an increase in labor force participation and productivity.

High-quality, relevant adult learning relies on (1) sound regulation and quality standards that promote autonomy and accountability (largely missing in all but a few ECA countries), including recognized qualifications frameworks and certificate programs, and (2) financing incentives that promote a competitive market and overcome the obstacles and market failures associated with the provision of adult learning. Overcoming information barriers for individuals and firms is central to both policy levers.

Unlike pre-university and university education, adult education systems are highly underdeveloped in most ECA countries. Building such systems will require a shift away from government-defined programs towards a well-regulated market of private and public providers that deliver training services to both working and unemployed adults. The preconditions for successful adult education systems are a high degree of coordination and partnership between government agencies and the private sector, as well as a strong voice for businesses and individuals—that is, the demand side of training—in determining training policy and content. Governments in the region will continue to have a role in education and training for the unemployed, but once a solid adult learning sector has been established, governments can then "steer" it according to the policy framework outlined previously: by monitoring data, promoting autonomy, and improving efficiency.

Although adult learning is of growing significance for all ECA countries, its relative importance depends on a country's level of economic development and demographic outlook. For some countries, such as the EU10 and Croatia, moving quickly to build or improve this sector will be essential; for others, such as low-income CIS countries, problems in other parts of the education system will be a greater priority in the near term.

Building the Foundations for Adult Learning Systems

Adult education and training is a relatively new concept in the ECA region. The experience of OECD countries suggests that developing this part of an education system calls for a common understanding and approach, shared strategic objectives, and functioning communication channels among a multitude of heterogeneous players. On the part of governments, it will require increased coordination between the ministries of education, labor, and finance, other relevant government agencies (e.g., employment services), and regional authorities. Functioning policy coordination mechanisms are needed to give the private sector a genuine voice in adult education, thus making the sector responsive to economic and labor requirements. Creating such coordination mechanisms, however, takes time.

Step One: A Coherent Strategy

A typical first step in policy coordination and partnership is the elaboration of a coherent strategy for adult education and training. This strategy creates the basis for a practical legislative and regulatory framework. The EU, for example, has advised its member states to develop and implement strategies on lifelong learning to advance the education and training dimension of the Lisbon Jobs and Growth Strategy and its successor, the Europe 2020 Strategy. The EU10 have been adopting such strategies since 2005 (see box 6.1 for a case study).

Box 6.1

Lifelong Learning Strategy of the Czech Republic

After consultation with a wide range of stakeholders, the Czech Republic adopted a Lifelong Learning Strategy in 2007 that includes a prominent section on further—or adult—education. Building on an analysis of strengths and weaknesses, it identifies seven strategic directions.

Recognition of prior learning through the Act on the Recognition of the Results of Further Education, with the elaboration of a National Qualification Framework, qualifications standards, evaluation standards, and verification of professional qualifications.

Promotion of equal opportunities in further education, particularly for disadvantaged groups, through financial and nonfinancial instruments, including information and counseling services.

Development of functional literacy, including the ability to use information technology, language skills, and other general behavioral skills.

Introduction of a system of labor market monitoring, evaluation, and forecasting to harmonize educational opportunities with socioeconomic and labor market developments.

Stimulation of demand for lifelong learning through elimination of financial and nonfinancial barriers among individuals and employers, for example, through counseling support, assistance services, and the promotion of systems of human resource development in small and medium-size enterprises.

Measures to enhance the quality of educational opportunities, including a system of external and internal evaluations, certification of adult education teachers, and accreditation of educational programs.

Development of information counseling services.

The strategy is used as the guiding document for further reforms in adult education and training in the country, as well as for program financing by the European Social Fund.

Source: Czech Republic 2007.

The experience of EU and OECD countries suggests that ECA countries could establish multistakeholder commissions on adult learning and task them with drafting a plan for developing the sector. Such commissions typically convene national and regional stakeholders, including representatives of key government agencies, private sector employers, and trade unions. In drawing up a strategy, the tasks of such a commission typically involve taking stock of existing structures related to adult learning and determining the best way to make them more relevant to the current needs of labor markets and individual learners. In many cases, an entirely new system may not be necessary.

Step Two: Coordination Mechanisms

Once a coherent strategy has been elaborated, coordination between government and private sector actors is important to guide implementation. Coordination mechanisms can differ, depending on the context and type of training. In the Republic of Korea and the United States, for example, large multinational enterprises, together with relevant government institutions, industry associations, small enterprises, and education providers, have collaborated in creating "training consortia" and joint training centers that address the strategic training needs of workers. In the Slovak Republic and the Czech Republic, there have been similar efforts at collaboration between large multinational companies and government agencies to promote adult learning in the automotive sector.

In an effort to facilitate coordination, a number of countries worldwide have set up national adult learning bodies with broad responsibilities. The United Kingdom, for example, has established a Learning and Skills Council (LSC), which is responsible for overseeing nontertiary learning targeted at those over the age of 16 years. The LSC works at both the regional and national levels (see box 6.2). In Mexico, the National Council of Education for Life and Work (CONVEyT) is responsible for building a national system of education to serve adults over the course of their lives, including clarifying the role of different providers and conducting research and evaluations. Bulgaria has established a National Agency for Vocational Education and Training (NAVET) that convenes government, education providers, and social partners (e.g., parent associations, NGOs, chambers of commerce, etc.) to define vocational education and training policies.

Such organizations are, however, unlikely to be successful if the relevant governmental ministries are not prepared to fully cooperate with them and provide them necessary support (OECD 2005c). Creating new

Box 6.2

Policy Tools for Advancing Adult Learning in the United Kingdom

The Skills Alliance, a ministerial-led group of adult learning stakeholders, including employers, provides oversight of the Skills Strategy in England. Employers offer input to the Alliance through their representatives, together with the Skills for Business Network and the National Employment Panel (NEP). The provision of training is organized and funded by Learning Skills Councils (LSCs) at national, regional, and local levels in partnership with Regional Skills Partnerships, colleges, providers, and other key stakeholders. Providers include publicly funded bodies, nonprofit agencies, and private education providers.

The LSCs allocate funds based on "expected demand." The planning process involves taking stock of the existing learning environment, drawing on different sources of labor market intelligence, and dialoguing with key partners, including employers and providers. Implementation involves the securing of training through open bids and closed negotiations managed by LSCs. In an effort to make the system less supply driven, an independent review of the U.K. adult learning system, the 2006 "Leitch Review," laid out the following principles for adult education and training:

(1) demand-led funding, that is, routing public funds for adult vocational skills training through demand-led channels, thus ending supply-side planning of skills provision;
(2) strengthening the voice of employers by rationalizing the number of bodies that articulate the views of employers and creating a single Commission for Employment and Skills; and
(3) providing economically valuable skills by relying on reformed and relicensed Sector Skills Councils to ensure that vocational qualifications reflect the skills valued by employers (Leitch Review of Skills 2006).

Similar to other EU countries that have introduced National Qualification Systems, the United Kingdom established the National Vocational Qualification (NVQ) system to recognize a broad spectrum of vocational skills that can be acquired both on and off the job. Most critically, the NVQ system recognizes prior learning through an assessment process. The modular system allows participants to learn at a pace convenient to them. During the period 1988–2003, approximately 4 million NVQ qualifications were awarded, with the majority at Level 2 of

(continued next page)

Box 6.2 *(continued)*

the system (Dearden, McGranahan, and Sianesi 2004). Yet despite the growth in these qualifications, wage returns to NVQ Level 2 qualifications have to date largely been low or nonexistent, with a few exceptions (Dearden, McGranahan, and Sianesi 2004).

In addition, various projects provide information to workers to keep them better informed about market demands and the returns to training. A number of providers also offer advice to workers, particularly those who are unemployed or qualify as low skilled. These efforts include Jobcentre Plus work to identify the skill needs of Jobseeker Allowance recipients who have been unemployed and inactive for six months; Learndirect's personalized advice, information, and guidance tailored to the needs of adult clients at the skill level NVQ 2 or below; and the community outreach of Learning Ambassadors, local volunteers who have themselves undergone adult training, to identify and work with people in similar situations.

Individual Learning Accounts (ILA) in the United Kingdom provide funding to individuals with the lowest skill levels, making training accessible to a group that otherwise would not participate. ILAs make a maximum sum of between £100 and £200 available to low-skilled individuals, who may spend it on a qualification and provider of their choice. Individuals and their employers are also encouraged to contribute to ILAs. Opening an ILA comes with a guidance package that targets individuals who are least able to borrow from private financial institutions. In 2000, England implemented one of its largest ILA projects, with 1.4 million participants, but it was later closed due to irregularities. The project was found to suffer from significant deadweight loss, with more than half of participating individuals stating that they would have sought training without their ILAs (OECD 2005c). Subsequently, however, both Scotland and Wales implemented comparable schemes and since 2007, England again began to pilot a similar project.

Lastly, the government's Train to Gain Program helps employers identify training needs and then tailor corresponding training packages which are jointly or fully financed by the government. The program offers financial incentives to workers with paid time off and subsidies to employers to compensate for trainee wages. This intervention targets all market failures, from financing training to overcoming the time preferences of employees, who worry about the opportunity cost of training. The Train to Gain initiative was first piloted in 2002–2006 and covered 30,000 employers and 250,000 employees. It has now been mainstreamed across the country. Initial evaluations indicate a small positive impact on the take-up of training for both employees and employers (Abromovsky et al. 2005).

Sources: Abromovsky et al. 2005; Dearden, McGranahan, and Sianesi 2004; OECD 2005c; Leitch Review of Skills 2006.

bodies carries the risk of adding additional layers of bureaucracy; and some countries, such as the Czech Republic, have managed to enhance cooperation between ministries without forming new agencies.

Given the varying needs across an economy, sector- or industry-level councils can also be key components of successful adult learning systems, especially for defining the standards of vocational training and developing national qualifications frameworks (see below). Permanent regulatory bodies, on the other hand, help ensure that qualifications remain relevant to labor market requirements over time. The United Kingdom, for example, currently relies on a network of employer-led Sector Skills Councils (SSCs) to coordinate different market stakeholders and develop quality standards. The SSCs are monitored by the Sector Skills Development Agency, which also ensures that cross-sectoral skills are adequately covered by U.K. licensing systems (United Kingdom 2003).

Building on the United Kingdom's example, the Czech Republic has formed Sector Skills Councils with the involvement of social partners. The government convened the human resource experts from leading companies to help prepare a national occupations framework, which, in turn, laid the foundation for a national qualifications framework. In Croatia, sector councils—reporting to the Agency for Vocational Education—have recently been established to assess skills needs in specific vocational sectors and contribute to setting occupational standards (World Bank 2009a).

Building Adult Learning Systems in the ECA Region: Uneven Progress

Although many ECA countries, particularly the EU10, have made progress in developing the kinds of coordination systems described above, several challenges remain. First, the voice of labor market stakeholders in decisions on adult learning continues to be weak relative to that of the government. For example, in Hungary, education and enterprise representatives were involved in developing vocational qualifications and curricula, but employers viewed the qualifications as closely modeled on those of school education, too supply-driven, and insufficiently forward looking (Gunny and Viertel 2007). A large sample of top managers judged that the allocation of Hungary's employer-based training funds was influenced most by government institutions, followed by training institutions, and finally, by employers' associations. Not surprisingly, they felt that this order should be reversed (Godfrey 2003).

Second, coordination challenges, particularly across ministries, persist. In Hungary, for example, coordination between the ministries of labor and education is limited, evidenced by the fact that they operate separate adult education programs.[1] In Poland, the ministries of labor and education are statutorily required to cooperate on adult learning initiatives, which must be approved by the Council of Ministers. In practice, however, there has been little coordination (OECD 2005d).

The evidence for adult learning interventions to date is either limited or mixed; the success of their effectiveness depends on context, specific design features, and to whom they are targeted. Building adult learning systems thus requires carefully examining the successes and failures of existing international policies and programs. Moreover, governments in the region will benefit from rigorous monitoring and evaluation, including impact evaluations, of such programs to ensure that they meet desired objectives.

Promote Autonomy and Accountability of both Public and Private Providers

Autonomy

Adult education is perhaps most effective when it functions as a market for training. If informed well, consumers will demand programs of high quality that are relevant to their employment aspirations. If autonomous and agile, providers will respond to this demand and offer quality programs in a competitive environment. If providers are held accountable for the quality of the training provided, programs will meet the highest and latest standards. If, for example, a computer training provider delivers programs of limited quality and relevance, consumers will simply shift to another provider.

Arguably, private providers are already autonomous in their decisions regarding market entry and exit, as well as regarding investments and products. The same is not necessarily true for public providers if they receive institutional funding from the government and are bound by government rules. In order to truly compete in the adult education and training market and deliver useful, state-of-the-art programs, public providers also require autonomy to respond to changes in demand and other competitive pressures. For instance, to compete successfully, vocational training providers and tertiary education institutions will, similar to private providers, need to be autonomous in their decisions regarding market entry and exit, as well as regarding investments and programs. As an example, the Czech Republic is encouraging public vocational education and training schools to compete in the adult training market.

Accountability

Information is the key to accountability in adult education and training. Functioning accountability systems require government regulatory intervention to ensure that (1) adequate information is available for consumers of such education (so that they may make informed decisions), and (2) the suppliers of adult education and training programs maintain the quality and relevance of their program offerings. Thus, policies that set standards for and ensure the quality of adult learning opportunities both foster supply and stimulate demand. For example, national qualification frameworks can help to stimulate demand by allowing workers to obtain certified qualifications that prove their competencies to employers—and address a key information constraint. They can also make continuing vocational education and training (CVET) and retraining of unemployed workers more strategic and relevant to economic needs. Clearly, the regulation and certification of education providers—both public and private—and their programs is a key element of developing an adult learning system.

National qualification frameworks (NQFs) are being developed in many ECA countries to establish coherent quality standards for education and training systems and recognize prior learning, including that acquired through formal, nonformal, and informal learning methods. For many countries in the ECA region, NQFs—at least for the tertiary level—are a mandatory component of the Bologna process (see chapter 5). The development of such frameworks is, however, complex. NQFs require a strong legislative basis, a high degree of coordination and administrative capacity, and a great deal of time—countries such as Ireland and the United Kingdom have spent years developing and refining them (Gunny and Viertel 2007; Ireland 2003; United Kingdom 2003). Moreover, they are no panacea, and it is important to set realistic expectations as to what they can achieve in conjunction with other policy levers in adult education and training. A recent assessment of the experience with NQFs in 16 countries worldwide showed that they may not always result in the better matching of demand for and supply of adult education and training, nor in better training outcomes (Allais 2010). The success and failure of NQFs appear to depend, at least in part, on the extent of the constructive involvement of key stakeholders—and their willingness to eventually make use of frameworks devised.

As noted in the previous section, employer-led, sector-level councils often play a critical role in developing standards. For example, in the Czech Republic, sector skills councils have started to develop national occupational frameworks for each occupation, together with their required key competences and qualifications. National qualifications standards are also being developed based on this information. By early 2009 more than 160 qualifications standards were in place, with an additional 250 yet to be defined. According to the Ministry of Education, Youth, and Sport, the eventual number of qualifications could reach between 1,000 and 1,200. Given the magnitude of NQFs, it is practical for countries to begin defining standards for a few important occupational sectors before working towards a broader qualifications framework. The Kyrgyz Republic, for example, has begun piloting a qualifications system for the tourism sector as part of developing an NQF (ETF 2007).

In addition to setting appropriate standards and coordinating relevant stakeholders, some countries also face social barriers when implementing qualifications systems. For example, members of the formal education system sometimes believe that they are the sole legitimate providers of education and training, making them averse to systems that accredit formal and informal learning results on an equal basis (Hungary 2006). Similarly, a shift in thinking is also required on the part of employers, who, when hiring workers, will need to be open to considering not only recognized education degrees, but also partial certified qualifications—that is, an individual's job qualifications that do not necessarily stem from formal education degrees. Again, the actual use of NQFs is likely to depend on the extent to which key stakeholders have been an active part of their formulation.

In addition, some adult learners are intimidated by the process of obtaining qualifications. Although this does not appear to be a major barrier to adult education and training in many ECA countries, it may hinder less educated workers in particular. In order to attract these workers, regulators and providers can design learning programs in small units and ensure that testing methods are approachable. For example, computer-based testing, multiple assessment opportunities, and small group learning have all contributed to increasing the participation of low-skilled and immigrant workers in the United Kingdom as part of the London Open College System (United Kingdom 2003).

Quality standards and accreditation systems are also important for ensuring the quality of adult learning providers, especially those that receive public funding. Several OECD countries have developed quality assurance, inspection, and accreditation systems that can serve as models for ECA countries. For example, Denmark, Portugal, and Spain have developed institutes that evaluate adult learning programs with the aim of ensuring quality. The United Kingdom has established an Adult Learning Inspectorate that assesses hundreds of publicly funded programs every year and publishes the results; those that underperform often lose funding (OECD 2005c). Quality assurance systems in adult education and training can also involve the use of self-evaluations by providers alongside external evaluations, as in the case of Slovenia. In the Czech Republic, the Ministry of Education, Youth, and Sport certifies retraining programs for the unemployed that are financed by the Labor Office. The ministry is also beginning to pilot a quality assessment system and plans to institute a star rating scheme for quality based on a simple set of criteria, rather than complicated quality standards. If successful, this could be an interesting option for less advanced countries.

In ECA countries, programs that assess the quality of adult education and training may play an important role in helping adults, particularly those with little experience of these programs, make decisions. As noted in box 6.3, cost is a major barrier to adult education and training in the region: Polish providers have determined that learners are likely to choose a program based only on price, irrespective of quality (OECD 2005d). For providers that do not typically receive public funding, quality seals are an attractive means of assessment. Even though such seals rely on voluntary participation, providers have the incentive to meet standards in order to demonstrate the quality of their product to the market. Both Germany and Austria have developed quality seals. In Austria, the initiative was originally supported by nonprofit providers and in Germany by market providers, but both receive funds from the government (OECD 2005c).

Ensure the Efficiency of Sector Financing

Financing for adult education and training programs should largely be private, certainly for most continuing vocational education and training programs. However, public funding will be needed to address market failures in the sector, provide incentives to encourage the participation of underrepresented groups (e.g., older and less skilled workers), and finance programs for the unemployed. Governments already play a role in the financing of adult education and training in ECA, funding retraining for the unemployed through public employment services and providing incentives for private investments. The existence of market failures in the sector presents a rationale for continued and, occasionally, expanded

Box 6.3

Market Failures that Impede Adult Learning

Private investments lie at the heart of adult education and training in most countries, but governments can create an enabling environment for private investment through careful regulation that facilitates the flow of information and ensures educational quality. Firms and workers—not governments—should drive adult training decisions, as their main motivation for investing in training is the expectation of greater profits and higher wages, respectively. Governments, conversely, recognize both the social returns and overall economic benefits of increased human capital. Accordingly, it is in their interest to provide a certain amount of financing to overcome market failures associated with the provision of adult learning, including externalities, credit market failures, and information failures.

The economic literature identifies a range of market failures in adult education and training, suggesting that the participation of individual workers in such training may be below the socially optimal level, despite its considerable returns. In other words, individual workers and company managers are making rational and optimal decisions about training given the constraints that they face, but the sum of these decisions represents a less than optimal outcome for individual countries. First, *externalities* may hold back training. Economic theory suggests that because firms do not enjoy the full benefits of training—some of it will accrue to future employers—they may invest less in it. For example, the higher the risk that a worker will leave a company soon after training (i.e., the "poaching" of trained workers), the more firms will be cautious in investing in this area. While no evidence from firm surveys in the ECA region documents an externality barrier, anecdotal evidence suggests that it is an important concern for employers in the region, particularly in those countries that, until recently, faced a very tight labor market.

Second, individuals and firms may also be unable to generate the necessary funds to finance education and training (*credit market failure*). For example, firms may be unable to raise financing in the capital markets themselves, especially small firms with limited physical collateral. Survey data from the EU10 suggests that the cost of training is presently an important barrier to more training (see figure B6.3). Third, workers and firms may opt out of training because they *lack information*, for example, about the availability and quality of training providers. Lack of recognition or certification of learning will also reduce workers' interest in

(continued next page)

Box 6.3 *(continued)*

Figure B6.3 Barriers to the Expansion of Adult Education and Training in the ECA Region

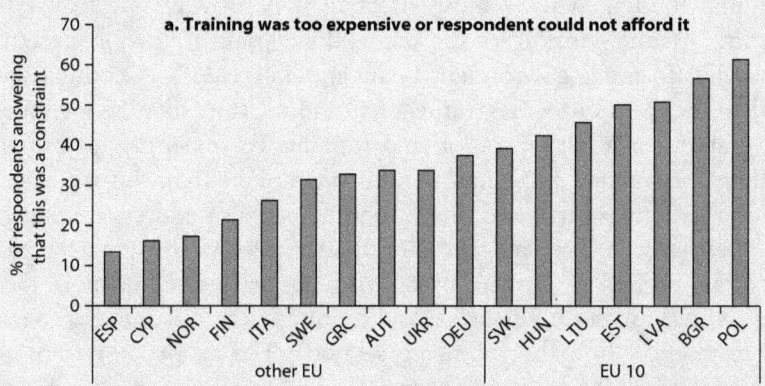

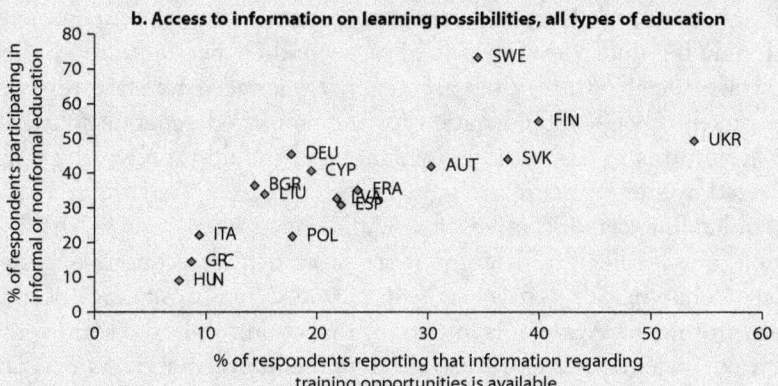

Sources: Authors' calculations based on AES data (2007).
Note: See "Abbreviations" for country abbreviations and groupings.

training because they cannot be sure that they can demonstrate their raised productivity to employers. Conversely, employers and workers in developing economies may not be fully aware of the productivity returns from training due to lack of information about the type and area of training, as well as a lack of managerial skills in small and medium-size enterprises. Survey data from ECA confirm a positive correlation between the incidence of training and the availability of information (see figure B6.3, panel b), with the information barrier particularly acute for less educated workers.

Source: Authors.

government investment in adult learning in the region (see box 6.3). Government financing is unlikely to make a difference, however, unless it is used strategically to support better partnerships and overcome the disconnect between different market players.

Public funding will be most effective if it provides incentives that promote quality, empowers the demand side, and follows competitive principles. To make government financing effective, ECA countries will need to focus on outcomes, rather than inputs, thus shaping a competitive market for adult education and training. For example, government funding for training programs for the unemployed can be made competitive and outcome-based. State funding can also address market failures that result in lower average participation rates, or lower participation by certain groups of workers, by offering the private sector more incentives to invest in adult education and training, such as voucher programs and tax breaks (see the following section). The scope of government financing for adult education and training will vary by the type of training and target group. Because retraining programs for the unemployed, including the underdeveloped field of "second-chance" education, generally have social returns, they are generally financed by state resources. Conversely, CVET and education for the employed generate substantial private returns to firms and individuals, and should therefore be largely financed by these groups.

Public financial incentives for CVET have been rare in the ECA region, but are likely to become more prominent as economies become more technologically advanced and the need for "upskilling" becomes more prominent. Again, it is important that countries in the region create the right incentives and focus on strengthening demand. As described earlier in this chapter, governments in many OECD countries use public financing both to promote more private investment in training and to overcome market failures. Two incentives for firms found in many OECD countries are tax deductions for training costs and payroll training levies. Some ECA countries have also begun experimenting with these tools. In addition, a number of EU10 countries have begun utilizing financing from the European Social Fund (ESF) to create grant programs for firms, while others have used demand-side financing, such as vouchers, to target individual workers to participate in training.

Offer Tax Deductions to Firms that Offer CVET

Allowing firms to deduct the costs of training from their taxes is one of the most common forms of training incentives for firms. Such tax deduction schemes have been implemented in some countries in the ECA region, particularly in the EU10 and the Russian Federation, and have been a useful first step for stimulating demand for training. Tax deductions for training costs are relatively simple for governments to administer and for firms to use, as they rely on existing tax systems. Although tax deductions generally benefit only firms that are profitable, this bias can be managed by allowing deductions to be spread over a period of years.

However, tax deduction systems can also result in deadweight loss and higher administrative costs. Deadweight loss occurs when individuals and firms take advantage of tax deductions even though they would have offered training without them. For example, large firms are generally most likely to take advantage of deductions and are more prone to use funds to train highly skilled workers (Cedefop 2009). This reality is why several OECD countries employ more complex, multilevel tax deduction systems that target financial incentives to those firms and individuals who face barriers to training. While such targeting is attractive in theory, it also increases administrative costs, invites manipulation by firms and makes the system more difficult to use. In an effort to reduce deadweight loss, for example, the Netherlands experimented with targeted tax deductions but decided later to abolish them because they were ineffective and too complex (OECD 2005c). However, despite these challenges, tax deduction schemes can be a valuable tool for giving an initial boost to adult education and training, particularly in environments where few firms and individuals currently provide training.

Consider Payroll Levies and Other Grant Mechanisms

Grant systems based on payroll levies can also create an effective funding source for training and allow for greater targeting of training funds. However, such systems can be challenging to implement. This type of grant system levies a payroll tax (typically of 0.5–2.0 percent) and disburses the funds collected to firms for training purposes, either in the form of reimbursements or grants (Dar, Canagarajah, and Murphy 2003; OECD 2005c). There is promising evidence from OECD countries that well-designed training levies can increase training rates, particularly for medium-sized firms (OECD 2005c; Tan 2001). By allowing grants to be targeted to firms and individuals who are less likely to seek training in the absence of a financial incentive, levy grant systems can in theory also be designed to limit deadweight loss. However, to implement an effective levy grant system, countries need to consider the preparedness of firms to participate in such a system, management of the funds, and ways to ensure the actual participation of small and medium enterprises (SMEs) in training programs. Careful communication and coordination with the enterprise sector is crucial, as such systems can be problematic in situations where firms complain of high payroll taxation and believe that they will have a low chance of successfully accessing and utilizing training funds.

Even in countries where payroll levy grant systems have had a generally positive impact on raising training participation, noncompliance rates are often a concern, particularly in less advanced countries and among small firms (Dar, Canagarajah, and Murphy 2003). Most existing levy grant systems rely on a central agency that manages the funds and awards them to firms—a role that can be filled by a government or social partners (Ok and Tergeist 2003). To be effective, levy grant agencies require strong capacity in administration, quality control, and training policy. Levy grant systems can also be managed by a firm itself; Poland, for example, has set up a combined training fund and subsidy based in individual firms, thus avoiding a central management structure. If a firm commits at least 0.25 percent of its total wage bill to a training plan designed in cooperation with employee representatives, the government will subsidize the training (OECD 2005e).

Despite the training benefits for medium-sized firms, one of the drawbacks of levy grant systems is that they tend not to benefit either SMEs or very small firms. The most effective way to implement a levy grant program may thus require additional targeting of SMEs and exempting the smallest firms (e.g., those with fewer than 50 employees), which are provided a different type of assistance. (For specific barriers to SMEs that are not alleviated by simple financial incentives, see box 6.4.) The Human Resource Development Fund (HRDF) in Malaysia is an example of a successful payroll levy program that alleviates the additional constraints faced by SMEs and reduces the administrative burden. For example, rather than requiring SMEs to develop their own training plans, established training providers are used to offer time-tested and preapproved training programs. This feature also helps stimulate supply by giving training providers the opportunity to market well-defined programs (Tan 2001).[2]

Grant schemes play an important role in many ECA countries, particularly in the EU member states, which have access to grants from the ESF. They use these grants to support lifelong learning programs in line with the EU Lisbon Jobs and Growth Strategy and its successor, the Europe 2020 Strategy. These funds, however, sometimes bolstered the supply, not the demand, side of adult education and training. Instead of providing workers with vouchers, they have often been channeled to training institutions. Some countries have utilized general budget funds

Box 6.4

Supporting Small and Medium Enterprises to Participate in Training

Small and medium enterprises often face a variety of constraints that make it difficult to provide and take advantage of training, such as obsolete technology, lack of access to finance, limited administrative capacity, poor management skills, and an inability to use training effectively. Programs that alleviate credit and financial constraints, however, may not be sufficient to stimulate more worker training—such programs must be designed to address additional constraints as well. The Integral Quality and Modernization (Spanish acronym CIMO) Program in Mexico was developed when it became clear that training subsidies alone were not effective in increasing worker training in many SMEs. Firms who participate in the program undergo a diagnostic process that identifies their production methods and assesses workers' skills needs and other firm constraints. CIMO then organizes clusters of enterprises (where possible), links firms to outside providers, and subsidizes up to half of the cost of training per firm—a set of policies that is likely to be more efficient than having the government provide the training directly.

An evaluation of the CIMO program suggested positive impacts on training participation rates and enterprise performance. In sectors with many SMEs, particularly where they partner or act as suppliers to larger firms, programs to pool resources are promising. For example, the Korean government has supported the development of large enterprise-led training consortia in response to the low take-up of payroll tax-funded training grants by SMEs. Large enterprises have developed training consortia in response to skilled labor shortages and low-quality partner organizations and suppliers. The consortia—which have had very high participation rates—can capitalize on training resources that already exist in large enterprises, benefitting from higher-quality inputs and more efficient relationships with partners. They receive some direct subsidies and also benefit from a higher uptake of existing training grants. In the ECA region, the Czech Republic is launching a similar SME retraining voucher program funded by the European Social Fund. The program will promote professional retraining, pooling resources from enterprises, municipalities, and the ESF.

Source: Tan and Lopez Acevedo 2005; OECD 2005c; OECD 2004a.

---

for grant schemes, especially to fund services for the unemployed. Bulgaria, for example, is now operating a grant cofinancing scheme to encourage in-service training of the workforces of private companies. Careful evaluations could help determine the effects of these efforts.

Alternative Financing Mechanisms: Provide Support Directly to Workers

Demand-side programs that offer incentives directly to workers are an alternative or supplement to supply-side programs that finance adult education and training providers. Since financial and time constraints are often cited by workers as hindrances to training (see box 6.3), programs that directly address these problems can be beneficial. These programs build on the individual motivation to learn, which may increase the chances of learning success, and also have the advantage of directly helping workers with the greatest skills deficits.

The simplest and most widely implemented demand-side program is a tax incentive that allows workers to deduct the cost of self-financed training. Such programs more effectively benefit targeted individuals than do tax incentives for firms; however, individual-based tax incentives only reach those workers who earn wages high enough to pay income taxes. An alternative is training leave, which provides workers reduced working hours or breaks from full-time employment with some degree of compensation, to enroll in training programs, combined with the guarantee of a job upon completion of the training. This type of program is used in many OECD countries and takes various forms in terms of targeting, length, and the level and source of financial compensation (see OECD 2005c, chapter 3).

Grants and vouchers are increasingly popular programs that provide incentives for workers to seek education and training. The advantage of these programs is that different levels of subsidies can be offered to different types of workers, based on need. For example, education and training voucher programs in Austria offer more generous support to older workers, while the Adult Learning Grant (ALG) in the United Kingdom offers an "allowance" that varies in size according to the means of the recipient (IFF Research 2008). Voucher and grant programs oriented towards shorter courses have been designed to cover only education and training costs, while programs geared towards higher qualifications must usually offer subsidies that provide living expenses in order to be effective (see OECD 2005c).

Like several other new EU member states, the Czech Republic is using financing from the ESF for a demand-side voucher program called "Pivo." The program targets both employed and nonemployed individuals aged 25–64 years to finance education and training in languages, information and communication technology (ICT), and entrepreneurship skills—all skills that have been identified as underdeveloped among the Czech workforce. However, training vouchers do have limitations. Recent evaluation evidence from the United States, for example, indicates that their effectiveness may be hampered by faulty information, as when up-to-date data on local skill needs are not available to either training providers or participants (particularly disadvantaged and low-skilled participants) (Barnow 2009). In addition, the effectiveness of vouchers can be affected by a limited supply of quality training providers, at least in more remote geographical locations—though the existence of vouchers can help stimulate the training market.

As noted earlier in this chapter, Individual Learning Accounts (ILAs) are another form of support for individual workers. Individually designated bank accounts that can receive financing from a firm, an individual, or the government, ILAs encourage investments in adult learning but can be onerous to administer. Like other demand-side financing schemes, ILAs are appropriate only where it is possible to safeguard against abuse and fraud. Indeed, England abandoned a large ILA program because of this very concern. Nevertheless, ILAs are appealing because they often rely on matching funds, sometimes in a (tax-sheltered) savings account. Although several OECD countries have found them difficult to implement, some of their large employers have independently started implementing ILAs to encourage employees to do training. Providing tax relief for firm-based accounts, where they exist, could also be a helpful way to encourage education and training in ECA countries.

Continued Government Role in Retraining and Education for the Unemployed

In most ECA countries, retraining and education programs for the unemployed are largely publicly funded and represent a significant share of government spending on active labor market programs. The record on the effectiveness of such training is mixed, but there is evidence that they can have positive impacts on employment if well designed, especially over the medium term (Betcherman, Olivas, and Dar 2004; Card, Kluve, and Weber 2009). Access to training for the unemployed in the ECA region is limited (see chapter 2), yet its importance is set to grow in light of shrinking populations and the increasing need to expand labor force participation. Retraining programs can make a crucial contribution to promoting employment by strategically reskilling laid-off workers for new jobs—an important agenda in the wake of the recent economic crisis.

When focused on basic skill gaps, these programs can also promote social inclusion (see box 6.5).

Although many ECA governments have long funded industrial training institutes that trained or retrained unemployed adult workers, in most instances, these institutes were not always designed to meet the needs of the modern work force. Governments today would be better

---

Box 6.5

Second-Chance and Remedial Education

The demographic decline being experienced in most ECA countries suggests that every person of working age needs to be brought into the labor force. This means that, in addition to the equity imperative, there is a growth imperative for greater skills. Many unemployed and economically inactive people in the ECA region face educational disadvantages as a result of leaving school early or a failure to acquire basic skills. Second-chance and remedial education and training are promising tools for addressing basic skills deficits that prevent adults and young adults from entering the labor force and becoming sustainably employed. These programs often involve basic literacy and numeracy training. Overall, second-chance education programs remain limited in many ECA countries, even though basic skills deficits often are a key barrier to the labor force participation of disadvantaged workers. Some countries in the EU10, such as Bulgaria, have recognized that literacy is a concern for a small but significant portion of the disadvantaged population, including the Roma minority, and have begun to extend their literacy programs in response.

Opening new pathways to employment through this type of education requires developing new outreach and delivery mechanisms. Employment services in many ECA countries have a poor record of effectively serving the most disadvantaged.[a] Basic skills gaps such as functional literacy are typically not even considered when identifying active labor market interventions for the registered unemployed, even if these people are highly disadvantaged. Second-chance education and training are thus ideally part of employment activation programs for the disadvantaged, long-term unemployed, and welfare-dependent adults. However, these programs require employment services and social welfare offices to integrate their efforts in partnership with NGOs and community-based organizations—both in order to reach beneficiaries and to deliver tailored support to them.

(continued next page)

> **Box 6.5** *(continued)*
>
> Second-chance education and training programs often involve behavioral and social skills training—especially for young people who have failed to enter the workforce and for other long-term unemployed who have attained some basic level of education. Many such individuals are from disadvantaged backgrounds and lacked the opportunity to develop the social and behavioral skills needed to effectively hold down a job. For example, Czech employers cited irregular job attendance and low work motivation as reasons for not hiring (especially young) Roma (World Bank 2008a). It is thus critical that job training for such groups take such concerns into account. The youth-oriented Jovenes program in Latin America, which was deemed successful in short-run evaluations, is an example of a program that successfully combines training in vocational skills with a curriculum aimed at improving communications, personal relations, and self-esteem.
>
> a. For evidence from the Czech Republic, see World Bank (2008a).

off by contracting out retraining services through a competitive bidding process, rather than relying on these training institutes. In this way, they would both foster the restructuring of formerly public providers and trigger the market entry of new, private providers. As a large purchaser of training services for the unemployed, a government can implicitly set the rules of the overall adult education and training market and thereby foster more private investment, including in CVET, if public financing is following competitive rules. The Czech Republic followed this approach in shaping its training market, which resulted, deliberately or not, in substantial market entry and a largely private-provider market.

Retraining programs in ECA countries can become more effective if they are designed to meet identified labor market needs; center on the needs and capabilities of individual job seekers; and are well linked to other active labor market programs, such as job referral services. Effective training and requalification efforts would also benefit from regular labor market assessments, including analysis of vacancy data, to gauge changes in labor demand and ensure that jobseekers become retrained in vocations that are actually in demand on the labor market.

As valuable as such analysis is, it can be difficult to implement in practice. In the Czech Republic, for example, labor offices conduct regular assessments of vacancies at the regional and municipal levels. However, the actual provision of training does not always respond to such assessments, as certain training programs are procured in bulk by the labor office. In Poland, it has been argued that regional labor offices lack the resources and training to conduct labor market assessments. Clearly, capacity building in this area is a critical to ensuring that such assessments take place (OECD 2005d).

When contracting out training to private providers, output-oriented incentives such as performance-based contracts can boost the relevance and effectiveness of the training. Turkey has had good experience with contracts that include built-in incentives for private providers to achieve high job placements rates. Until 2008, the Turkish Public Employment Service (ISKUR) followed this course to ensure that there was an actual demand for the skills that providers offer in their training classes.[3] Recent ISKUR data provided to the authors indicate significant differences in placement rates for in-class training programs between providers that have employment incentives (i.e., employment guarantees) and those that do not, highlighting the importance of contract design in placement intermediation (see figure 6.1).

Figure 6.1 Employment Placement Rates by Type of Retraining, Turkey, 2008

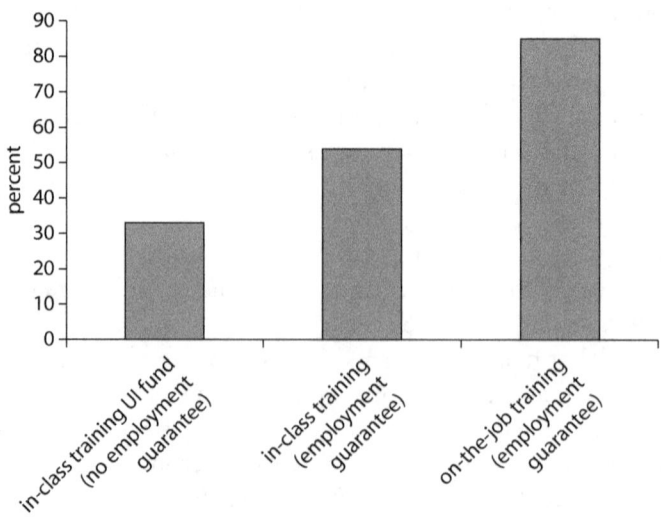

Source: Staff calculations based on administrative data for 2008 provided by the Turkish Public Employment Service (ISKUR).

Priorities for Adult Education and Training Systems in ECA Countries

Given that the development of modern adult learning systems is a complex and lengthy task, countries in the ECA region need to carefully prioritize their efforts in this sector. In many cases, improving the quality and equity of other levels of education may be of greater importance in the near term. Figure 6.2 suggests priorities for countries in the region based on their GDP per capita (as a measure of economic development) and demographic outlook. The figure groups ECA countries into three broad groups:

(1) Advanced economies facing a demographic decline that compete in highly competitive markets (i.e., the new EU member states, Croatia, and Russia);[4]
(2) Less advanced economies facing a demographic decline (i.e., many countries in South Eastern Europe plus several rapidly aging CIS countries); and

Figure 6.2 Adult Education and Training Priorities in the ECA Region

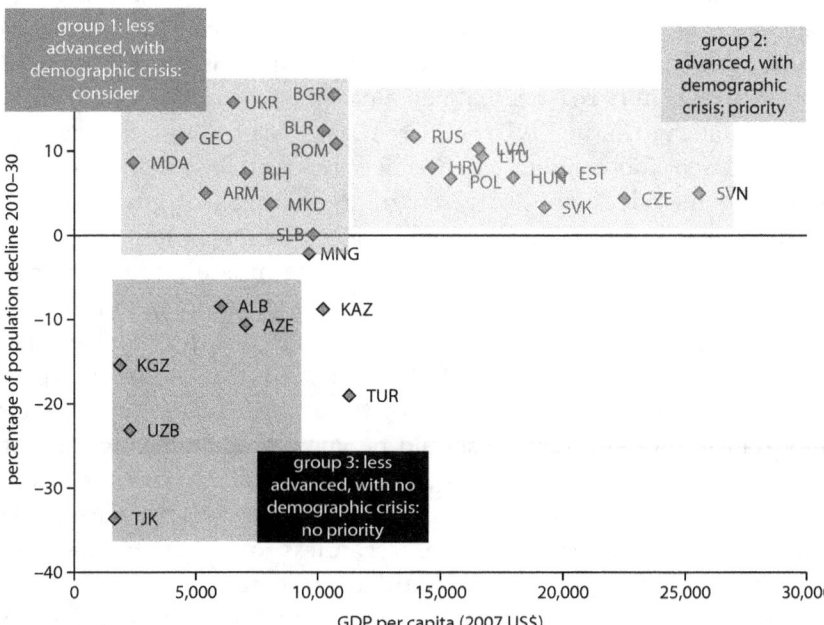

Source: Staff calculations based on United Nations 2006.
Note: See "Abbreviations" for country abbreviations.

(3) less advanced economies facing a demographic expansion, consisting of the majority of the Central Asian countries along with Albania.

Turkey and Kazakhstan do not fit well into any of these categories, but it can be argued that their priorities are the same as those of group 1.

Table 6.1 provides a rough policy framework for adult education and training in ECA countries, based on their respective economic and demographic indicators.

Advanced Economies in Demographic Decline

Expanding adult learning is a priority for advanced economies in the region that are facing a demographic decline. Their challenge is to ensure that existing coordination mechanisms function well and that regulation and financing are used to facilitate the emergence of a private sector-oriented adult education and training market. As shown in chapter 2, some EU10 countries are relatively advanced and on par with many older EU member states in terms of training participation. The Europe 2020 Strategy places a strong emphasis on lifelong learning and has served as an engine for policy change and the programming of EU funds. These funds, in turn, have stimulated greater promotion of adult education and training. The strategies in these countries are in place, supported by multistakeholder coordination bodies, and legislation is being introduced alongside regulatory regimes and new financing schemes.

The challenge in the EU10 and Croatia is to ensure that the demand for education and training emanating from the labor market can be served by flexible, high-quality programs. Within this group, certain countries, such as the Czech Republic and the Slovak Republic, have high training participation rates and a culture of adult education and training has taken root. Here, the task is to make training more effective and strategic, improve quality through autonomy for providers and accountability mechanisms, carefully evaluate outcomes, and use government financing in a tactical way. Across the region, given their importance, special attention should be given to encouraging training in small and medium enterprises. A particular challenge will be ensuring that less educated, older, and disadvantaged workers can participate more in education and training, regardless of whether they are employed, unemployed, or outside the labor force.

Turkey and Kazakhstan might also consider following this agenda for adult education and training. Although neither country fits well into the country groupings used in this chapter, both countries have expanding

Table 6.1 Recommended Policy Framework for Adult Education and Training in the ECA Region

	Advanced economies with demographic challenge	Less advanced economies with demographic challenge	Less advanced economies with no demographic challenge
	EU10, HRV, RUS	ARM, BIH, BLR, GEO, MDA, MKD, MNE, SRB, UKR	ALB, AZE, KGZ, TJK, UZB
Policy and institutional foundation			
Multistakeholder skills task force			
National strategy on adult learning			
Coordination mechanisms			
Autonomy			
Promote autonomy of training institutions			
Accountability			
National qualifications framework			
Regulation and certification regime			
Certification and quality control agency			
Strategic financing			
CVET—firms			
Training tax deductions for firms			
Training grant schemes based on payroll levy			
Grant schemes			
SME support schemes, with training focus			
CVET—individuals			
Worker tax deductions for training			
Subsidies or vouchers for individuals			
Training leave			
Individual learning accounts			
Loan schemes for individuals			
Retraining and education for the nonemployed			
Job training for the unemployed			
Second-chance education programs			

Source: Author's assessment.
Note: Color key: priority, consider, not a priority. See "Acronyms" for country abbreviations and groupings.

populations and aspire to develop more advanced economies. In the case of Turkey, the EU accession process will also focus on the Europe 2020 Strategy and thus, lifelong learning. In addition to developing effective policy coordination mechanisms and strategies for adult education and training, both countries should consider introducing regulatory systems that use accountability and financing schemes to promote more labor market-relevant adult learning programs.

Less Advanced Economies in Demographic Decline
The principal priority of less advanced economies in the region experiencing a demographic decline (i.e., many of those in South Eastern Europe and the middle-income CIS countries) is to introduce a strategic framework for adult learning and create the tools needed to implement this strategy (e.g., coordination mechanisms, plus initial steps toward regulation). Their demographic challenge and less advanced level of economic development make adult learning critical for these countries. However, in view of resource constraints, the competing claims of other parts of the education system, and limited administrative and policy planning capacities, these countries should initially focus more on introducing a strategy for adult education, and less on financing and regulation. At the same time, this group can benefit from the experience of the EU10 (e.g., the Czech Republic) to learn how to foster competitive, private sector-driven adult education and training markets.

Less Advanced Economies with Growing Populations
For the less advanced economies in the region that are not facing a demographic decline (i.e., those of low-income CIS countries and Albania), it may be more productive to limit efforts to establish strategic frameworks and coordination mechanisms for adult education and training. It is suggested that this group of countries refrain from creating and piloting financing schemes or implementing regulations until other educational challenges, including the achievement of high secondary completion rates, are adequately addressed. The more limited scope of action proposed for this group is a specific reflection of the fact that (1) low-income CIS countries face significant impediments to improving learning outcomes in other education sectors, which will absorb much of their fiscal and policy-planning capacity and (2) the relevance of adult education and training to their economies is presently more limited, due to their different demographic outlook and the greater distance of their economies

from advanced technology compared to the EU10 and middle-income CIS countries.

Summary

Lifelong learning and adult education and training are growing in importance across the ECA region. Increasing demand for skilled labor, accelerating technological change, and significant demographic decline are all contributing factors. Although building adult learning systems is critically important, its overall priority in individual ECA countries depends on economic and demographic conditions and their most pressing education challenges.

Successful adult education and training systems are based on a high degree of policy coordination and partnership between government agencies and the private sector, with a strong voice for the demand side—businesses and individuals—in determining training content. Once a solid policy foundation has been created, governments can "steer" adult education and training through tracking data on program quality (derived from both routine monitoring and evaluation and impact studies), promoting autonomy and accountability, and ensuring efficient government financing.

Across the board, private investment lies at the heart of adult education and training, though governments will need to provide a certain amount of financing to overcome market failures. In the case of CVET programs for the employed, governments will mainly need to create an enabling environment for private investment through appropriate regulation and the provision of information. In addition, various financial incentives for more private investment can be targeted to both firms and workers. For the unemployed, retraining and education programs are an important part of active labor market policies in most ECA countries; in this case, governments can use their role as purchasers of retraining services to shape the overall adult training market.

Notes

1. For a discussion of regional variation in SEE countries, see Gunny and Viertel (2007). See also OECD (2005d) and Hungary, Ministry of Education and Culture (2006).
2. The program also supports SMEs with training needs analysis and provides opportunities for group training with other SMEs.

3. Despite its evident effectiveness, Turkey's new Law on Labor Force Training, adopted in 2008, abolished the placement incentive scheme.
4. Bulgaria, Romania, and Belarus lie close together in terms of GDP per capita and the scale of their demographic decline. However, Bulgaria and Romania should consider adult education and training more of a priority than should Belarus, given the former countries' membership in the EU, participation in the Lisbon Agenda, and access to financing for lifelong learning from the ESF.

CHAPTER 7

Extended Summary: The Path for Education Reforms in the ECA Region

The countries of Europe and Central Asia are coming out of a deep economic crisis—the worst since the economic transition-induced recession of the early 1990s and the deepest recession among all developing regions. Post-crisis conditions look very different from those of preceding years. Previously, growth in the region was fueled by cheap borrowing from abroad, growing exports of goods and services (including labor services), and, in the case of natural resource exporters, rising global demand. The world of 2011 is a changed one. Borrowing is significantly more expensive and export growth is restrained by potentially slower growth in destination countries. Restoring and sustaining growth in this context requires boosting competitiveness and increasing labor productivity—the very reforms that were postponed in the boom years. These reforms are all the more important given a shrinking working-age population in many countries of the region.

The boom years also exposed significant bottlenecks to growth in the ECA region, particularly with respect to the skills of the labor force (Mitra, Selowsky, and Zalduendo 2010). Paradoxically for a region with relatively high educational attainment, a shortage of worker skills emerged as one of the two most important constraints to firm expansion (the other being the tax regime). This finding makes it crucial for countries to undertake reforms to reduce skills shortages as they plan for recovery. Education systems play a very important role in creating the right skills.

This book investigated two primary questions: Are education systems in the ECA region able to inculcate the right skills in their graduates and what can they do to improve on their performance? In answering these questions, a fundamental problem emerged: data exist on the number of students who graduate (i.e., how many diplomas are issued) in ECA countries, but internationally comparable information on whether graduates of upper secondary and tertiary institutions (from which the bulk of ECA graduates now enter the labor market) have the right skills and competencies for the job market is not available.

A range of available data sources was examined to argue that there is significantly more that education systems can do to improve the quality and relevance of education and thereby enhance the skills of their student populations. Although ministries of education are constrained in a number of ways from effectively managing their education and training sectors for results—that is, with an eye to student skills and competencies—greater efforts should be made to reduce and eventually eliminate the three most important and interrelated impediments to educational success: the lack of systematic data on key skills-related performance issues, the legacy of central planning, and the inefficient use of resources.

Education and training systems in the region have simply been slow in making the transition from teaching the basics (i.e., factual content, often via rote learning) to inculcating the kind of higher-order skills increasingly required in a modern economy. The ECA countries should therefore view the reform of their education systems—at all levels and for all ages—to be critical to their future economic success.

The following is an extended summary of the findings and policy recommendations of this study.

The Skills Challenge in the ECA Region

The ECA region had a well-regarded education system prior to the end of central planning. Not only did countries in the region succeed in providing mass basic education, they had a number of highly regarded universities and research institutes, particularly in the basic sciences and mathematics. While the intervening years have taken some of the shine off this reputation, these countries continue to have strong achievements. Notably, enrollments are high at all levels of education. Primary enrollment rates are above 90 percent and primary completion rates are also very high throughout the region. Although secondary enrollment rates in many countries suffered a decline in the 1990s, they have since climbed and are now at or above what might be expected in all ECA countries, given their respective income levels.

The socialist legacy is particularly visible in low-income countries in the region, which have the highest secondary enrollments in the world for their income level. Tertiary enrollments, which have grown rapidly in the past two decades, are also high relative to income levels, with the few exceptions of certain low-income CIS countries, such as Azerbaijan and Uzbekistan.

In addition to attainment, ECA countries also do well in delivering a relatively good-quality education, particularly in the lower grades. In fact, many younger students in the region outperform their Western European students in reading at the fourth-grade level, scoring above the scale average on the Progress in International Reading Literacy Study (PIRLS) in both 2001 and 2006.[1] These results are not uniform across ECA, however. Countries that have not joined the European Union (EU), for example, scored below the average, with the marked exception of the Russian Federation, which scored well above the average and demonstrated the greatest improvement between 2001 and 2006 (see figure 7.1). The commendable performance in reading at the elementary level indicates that schools in ECA countries are very capable of providing a quality education at the early stages.

Many ECA countries, though certainly not all, continue to do well on international reading assessments such as PISA and TIMSS at or near the end of lower secondary education, but only relative to the performance of other countries at the same income level. Figure 7.2 provides a scatter plot of 2008 per capita GDP against the PISA 2009 reading scores of countries participating in PISA (with ECA countries highlighted by their letter acronyms). The figure shows a positive relationship between the two values, suggesting that 15-year-olds in countries with higher national incomes tend to perform better on the reading component of the PISA. Significantly, the ECA region seems divided. Many of the new EU member states (including Poland, but also Turkey and Serbia) lie above the regression line, demonstrating that their students apparently read better than would be predicted on the basis of GDP per capita alone. Others lie below the regression line, including Romania, Montenegro, Bulgaria, Azerbaijan, and the Kyrgyz Republic. Students in these countries scored lower on the reading component of the PISA than their GDP per capita would have predicted.

Figure 7.1 Assessing a Skill—Reading Performance in the Fourth Grade: PIRLS Performance of ECA Countries, 2001 and 2006

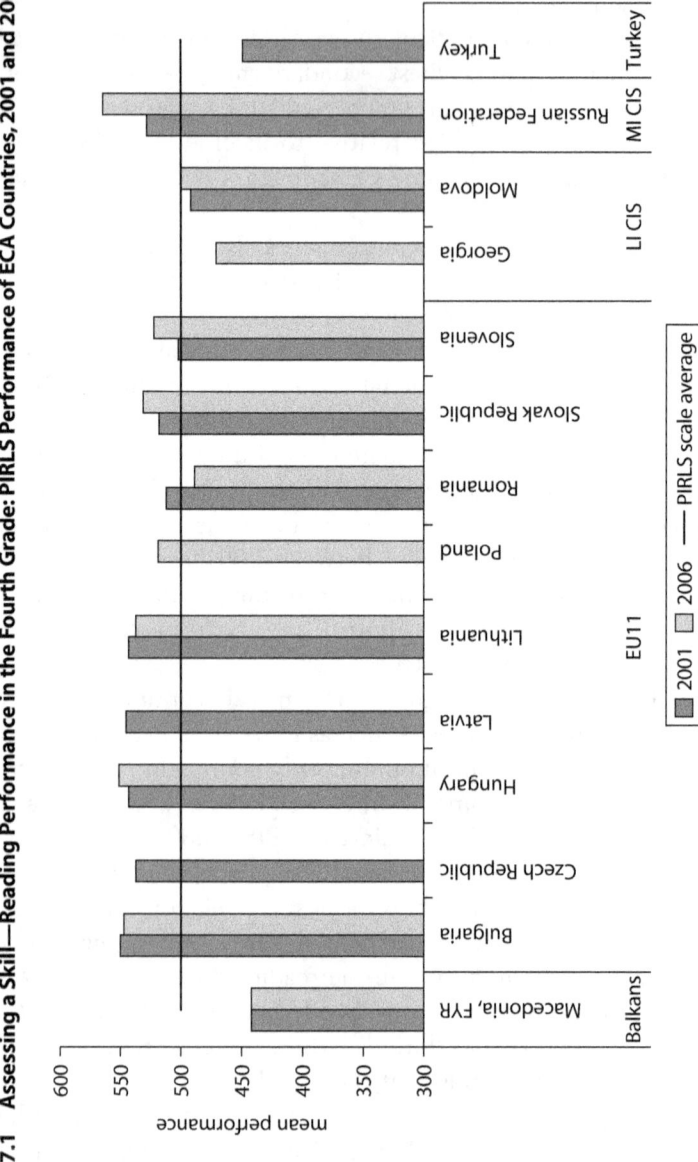

Sources: World Bank staff calculations based on PIRLS test score data downloaded from EdStats Database.
Note: LI = low-income, MI = middle income.

Figure 7.2 Analysis of Reading Competency of 15-Year-Old Students on the PISA 2009

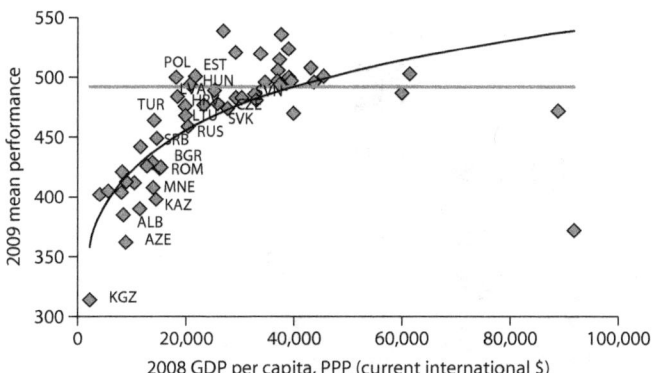

Sources: PISA 2009 Database and World Bank staff calculations based on World Development Indicators Database.
Note: The figure shows a regression line representing countries' predicted PISA reading scores based solely on GDP per capita, compared to the OECD mean reading score (horizontal line) on the assessment and GDP per capita in 2008. See "Abbreviations" for a key to country abbreviations.

In spite of these positive achievements of ECA education systems, the EBRD-World Bank Business Environment and Enterprise Performance Surveys (BEEPS) show that ECA firms' perception of skills constraints changed dramatically around 2005.[2] By 2008, skilled labor shortages had become one of the most commonly reported constraints to growth in the BEEPS survey across all countries in the region, second only to tax rates (see figure 7.3). On average, 30 percent of firms considered education and skills to be a major or severe constraint in 2008. The highest proportion of firms reporting constraints were found among the middle-income CIS countries, where upwards of 40 percent of firms were dissatisfied with the availability of skilled workers. A smaller proportion of firms in the Western Balkans reported similar levels of dissatisfaction, with significant variability in the dissatisfaction levels of firms in the EU10+1 countries and Turkey (BEEPS dataset 2008).

Why Are Skills an Emerging Problem if Education Systems Are Delivering?

Despite generally high average enrollment and attainment rates, as well as respectable quality education for their income levels, especially at lower levels of education (and even at lower secondary, where two-thirds of participating countries "punch" at or above their weight), skills shortages

Figure 7.3 Distribution of Firms in ECA Region That Consider Worker Skills a "Major" or "Very Severe" Constraint, 2008

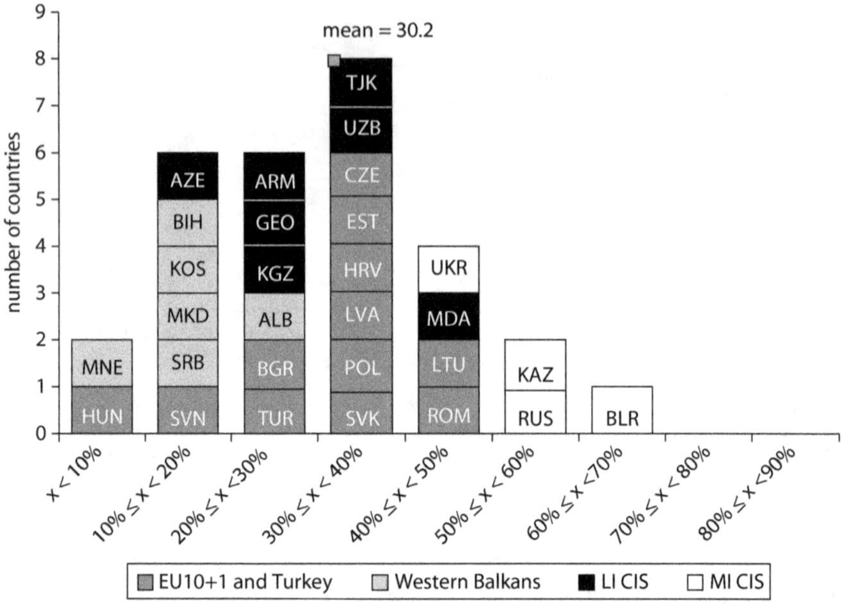

[Stacked bar chart: number of countries (y-axis, 0–9) by percent bins (x-axis). mean = 30.2]

- x < 10%: MNE, HUN
- 10% ≤ x < 20%: AZE, BIH, KOS, MKD, SRB, SVN
- 20% ≤ x < 30%: ARM, GEO, KGZ, ALB, BGR, TUR
- 30% ≤ x < 40%: TJK, UZB, CZE, EST, HRV, LVA, POL, SVK
- 40% ≤ x < 50%: UKR, MDA, LTU, ROM
- 50% ≤ x < 60%: KAZ, RUS
- 60% ≤ x < 70%: BLR
- 70% ≤ x < 80%: (none)
- 80% ≤ x < 90%: (none)

Legend: ■ EU10+1 and Turkey   □ Western Balkans   ■ LI CIS   □ MI CIS

Sources: BEEPS 2008; Mitra, Selowsky, and Zalduendo 2010.
Note: LI = low-income; MI = middle-income; x = % of firms (in respective countries) that consider education as an obstacle. See "Acronyms" for a key to country abbreviations.

were constraining growth in ECA countries before the onset of the current downturn. This is a puzzle that this book could not fully resolve, mainly because crucial information is missing. International assessments provide information about student competencies up to the age of 15 (usually the end of lower secondary education), but beyond that age, no information exists on student competencies. Nor does information exist on the quality of upper secondary or tertiary education or the relevance of education at these levels. Moreover, no information exists on students' noncognitive (or socioemotional—"soft"—skills) (see World Bank 2011b for an example of testing noncognitive skills in Peru). For policy makers to better understand the role of education in contributing to skills bottlenecks—and how to address it—this informational gap needs to be addressed.

Although the education offered in ECA countries at the end of lower secondary is respectable relative to levels of income, it does not appear to be adequate (or of the right relevance) to meet the demand for skills in the region. In addition to higher levels of education, firms are demanding *higher-order skills* that higher education alone does not guarantee, including cognitive skills such problem solving, together with behavioral skills such as teamwork (see box 7.1). Such skills are increasingly a part of the landscape of work in modern economies. Figure 7.4, which illustrates findings from the European Work Conditions Survey, demonstrates how the cognitive demands of work have risen relative to more routine tasks.[3]

The need for higher-order skills is not, moreover, confined to a few high-technology sectors, even construction—which is not normally viewed as a highly skilled industry—requires the ability to learn on the job, work independently, and solve complex problems. Nor are higher-order skills a requirement only of upper-middle income countries. Surveys of employers in lower-middle income countries, such as Kazakhstan and the former Yugoslav Republic of Macedonia, point in the same direction: the skills that are lacking include communication, thinking skills, problem-solving skills, and the ability to work independently (Ivaschenko 2008, World

---

Box 7.1

Higher-Order Skills for the World of Work in the 21st Century

It is now recognized that beyond formal qualifications, what is needed to function effectively in 21st century economies is the ability to *use* knowledge and other personal and social skills to complete tasks and solve problems as they arise. This broad group of abilities is generally called "skills" or "generic skills" because they are not specific to a job and are transferrable across employers. While there is no international consensus on key generic skills, most experts would agree that they include both basic and higher-order skills. Basic skills include reading, writing, computation, and the ability to use technology. Higher-order skills can be cognitive (e.g., learning to learn, problem solving, and creative thinking) or behavioral (e.g., communication, negotiation, and teamwork). The OECD list of key "competences" includes, in addition, the ability to act autonomously—that is, to perform and conduct one's own life plans—a skill that is particularly important in the modern world, where stable lifelong employment is less common. At present, standardized tests of secondary school students measure basic skills and some higher-order cognitive skills, but not behavioral skills. Recent research in Peru provides an example of how to incorporate the testing of behavioral skills into regular household surveys (see World Bank 2011b).

Sources: Authors, based on OECD 1999a and materials available on the following websites: State Secretariat for Economic Affairs of Switzerland (www.seco.admin.ch), Australian National Centre for Vocational Education Research (www.ncver.edu.au), American Society for Training and Development (www.astd.org); all URLs accessed September 2010.

Figure 7.4 Worker Responses to Survey on Working Conditions in Europe, 2005

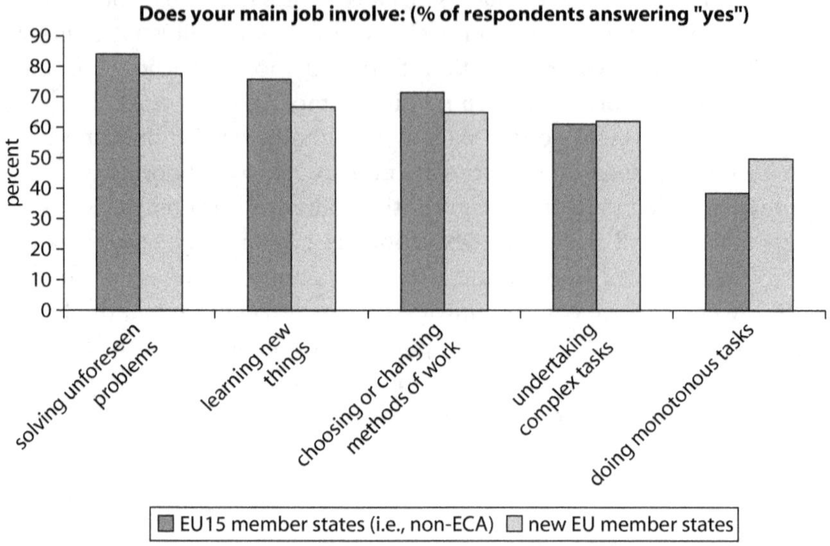

Does your main job involve: (% of respondents answering "yes")

Task	EU15 member states (i.e., non-ECA)	new EU member states
solving unforeseen problems	84	78
learning new things	76	66
choosing or changing methods of work	71	65
undertaking complex tasks	61	62
doing monotonous tasks	38	50

Source: Authors' calculations based on data obtained from Eurofound 2007.

Bank 2010b). These findings mirror longer-term trends observed in other parts of the world (see chapter 1).

Many Students are Failing and Problem-Solving Skills are Weak

Two problems related to quality seem particularly acute in the ECA region: too many students are failing and education systems have difficulties imparting problem-solving skills. A closer look at ECA countries' performance in international assessments show a large number of underperformers: 15-year-olds with such weak math and literacy skills that their ability to succeed in today's workplace is highly questionable (see box 7.2). As work becomes more demanding even for this group, their poor skills will become more apparent. Although ECA countries perform reasonably well on international assessments that measure students at the primary level (grade 4), their performance is weaker on assessments of students around the end of lower secondary education (grade 8), suggesting that their education systems are adept at imparting basic skills, but have problems imparting problem-solving skills—the very skills that firms increasingly seek.

Another reason why firms are increasingly complaining may be that the quality of education in the ECA region has not shown consistent improvement. In many countries, the quality of education appears to be

Box 7.2
A Large Proportion of Students Are Failing

Despite PISA scores that are largely in keeping with countries at the same income level, a large proportion of students in many ECA countries still achieved only a basic level of competency (Level 1) or less on the reading part of the PISA 2009 (see table B7.2). This level means that a student can complete a basic reading task, such as locating a piece of information or identifying the main theme in a text, but cannot necessarily use this information in problem solving. The factors underlying this poor performance vary. In Turkey, a nontransition country, a very selective academic system leaves many graduates of vocational and general high schools with poor basic skills. In Azerbaijan, poor reading competencies co-exist with strong competencies in mathematics, largely because the transition from a Cyrillic to Latin alphabet in the post-independence period left a generation of students and their parents without adequate reading materials to build reading skills.

Table B7.2 Proportion of 15-Year-Old Students in ECA Who Achieved Only Basic Reading Competency on PISA 2009

Students scoring at or below Level 1	Country
< 10 %	
10–20 %	Estonia, Poland, Latvia, Hungary, OECD average
20–30 %	Croatia, Czech Republic, Lithuania, Slovak Republic, Slovenia, Russian Federation, Turkey,
30–40 %	Serbia
40–50 %	Bulgaria, Montenegro, Romania
50–60 %	Albania, Kazakhstan
> 60 %	Azerbaijan, Kyrgyz Republic

Source: PISA 2009 Database.

getting worse, not better. Rather than narrowing the gap between their scores and OECD mean scores, many ECA countries that participate in international learning assessments at this level—which are likely the better-managed countries—either seem stuck or have regressed in terms of their scores. It is probable, moreover, that the situation is even worse in ECA countries that do not participate in efforts to measure and compare the academic performance of their students. In fairness, the latest round of PISA (2009) showed some improvements for 11 ECA countries, compared to their 2006 performance (including big increases in Bulgaria, Romania, Serbia, the Kyrgyz Republic, and Turkey). However, seven ECA countries experienced a deterioration compared to their 2006 performance.

The Quality and Relevance of Upper Secondary and Tertiary Education Is of Concern

An additional explanation of the skills gap perceived by employers may be that the quality of upper secondary and tertiary education in the region is not keeping up with changing skill demands, although the lack of data makes it hard to confirm this suspicion. With educational quality failing to show consistent improvement at the lower secondary level, this weakness is probably mirrored at the upper secondary level (although with a delay). Moreover, enrollments at the tertiary level used to be tightly controlled and reserved for the few, best performers. In the past two decades, however, enrollments have doubled, tripled, or quadrupled in an environment with the expansion of new programs, institutions and types of students. This growth has taken place without the benefit of quality assurance mechanisms and without the kind of information students and parents need to make informed choices. There is also evidence of widespread unethical behavior, such as purchasing admission, grades, and even degrees (see figure 7.5). Educational quality at the tertiary level is thus unlikely to have improved. Weaknesses in the quality of upper secondary and tertiary education is particularly problematic from a skills perspective because, most of ECA's new labor market entrants now enter the labor market after having completed either an upper secondary or a tertiary degree (see chapter 3, figure 3.1).

Finally, graduates of upper secondary and tertiary education may also be graduating with the wrong set of skills. During the early years of the transition, the vocational school system—which once produced more than half of all secondary graduates in most ECA countries—rapidly declined. Since then, students have left vocational schools in favor of general secondary education and the prospect of pursuing a tertiary degree. However, ECA firms still value technical and vocational skills, judging by the better employment prospects of graduates with technical skills (see chapter 1). Thus, the pendulum may have swung too far in one direction, with the vocational sector having retrenched too far. Nevertheless, as the region's vocational schools remain unable to produce graduates with appropriate skills, it is likely too soon to be promoting a return to this sector.

Figure 7.5 Students Report Unofficial Payments Are "Usually" or "Always" Needed in Public Technical Colleges and Universities, 2006

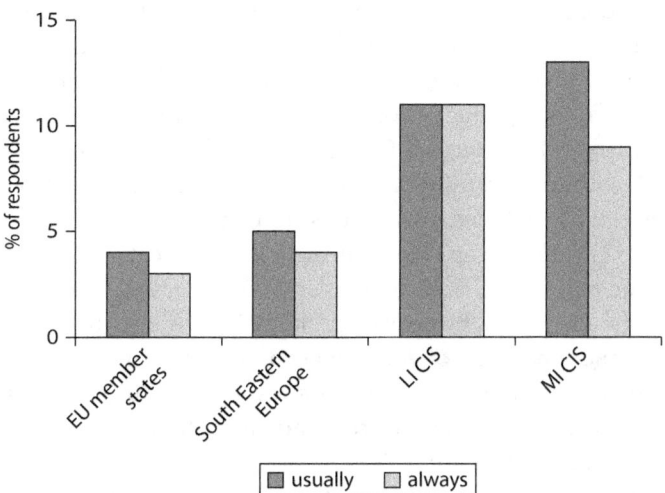

Source: Raw dataset from EBRD-World Bank 2006.
Note: LI = low-income, MI = middle-income. The graph reflects the answers from Question 3.13 of the Life in Transition Survey in ECA countries, which can be downloaded at http://www.ebrd.com/downloads/research/economics/litsques.pdf (accessed January 2011). The exact question asked was: "In your opinion, how often is it necessary for people like you to have to make unofficial payments/gifts in these situations?" One of the response options was: "Receive public education (university, college)." Thus, it is unclear whether the response refers to grades or admission, or simply to regular payments.

Adult Learning Remains a Blind Spot

The skills deficit relates not only to the uneven quality and uncertain relevance of formal education. It also involves too little progress in providing workers with options for additional training. Since continuous adult education and training have been shown to foster employment and greater productivity, the development of this sector should be central to the region's economic growth strategy, particularly in more advanced ECA countries and those that are facing a significant demographic decline. Yet many of these countries have only started to plan for the development of this sector. In light of the growing skills shortage, adult education and training in ECA countries can no longer be neglected.

Priority Areas for Action

As noted previously, three major impediments are inhibiting the creation of flexible and responsive education systems in the ECA region. First, these systems have been operating "in the dark" because they do not systematically collect data on the learning and employment outcomes of all students. Second, the legacy of central planning has kept the governance and management of school systems highly centralized, with central policy makers deeply involved in operational details. While virtually all OECD countries have embraced performance-oriented management in education since the 1980s (see OECD 2005c)—albeit at different speeds—most ECA countries continue to use management practices that focus on compliance with detailed regulations and financing schemes based on inputs, not outputs. This means that most local education authorities and school principals in the ECA region lack the autonomy and authority to make crucial management decisions for their own institutions, including how much and what type of vocational content students can choose from and how many teachers to employ. As a result, the education and training system is inflexible and does not respond either to labor market needs or to changes in student numbers.

Third, financial resources are ineffectually used in the region, particularly in the pre-university sector, where few countries have adjusted teacher staffing levels in response to falling student numbers over the past 20 years. As a result, student-teacher ratios (STRs) have fallen sharply as per student costs have risen—more so than in any other region in the world (see figure 7.6). This implies that scarce resources are misused by paying meager salaries to too many staff members and heating half-empty buildings.

With few exceptions (notably Turkey), class sizes in ECA are also smaller than those in other parts of the world. For instance, the average class size at the primary level in Poland, Serbia, and Azerbaijan is 20, 14, and 12, respectively, compared to 23 in France, 26 in the United Kingdom, and 31 in Chile and the Republic of Korea (see figure 7.7). Although the ECA region also has a large number of small schools, relatively small class sizes are prevalent even in the largest schools, with the possible exception of Armenia.

Small class sizes and lower STRs in the ECA region have not, however, improved educational quality—as the cost per student has increased, student learning outcomes have not improved. Instead, these conditions have led to poor teacher remuneration—especially at the entry level, but also relative to other professions—and ultimately, to the demoralization of the teaching workforce. This has discouraged talented young students from becoming teachers, while simultaneously encouraging those already in the profession to stay on as long as they can to benefit from seniority-related pay. As a consequence, the profession as a

Figure 7.6 Primary School Student-Teacher Ratios in ECA Compared to Other Regions of the World, 1990–2008

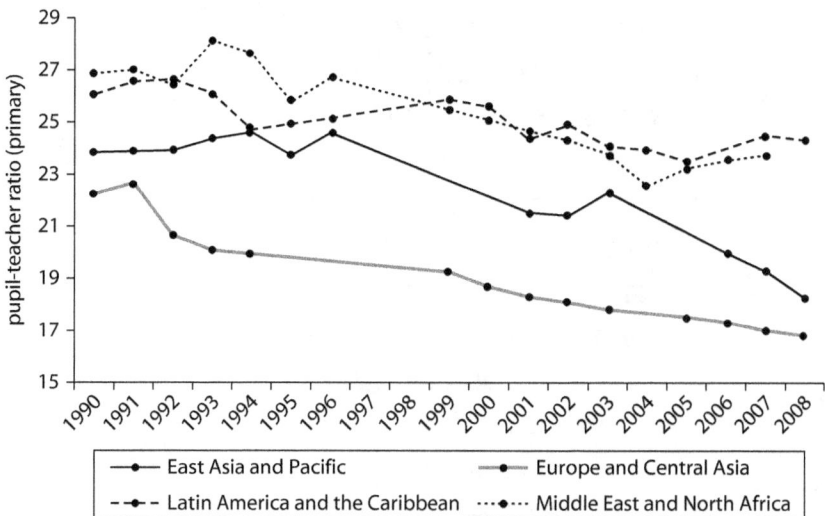

Sources: EdStats Database, plus authors' linear interpolations for missing years.
Note: Actual data are marked with dots. One of the problems with international data on student-teacher ratios (in both the World Bank's EdStats Database and other international education databases) is that it is unclear whether or not data for a particular country are reported on a full-time equivalent basis.

whole is failing to renew itself: few new recruits are entering the system and the teaching cadre is aging (see figure 7.8). As the wage bill squeezes out other spending, less resources are available for training and the training received is often of questionable value. Given the importance of effective teaching, especially for inculcating higher-order cognitive skills, ECA countries are thus poorly positioned to improve student learning with their existing teaching workforce.[4]

To be fair, these impediments affect ECA countries differently and vary accordingly to the level of education. However, no ECA country has fully escaped the legacy of central planning.[5] That system focused on generating data on inputs—that is, it checked whether local actors were in compliance with detailed norms for all inputs. Education ministries remained in the dark, however, about the return on those inputs, that is, whether students actually acquired skills and competencies.

In terms of how these impediments affect the different levels of education, they are most clearly apparent at the pre-university level, which absorbs two-thirds of total education funding in the ECA region. The

Figure 7.7 Comparison of Average Size of Primary School Classes Worldwide, Various Years

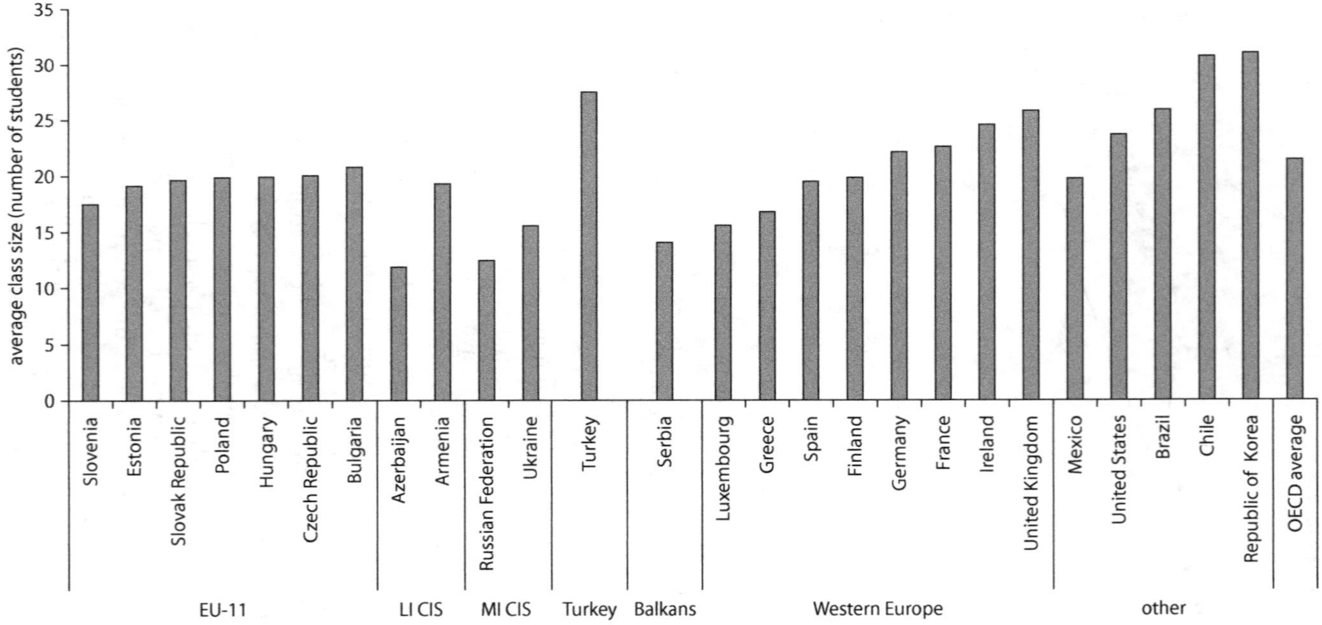

Sources: OECD Education At a Glance Database for OECD and partner countries; authors' calculations based on Ministry of Education data (from education management information systems) for Azerbaijan, Serbia, and Romania, and on Statistical Institute school-level data for Bulgaria.

Note: LI = low-income, MI = middle-income. Most recent data for each country (2005, 2006, 2007, or 2008).

Figure 7.8 Percentage of Students with a Teacher Over 50 Years Old in ECA Countries, Selected Years

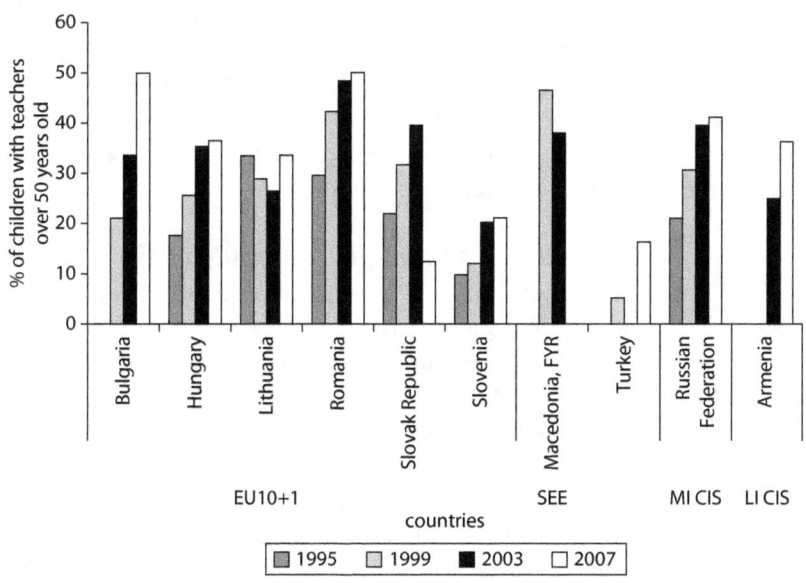

Sources: IEA (1995, 1999, 2003, and 2007): Mathematics and Science Teacher Background Data Almanacs.
Note: LI = low-income, MI = middle-income.

same three impediments affect tertiary education in a slightly different way, as this sector has already undergone significant reform over the past 20 years, during which time it has doubled or tripled in size in many countries (see chapter 5). Because most ECA countries do not yet have adult education sectors in the modern sense, these impediments cannot be fairly characterized as problems of this sector. However, the policy recommendations offered in this book do apply to adult education and offer ideas and principles for how this subsector could be developed and managed in the region (see chapter 6).

Managing Education Systems for Results

This book argues that in order to address the three constraints outlined above, countries in the ECA region need to manage their education systems for results. First and foremost, they need to collect more information on "performance," that is, what are students learning, what jobs they are finding, and what salaries graduates are earning. In addition, ECA countries need to follow the lead of OECD countries and replace input-oriented management of the education sector with performance-oriented management. This change implies devolving more autonomy to frontline providers and putting in place accountability mechanisms—for instance, performance contracts and performance-based budgeting—that emphasize results and performance, not compliance with norms. With greater availability of performance data and frontline providers empowered with greater decision-making power, the preconditions will be in place for education systems in the region to become both more responsive to labor market needs and more efficient.

Focus Attention on Learning and Employment Outcomes

Better data alone does not lead to better-quality education. Partly due to difficult demographic trends and partly due to history, ECA education systems have wound themselves in a knot that will be very difficult to untie without devoting greater attention to results. The legacy of central planning has created a system where bureaucrats manage the sector, and schools in particular, by writing detailed norms into legislation and then micromanaging principals so that they comply with these norms. Generations of managers have lived with this system for their entire lives. When asked to improve education system performance, they therefore reach for the tools that they have always used, either by revising norms or ramping up inspections. This chapter argues that the solution is not to rewrite norms or expand the inspectorate. Rather, the solution is to reach for different tools. However, none of these "new" tools will work without better data on performance, data that answers the question: What are students learning and are graduates finding jobs?

The good news is that there is significant consensus on the key skills and competencies that basic education is expected to deliver, as well as standardized tests to measure them. Many countries in the region already participate in international assessments, which are more useful when complemented by national assessments. Although all school systems in the region have national assessment systems, many of these systems are in the early stages of development (see figure 7.9) and there is very little evidence to date that ECA countries are using these assessments to inform policy. Rather, national assessments continue to be seen as a certification mechanism, one that confirms a student has gained a mastery of a predetermined curriculum, thus enabling a diploma to be issued or the student to progress to upper secondary or tertiary education. Student assessments are rarely seen as an opportunity to identify the strengths and weaknesses of an education system.

When students graduate, ministries of education in the ECA region do not systematically collect, analyze, and disseminate information on their

Figure 7.9 Status of Measuring and Using Data on Student Learning Outcomes in the ECA Region, 2009

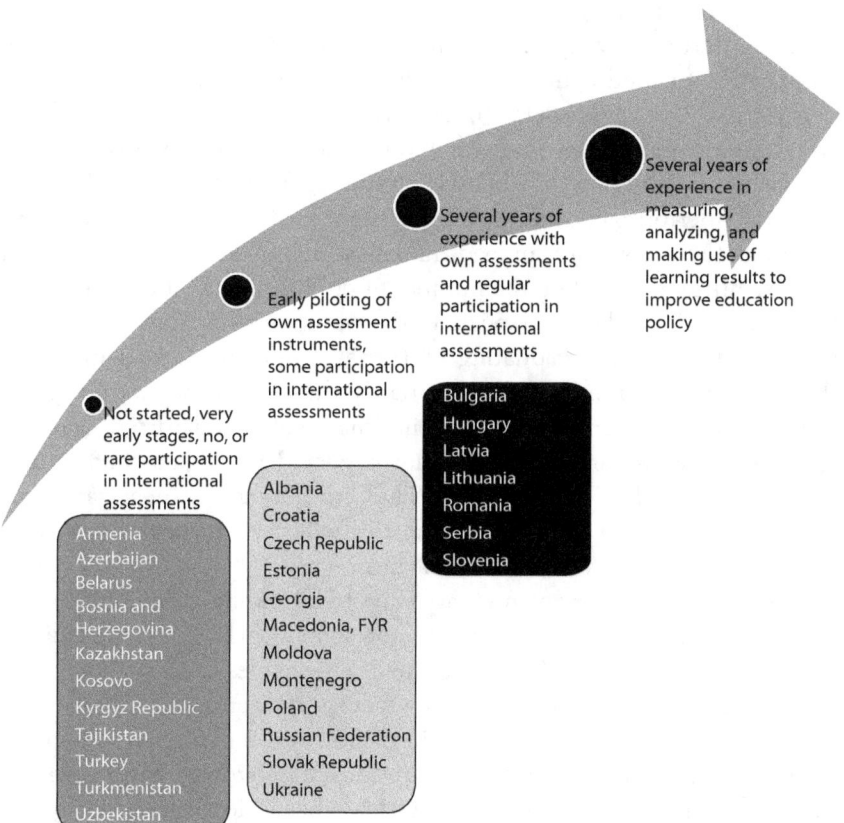

Sources: Authors' assessments based on data from UNICEF (2007, table 2.1); the extent of countries' participation in PISA, PIRLS, and TIMSS since 1995; and inputs from World Bank country experts. The UNICEF data is drawn from "Table 2.1: Status of Reforms of Assessment and Examination Systems, 2006," regarding "Introduction of other school exams or assessments (e.g., basic school)" and "Introduction of sample-based national assessment." In this table, UNICEF scores the progress of countries on a range of 0 to 4, with 0 representing "not planned or started" and 4 representing "operational." In addition, the figure uses World Bank staff compilations on the number of international assessments in which each country has participated.

employment outcomes. Such information is, however, critical for policy makers and higher education institutions because it helps them detect which programs and fields of study are in high demand among employers. Moreover, these data can help students make better choices about which university and field of study to pursue. Again, some member countries of the OECD (including Hungary, Italy, and the Netherlands), together with Romania, provide examples in this area for others to emulate. Using the example of the tracer study in the Netherlands (which has been in place since 1989), table 7.1 provides an example of the types of information such surveys can provide.

At the tertiary level, data on employment and learning outcomes are also needed to shed light on how the sector is performing from a skills perspective. Currently, data on tertiary outcomes (both in ECA and around the world) focus on research outcomes, such as how many publications the faculty of a university is producing. Unfortunately, when this is the only performance indicator available, it inadvertently receives more attention than it should. Indeed, rankings of universities in the region place significant weight on the number of publications that they produce. However, from a skills perspective, the outcome that matters most is whether students are graduating with the competencies in demand on the job market and finding jobs. Currently, these outcomes are not being measured, and, unfortunately, an international standardized learning assessment for tertiary students is not expected to be launched by the OECD until 2016 (see box 5.1). Thus, to gather the necessary data now—when it is needed—ECA countries will need to begin with their own, domestically developed approaches.

There are several complementary ways of providing more information on the performance of the tertiary sector, some of which are more direct than others. These include rankings or league tables, tracer studies, and direct measurement of student competencies via standardized tests. One way that ECA countries might begin to measure the learning outcomes of tertiary students would be to introduce standardized testing within fields of study where these outcomes have been clearly defined by the National Qualification Frameworks which have been built in most countries (e.g., for graduates of nursing programs). Alternatively, ECA ministries of education might define and measure a set of broad competencies that all tertiary graduates are expected to have. The OECD's DeSeCo project (OECD 2005c), discussed in chapter 2, could provide a starting point for the definition of such broad competencies.

Introduce Autonomy and Accountability Based on Results
Overcoming the legacy of central planning involves moving away from detailed norms and instead holding actors accountable for *performance* (or results). At the central level, this implies that policy makers in the ECA region would relinquish certain duties and assume others so that education systems may innovate and improve student learning outcomes. The opportunity before central governments in these countries is to

Table 7.1 Information Collected from Tracer Study of Dutch University Graduates, 2007

	Duration of job search (in months)	Full-time employment (%)	Unlimited term contract (%)	Monthly gross income (euros)		Managerial or professional (% ISCO 1 or 2)	High utilization of skills (%)	High job satisfaction (%)
	Mean	Mean	Mean	Mean	Median	Mean	Mean	Mean
Science and math	0.7	88.4	45.6	2499	2429	83.6	71.0	77.5
Medicine and health	0.7	79.0	41.0	2904	2783	82.6	78.9	81.7
Engineering	1.0	94.4	66.2	2772	2631	87.4	75.2	72.8
Economics	1.0	96.1	71.3	2954	2783	70.3	65.6	70.1
Law	1.2	92.7	57.5	2864	2732	87.8	66.0	70.2
Humanities and arts	1.2	59.1	43.0	2188	2226	66.0	50.4	61.3
Social sciences	1.3	60.6	45.4	2317	2350	72.0	63.9	65.4
Agriculture	1.5	86.7	45.6	2137	2328	84.2	73.2	71.2

Source: Table provided by the Research Centre for Education and the Labour Market (ROA), The Netherlands, 2008, at request of the authors.

move away from micromanaging schools and classrooms and focus instead on setting goals, policies, and standards; defining responsibilities; mobilizing financial resources; ensuring political consensus; targeting poor and excluded students; and monitoring and evaluating service delivery and system quality.

Extending autonomy throughout education systems means placing authority and responsibility in the hands of the people most able to innovate and improve the quality of education: local managers and education authorities (see Osborne and Gaebler 1992). It also means holding these actors accountable for improving the learning outcomes of the bulk of their students. Aligning the incentives of these stakeholders with the student learning outcomes desired by policy makers requires education ministries to set overall performance goals; articulate who is responsible and accountable to whom and for what; and ensure that these responsibilities are agreed, accepted, and understood.

At the pre-university level, policy makers can expand the autonomy of lower-level actors in the school system by granting them greater decision-making power over school operations and budgets and relaxing norms on class sizes. Greater autonomy is particularly needed in vocational education and training, where programs and institutes need the ability to expand or contract course offerings in response to student and employer demand, not rigid governmental norms.

Simultaneously, policy makers will need to implement a range of accountability mechanisms to hold schools accountable for results. Potential mechanisms include the creation of school councils that involve parents and local communities in school decision-making processes; requiring schools to prepare school development plans that outline each school's strengths and weaknesses, together with an action plan for making improvements; preparing "school scorecards" that include basic indicators on a school's performance; as well sanctioning low-performing schools and rewarding high-performing schools (see chapter 4 and box 7.3). Here, however, it is important to define a high-performing school as one that delivers improved learning outcomes to all types of students, including those from low-income and minority households.

In general, the weaker a country's national assessment system, the more it will need to rely on more qualitative measures to assess school performance. It is important to stress here that utilizing information on student learning outcomes to strengthen accountability does not necessarily imply "paying for performance" or conducting tests that have very high stakes for principals, local authorities, and teachers. If not carefully

> **Box 7.3**
>
> **Options for Making Schools More Accountable for Learning Outcomes**
>
> Administer national student assessments at key stages of the education cycle (e.g., after 4th, 7th, and 12th grades) and include such data in school "scorecards."
>
> Require schools to prepare school development plans that outline each school's strengths and weaknesses, together with a vision and action plan for making improvements. Support implementation of these plans and monitor their outcomes.
>
> Reward schools that show improvement in student performance.
>
> Prepare school "scorecards" for all schools that include information that enables parents and students to get a sense of their performance. Make such scorecards available on the website of the ministry of education, as well as disseminated to local authorities and schools.
>
> Agree on criteria that objectively identify schools in need of improvement and decide what actions should be taken to support such schools.
>
> Sanction schools that show low or no improvement in student performance.
>
> Require all school principals to be trained and licensed and be held more accountable for learning outcomes of the school's pupils.

designed, such an approach could create exactly the wrong incentives for improving learning. Rather, policy makers should use performance data to identify both schools that need greater support and schools that offer successful models for innovation.

Significant improvements in the direction of greater autonomy and accountability will, however, be difficult to achieve in the school system unless policy makers in the region address the demoralization of the teaching force, an effort that will involve resolution of serious overstaffing and improving the pay, professional development, and work conditions of teachers.

Most countries in the region have shied away from adjusting teaching staff levels in response to declining student numbers, even in contexts where per student financing provides powerful incentives to reduce teacher numbers. Addressing this inefficiency will free up funds for more classroom learning materials. Judicious use of retirement incentives for older teachers and stronger redundancy or retraining packages for departing teachers or both may make departures more acceptable. Countries now in the process of reducing teacher numbers (e.g., Bulgaria, Latvia, and Romania) may provide valuable lessons in this area.

At the tertiary level, policy makers in most of the ECA region have already granted substantial autonomy to institutions of higher learning, which now manage their own budgets and make important managerial decisions about their respective institutions. This autonomy has helped create some (but not all) of the conditions needed to improve the quality of course offerings and pedagogy with the goal of preparing students for the world of work. Policy makers have also begun to use financing incentives to "steer" these institutions towards education of greater quality and relevance to employer needs. In fact, considerably more countries in the region have adopted per student financing in the tertiary sector than in the pre-university sector. In terms of accountability, all countries in the region (with the exception of four central Asian countries and Kosovo) have become signatories to the Bologna Process, which aims to make academic degree and quality assurance standards more comparable and compatible across Europe.

Today, the challenge of tertiary education systems in ECA is to wield the instruments of autonomy, accountability, and performance-based financing more effectively with the goal of rapidly improving the quality and relevance of higher education. As noted earlier, most of new EU member states and, to a lesser extent, countries in SEE, the Russian Federation, and Ukraine, have devolved a fair degree of autonomy to tertiary institutions and have taken initial steps toward flexible financing. However, this group has lagged behind in establishing effective accountability frameworks. Certain countries in SEE and low-income countries in the CIS have retained more centralized control over tertiary education systems and would benefit from moving ahead to introducing greater autonomy, flexible financing, and accountability mechanisms.

Indeed, it makes little sense to delay in enhancing accountability in the tertiary sector. In the first place, greater autonomy and flexible financing will be ineffective without mechanisms that hold education providers accountable for the quality of the education that they provide. In the second place, it takes considerable time to develop and implement these mechanisms effectively. Many countries that have moved ahead on flexible financing and autonomy without strengthening accountability have later had to claw back control over tertiary institutions—a process that can be politically difficult.

Strengthening accountability at a minimum means safeguarding basic integrity in higher education. On the financial side, this means preventing embezzlement, fraud in public tenders, collusion, and the hiring of unqualified family members, among other practices. On the academic side, this means preventing examination fraud, unethical faculty behavior, noncompliance with admission standards, research fraud and plagiarism, and fraud in the quality assurance process (Salmi 2009). With the exception of a few new EU member states, evidence suggests that higher education institutions across the region continue to struggle with these basic integrity issues.

While integrity problems are widespread, that does not mean that policy makers need to resolve these problems *first*, before they make progress on accountability in other areas. The great temptation in the region—given its tradition of central planning and central control of universities—is to fix integrity problems through even stronger centralized control and management (e.g., requiring that every hiring and procurement decision be reviewed by the central education ministry). Rather, policy makers need to embrace solutions that show promise in terms of addressing basic integrity *and* strengthening accountability. The good news is that most of the instruments that help improve basic academic and fiscal integrity also strengthen accountability for desired outcomes and the efficient use of resources.

Looking at the different options illustrated in table 7.2, it is clear that strengthening accountability in the tertiary sector can be a long and

Table 7.2 Tools for Strengthening Academic and Fiscal Integrity in University-Level Institutions

Tools that strengthen academic integrity…	Tools that strengthen fiscal integrity…
• Licensing	• Financial audits
…and educational quality	…and efficiency of spending
• Accreditation/academic audits/evaluations	• Public disclosure laws
• Public disclosure laws	• Strategic budget plans
• Fostering outsiders to review academic integrity (e.g., Romania)	• Performance contracts based on performance indicators
• Performance contracts based on performance indicators	• Student loans/scholarships/vouchers
• Creation and dissemination of rankings/benchmarks	• Embedding incentives into allocated resources (e.g., tying funding to the number of students enrolled or graduated, rewarding good performers, etc.)

Source: Authors' review of available instruments, as presented in Salmi (2009).

difficult process. Building an effective accreditation agency or a national quality assurance system, for example, is a long-term proposition. Building the capacity of a national quality assurance agency to fully meet its mandate is a challenge for all countries in the ECA region. Many smaller countries, for example, simply do not have the in-country capacity to conduct effective national quality assurance. Here, coordination across countries and closer integration with external quality assurance agencies may be important to support the development of national capacity.

In light of these challenges, countries would be well-advised to follow a two-pronged process to strengthen accountability: first, build an effective quality assurance system that ensures tertiary institutions have the minimum levels of inputs and processes needed to provide a quality education; and second, emphasize greater transparency and information dissemination, so as to strengthen student choice (e.g., by developing rankings). These two approaches are complementary to one another.

As noted earlier, most ECA countries are signatories to the Bologna Process. Proper implementation of its 2005 Standards and Guidelines for Quality Assurance would go a long way to putting in place the building blocks of an adequate quality assurance system. A large number of countries in the region have not, however, begun the process of strengthening external quality assurance. In fact, a number have treated the strengthening of quality assurance within higher education institutions (so-called internal quality assurance) in a rather cavalier fashion. For the five ECA countries that are not yet signatories, aligning themselves with the Bologna Framework would be beneficial.

Improve the Efficiency of Resource Use through Performance-Based Financing

Managing school systems for performance means moving away from inflexible line-item budgeting towards greater use of delegated budgets, with incentives for maintaining enrollment and attendance (i.e., per student financing—a path on which the majority of ECA countries have already embarked). More flexible, smarter financing in the form of block grants (i.e., contract- or performance-based) can also provide funding to local education in return for meeting agreed learning outcomes. Not only does this type of financing give local education authorities much-needed flexibility that input-based budgets do not permit, it keeps them focused on student results.

At the pre-university level, countries in the ECA region are at different stages of introducing per student financing (see figure 7.10); the experience of those that have gone farther can provide lessons for countries that have yet to start on this path. Whether per student financing actually results in greater fiscal efficiency and an increased focus on student learning outcomes depends on the financing formula used and the broader context in which it is implemented. If, for example, a financing formula

Figure 7.10 Progress Towards Results-based Education Financing in the ECA Region, 2009

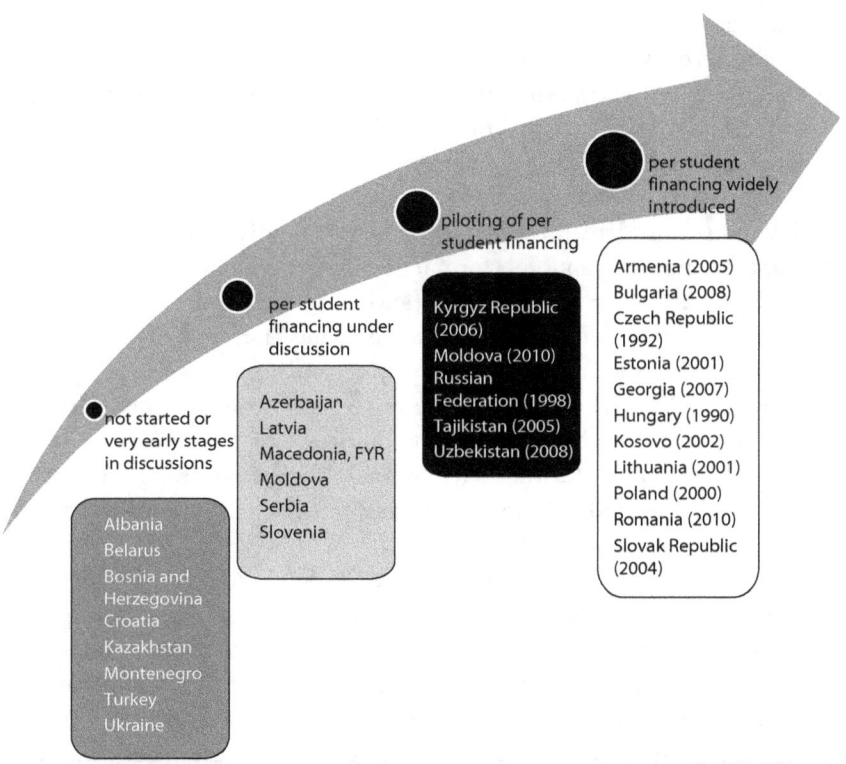

Source: Authors' assessment.
Note: The "result" referred to in this table is a student enrolled. As discussed in chapter 6, a more desirable per student financing scheme would be to finance a student who is graduating, or better yet, a student who is graduating with a desired level of competencies. However, even the most advanced ECA countries (in terms of moving to school financing based on results) still base financing on the number of students enrolled (an intermediate result, at best). This report therefore intentionally distinguishes between the inputs of teachers, classes, and finances, and between students "enrolled," "graduating," "graduating with a desired level of competencies," or "graduating and finding a job" as results (or outputs).

mirrors current unit costs of different localities, it may simply perpetuate an inefficient delivery model. In the Slovak Republic, per student recurrent costs are 100 percent higher for upper secondary vocational education and sports education schools than for gymnasia (upper secondary academic schools). These differences in unit costs, however, are largely caused by differences in class sizes and teaching loads, factors that should not necessarily be encouraged to continue (World Bank 2009b). By contrast, countries that have devised simple, transparent formulas which reflect the real costs of schooling have created strong incentives for school consolidation, increased class sizes, and a rebalancing of educational spending from wage to nonwage components (see the discussion of Bulgaria in chapter 4).

At the tertiary level, several ECA countries (for example, Poland and Romania) have already adopted per student financing, shifting their focus away from inputs and toward outputs. The remainder of countries in the region will need to introduce performance-based financing to improve the efficiency of spending in this sector.

Beyond per student financing, there is still relatively little use of "performance contracts" and "performance-based budgeting" in the region (see OECD 2007c). Such contracts (and budgeting arrangements) could be put in place between the ministry of education and universities, or simply between the ministry of education and its key agencies (which are charged with various roles in the management of the university sector) as discussed in chapter 5. Most ministries of education in OECD countries have moved toward such arrangements to enable ministries to focus on strategy and system monitoring rather than day-to-day operational details.

Another important move in terms of financing would be for ECA countries to consider more cost sharing at the tertiary level. Indeed, if ECA countries want to simultaneously raise participation rates and increase the quality of tertiary education, more private resources will also be needed—the cost pressures facing higher education in the region are simply too great. Mobilizing private resources will help strengthen results-oriented outcomes in the tertiary sector in two fundamental ways: (1) by increasing competition, as more nimble and innovative private providers help bring innovations to public providers; and (2) by increasing students' connection to the education process. When students and parents pay tuition fees—whether to a public or a private provider—they are generally more demanding about the quality and relevance of the education provided. There is no single ideal level of funding for higher education and no single ideal mix of public and private funding sources. Different countries will make different kinds of trade-offs.

Build the Foundations of Adult Learning Systems

The reskilling of the work force in the ECA region is needed not only to compete in the global economy, but also to address the lag effects of the transition to market economies. Significant segments of the labor force—often comprising less skilled and more disadvantaged workers—remain inactive in many of these countries. Given the rapid demographic decline occurring in many ECA countries, achieving and sustaining high rates of growth suggests that labor force participation will have to increase and each individual will have to become more productive—and stay so for a longer period of time.

Unlike pre-university and university education, adult education systems in the modern sense are largely nonexistent in most ECA countries. Building such systems will require shifting away from government-defined programs towards a well-regulated market of private and public providers that deliver training services to both working and unemployed adults. Governments in the region will, however, continue to play a role in education and training for the unemployed, often by contracting private providers to deliver needed services. Policies that address market failures in this sector are especially important for laying the groundwork for effective adult education systems. In general, successful systems require a high degree of coordination and partnership between government agencies and the private sector, as well as giving the demand side of training—that is, businesses and individuals—a strong voice in determining training policy. Once a solid adult learning sector is established, governments can then "steer" it by monitoring data on program quality, encouraging autonomy and accountability, and improving the efficiency of government financing in the sector.

Expanding adult learning is a priority for advanced economies in the region that are facing a demographic decline. Their challenge is to ensure that existing coordination mechanisms function well and that regulation and financing are used to facilitate the emergence of a private sector-oriented adult education and training market. The principal priority of less advanced economies in the region experiencing a demographic decline (i.e., many of those in South Eastern Europe and the middle-income CIS countries) is to introduce a strategic policy framework for adult learning and create the tools needed to implement this strategy (e.g., coordination mechanisms, plus initial steps toward regulation). Less advanced economies in the region that are not facing a demographic decline (i.e., low-income CIS countries and Albania) may find it more productive to limit efforts to establishing a strategic policy framework and coordination mechanism for this sector. For many countries, participating in the OECD's Programme for International Assessment of Adult Competencies (PIAAC) would be an important first step in understanding the current skills and competencies of their work forces.

Summary

Reforming education systems in the ECA region so that they deliver higher-quality and more relevant education to the majority of students will go a long way towards addressing the skills gap that many countries in the region face. Although the recent economic downturn has diminished the demand for labor and skills. Skills shortages will likely reemerge once growth picks up again. The process of reforming education will take time; consequently, ECA countries should not wait to begin.

Many needed changes—assessment systems that measure what students learn, changes in the size and remuneration of the teaching force, and strong quality assurance systems—are not without cost. Given that economic growth is expected to be lower and fiscal constraints tighter in the near to medium term, ECA countries will have little choice but to free up resources that are currently funding existing inefficiencies in their education systems, particularly those associated with school infrastructure and staff levels designed for much larger student populations. More resources will also need to be raised from outside the education system, especially at the tertiary level. Putting off the policy reform directions discussed in this book—whether for financial or political reasons—risks the deterioration of a fundamental source of national competitiveness: a skilled workforce. This is clearly not an acceptable option for any country in the region.

For movement of education systems away from an emphasis on inputs and processes to an emphasis on improving the learning outcomes of the majority of students, much more measurement of student learning outcomes is needed at all levels of education. This data must then be used in the policy process to identify strengths and weaknesses and help formulate appropriate policy responses. As the role of central governments is redefined to focus on strategic policy, system goals, and regulation, central policy makers can articulate clear goals for their education systems and use incentives to manage lower-level actors in these systems to meet these goals. In schools, this means greater use of per student financing, more autonomy, and greater accountability for learning outcomes. At the level of higher education, this means strengthening national quality assurance mechanisms in the short and long term, greater dissemination of information (e.g., rankings) to inform student choice, greater performance-based budgeting, and, where warranted, greater institutional autonomy.

It is difficult to draw conclusions about which reform options are the most relevant to the various subregions of Europe and Central Asia, as there is enormous variation in their current conditions. What is clear is that some member countries of the EU, together with certain countries in South Eastern Europe and the Commonwealth of Independent States, have not yet begun to systematically measure student learning. What is also clear is that virtually all countries in the region are not yet using assessment results to design education policy, a process that is complicated by the fact that assessment data—where it exists—often cannot be sufficiently disaggregated to identify problem schools and groups of students. A similar situation holds for per student financing: the greatest progress has been made in this area by the EU10, but progress has been highly variable in other subregions. It is also clear that all countries in the region need improved accountability mechanisms in the tertiary sector.

The economic crisis provided many countries in the region a reason to initiate reforms, particularly those linked to the financing of education. Under pressure to reduce spending, countries such as Romania, Poland, Serbia, and Latvia introduced per student financing in their general education sectors (covering primary and secondary education). This policy is likely to result in greater efficiency and open the way for future spending increases to focus on improvements that enhance the quality of education. These countries will, we hope, establish a path that can be followed by countries that have not yet focused on increasing the efficiency of educational spending.

Increasing demand for skilled labor as growth picks up, accelerating technological change, and significant demographic decline will soon make modern adult education and training systems an imperative in many countries in the region. Although building such systems is critically important for reskilling adult workers and retaining workforce productivity, its overall priority in individual ECA countries will depend on their specific economic and demographic conditions.

While the economic crisis offered opportunities for reform, it also made certain reforms more difficult. Both Bulgaria and Romania, for example, slowed the introduction of student loan programs, which are important for raising tuition fees and diversifying the sources of tertiary funding. Whatever measures countries in the region decide to adopt, it is important that they continue to build learning assessment systems and monitor and evaluate the impact of reforms on desired learning outcomes. This approach offers the only way to determine whether reforms have the intended effect, whether course corrections are needed, and whether funding is achieving the ultimate goal of education systems in the region: delivering the skills and competencies needed in the labor market.

Notes

1. The PIRLS scale average is a metric established by setting the mean scores of participating countries to 500 and the standard deviation to 100, thus enabling comparisons over time, since all cycles are placed on this metric so that scores are equivalent from cycle to cycle. In contrast, the international average, obtained by averaging across the mean scores for each of the participating countries, needs to be recomputed for each new cycle, based on the set of participating countries and changes from cycle to cycle, depending on the set of countries taking part. For more information on PIRLS 2006, see its website at http://timss.bc.edu/pirls2006/index.html (accessed January 2011).
2. The EBRD-World Bank Business Environment and Enterprise Performance Surveys (BEEPS) provide successive snapshots of the self-reported constraints to expansion by firms in the ECA region. The surveys were conducted in virtually all ECA countries in 1999, 2002, 2005, and 2008. Survey samples are constructed by random sampling from the national registry of firms (or equivalent) and cover both industry and service sectors.
3. The Fourth European Work Conditions Survey conducted in 2005 covers the EU-27 countries, Norway, Switzerland, Croatia, and Turkey (see Eurofound 2007).
4. The importance of effective teaching for learning is now increasingly recognized. A good teacher can make a huge difference, with high-quality teachers able to "get an entire year's worth of additional learning out of their students compared to those near the bottom" (Hanushek 2006, 3). That is, a good

teacher will get a gain of 1.5 grade-level equivalents, while a bad teacher will get only the equivalent of 0.5 years for a single academic year. When considered over the entire school cycle, such differences accumulate rapidly and make the impact of other variables small in comparison.

5. Although Turkey comes from a different tradition, education management remains highly centralized. The impediments identified in this section—specifically, too little information on student skills and competencies and too little autonomy and accountability—apply with equal measure to Turkey.

References

Abromovsky, Laura, Erich Battistin, Emla Fitzsimons, Alissa Goodman, and Helen Simpson. 2005. *The Impact of the Employer Training Pilots on the Take-up of Training Among Employers and Employees.* London: Department for Education and Skills, Government of the United Kingdom.

Acemoğlu, Daron. 1998. "Why Do New Technologies Complement Skills? Directed Technical Change and Wage Inequality." *Quarterly Journal of Economics* 113: 1055–89.

Acosta, Pablo, and Leonardo Gasparini. 2007. "Capital Accumulation, Trade Liberalization, and Rising Wage Inequality: The Case of Argentina." *Economic Development and Cultural Change* 55 (July): 793–812.

Adelman, Clifford. 2003. "Learning Accountability from Bologna: A Higher Education Primer." Institute for Higher Education Policy, Washington, DC.

AES (Adult Education Survey) (dataset). 2007. Eurostat, Luxembourg. http://epp.eurostat.ec.europa.eu/portal/page/portal/microdata/adult_education_survey.

Airola, Jim, and Chinhui Juhn. 2005. "Wage Inequality in Post-Reform Mexico." IZA Discussion Paper 1525, Institute for the Study of Labor, Bonn.

Allais, Stephanie. 2010. *The Implementation and Impact of National Qualifications Frameworks: Report of a Study in 16 Countries.* Geneva: International Labour Organization.

Alam, Asad, Mamta Murthi, Ruslan Yemtsov, Edmundo Murrugarra, Nora Dudwick, Ellen Hamilton, and Erwin Tiongson. 2005. *Growth, Poverty, and*

Inequality: Eastern Europe and the Former Soviet Union. Washington, DC: World Bank.

———. 2010. "When They Come to School, I Will Teach Them: When Equality Leads to Inequality." English translation of a Serbian-language PowerPoint presentation delivered to the Serbian Academy of Sciences and Arts conference, "The Change of Roman Identity, Culture, and Language Conditioned by Planned Socioeconomic Integration," Belgrade, December 6–8.

Alam, Asad, Paloma Anós Casero, Faruk Khan, and Charles Udomsaph. 2008. *Unleashing Prosperity: Productivity Growth in Eastern Europe and the Former Soviet Union*. Washington, DC: World Bank.

Alvarez, Jesus V., Garcia Moreno, and Harry A. Patrinos. 2007. "Institutional Effects as Determinants of Learning Outcomes: Exploring State Variations in Mexico." *Well-Being and Social Policy* 3 (1): 47–68.

Amaral, Alberto, Glen A. Jones, and Berit Karseth, eds. 2003. *Governing Higher Education: National Perspectives on Institutional Governance*. New York: Springer.

Autor, David H., Lawrence F. Katz, and Melissa S. Kearney. 2005. "Trends in U.S. Wage Inequality: Re-Assessing the Revisionists." NBER Working Paper 11627, National Bureau of Economic Research, Cambridge, MA.

Autor, David H., Frank Levy, and Richard J. Murnane. 2003. "The Skill Content of Recent Technological Change: An Empirical Exploration." *Quarterly Journal of Economics* 118 (4): 1279–334.

Barnow, Burt S. 2009. "Vouchers in U.S. Vocational Training Programs: An Overview of What We Have Learned." *Zeitschrift für Arbeitsmarktforschung* 42 (1): 71–84.

Barrera-Osorio, Felipe, Tazeen Fasih, Harry Anthony Patrinos. 2009. "Decentralized Decision-Making in Schools: The Theory and Evidence of School-Based Management." Report 48740, World Bank, Washington, DC.

Bartelsman, Eric, John Haltivanger, and Stefano Scarpetta. 2004. "Microeconomic Evidence of Creative Destruction in Industrial and Developing Countries." Policy Research Working Paper 3464, World Bank, Washington, DC.

Bartlett, William. 2007. "Economic Restructuring, Job Creation, and the Changing Demand for Skills in the Western Balkans Area." In *Labour Markets in the Western Balkans: Challenges for the Future*, ed. Anastasia Fetsi, 19–50. Turin: European Training Foundation.

Baucal, Aleksandar. 2006. "Development of Mathematics and Language Literacy of Roma Students." *Psihologija* 39 (2): 211–35.

———. 2010. "When They Come to School, I Will Teach Them: When Equality Leads to Inequality." English translation of a Serbian-language PowerPoint presentation delivered to the Serbian Academy of Sciences and Arts conference, "The Change of Roman Identity, Culture, and Language Conditioned by Planned Socioeconomic Integration," Belgrade, December 6–8.

Baucal, Aleksandar, and Dragica Pavlović-Babić. 2009a. "Quality and Equity of Education in Serbia: Educational Opportunities of the Vulnerable—PISA Assessment, 2003 and 2006 Data." Draft paper.

———. 2009b. "Kvalitet i pravednost obrazovanja u Srbiji: obrazovne šanse siromašnih." Ministarstvo prosvete Republike Srbije i Institut za psihologiju, Beograd.

BEEPS (Business Environment and Enterprise Performance Survey) (dataset). 2005, 2008. EBRD (European Bank for Reconstruction and Development), London, and World Bank, Washington, DC. http://go.worldbank.org/I4ZRB5O300.

Behn, Robert D. 2001. *Rethinking Democratic Accountability.* Washington, DC: Brookings Institution.

Berman, Eli, John Bound, and Stephen Machin. 1998. "Implications of Skill-Biased Technological Change: International Evidence." *Quarterly Journal of Economics* 113 (4): 1245–79.

Berman, Eli, and Stephen Machin. 2000. "Skill-Biased Technology Transfer Around the World." *Oxford Review of Economic Policy* 16 (3): 12–22.

Betcherman, Gordon, Karina Olivas, and Amit Dar. 2004. "Impact of Active Labor Market Programs: New Evidence from Evaluations with Particular Attention to Developing and Transition Countries." Social Protection Discussion Paper 0402, World Bank, Washington, DC.

Bologna Working Group on Qualifications Frameworks. 2005. "A Framework for Qualifications of the European Higher Education Areas." Danish Ministry of Science Technology and Innovation, Copenhagen.

Bound, John, and George Johnson. 1995. "What are the Causes of Rising Wage Inequality in the United States?" *Economic Policy Review* 1 (1): 9–17.

Bourguignon, François, and F. Halsey Rogers. 2008. "Global Returns to Higher Education: Trends, Drivers, and Policy Responses." Keynote address at the Annual World Bank Conference on Development Economics, Cape Town, South Africa, June 9–11.

Breshnan, Timothy F., Erik Brynjolfsson, and Lorin M. Hitt. 2002. "Information Technology, Workplace Organization, and the Demand for Skilled Labor: Firm Level Evidence." *Quarterly Journal of Economics* 117 (1): 339–76.

Bulgaria, Government of. 2007. Raw dataset from Bulgaria 2007 Labor Force Survey. National Statistical Institute, Sofia, Bulgaria.

Brunner, Jose Joaquin, and Anthony Tillett. 2007. "Higher Education in Central Asia: The Challenge of Modernization." World Bank, Washington, DC.

Campos, Nauro, and Aurelijus Dabušinskas. 2008. "So Many Rocket Scientists, So Few Marketing Clerks: Estimating the Effects of Economic Reform on

Occupational Mobility in Estonia." IZA Discussion Paper 3886, Institute for the Study of Labor, Bonn.

Campos, Nauro, and Dean Jolliffe. 2007. "Earnings, Schooling, and Economic Reform: Econometric Evidence from Hungary (1986–2004)." *World Bank Economic Review* 21 (3): 509–26.

Campos, Nauro, and Dana Žlábková. 2001. "The Wrong Mix: A First Look at Occupational Mobility during the Hungarian Transition." Discussion Paper 56, Center for Economic Research and Graduate Education-Economics Institute (CERGE-EI DP), Prague.

Card, David, Jochen Kluve, and Andrea Weber. 2009. "Active Labor Market Policy Evaluations: A Meta Analysis." IZA Discussion Paper 4002, Institute for the Study of Labor, Bonn.

Carey, David. 2007. "Improving Education Outcomes in the Slovak Republic." OECD Economics Department Working Paper 578, Organisation for Economic Co-operation and Development, Paris.

Carey, Kevin. 2010. "That Old College Lie: Are Our Colleges Teaching Students Well? No. But Here's How to Make Them." *Democracy* 15 (Winter): 8–20.

Carnoy, M., and S. Loeb. 2002. "Does External Accountability Affect Student Outcomes? A Cross-state Analysis." *Educational Evaluation and Policy Analysis* 24 (4): 305–31.

CEDEFOP (European Centre for the Development of Vocational Training). 2009. "Using Tax Incentives to Promote Education and Training." Cedefop, Thessaloniki.

Chawla, Mukesh, Gordon Betcherman, and Arup Banerji. 2007. From Red to Gray: The "Third Transition" of Aging Populations in Eastern Europe and the Former Soviet Union. Washington, DC: World Bank.

CIE (Center for Innovations in Education). 2009. "Math and Reading Skills of Azeri Students: Possible Reasons for Relatively High Performance in Math and Poor Performance in Reading in PISA 2006." Draft report prepared for the World Bank, CIE, Baku. Text available on the Curriculum Portal, Ministry of Education of the Republic of Azerbaijan, Baju, http://www.kurikulum.az/files/Analysis%20of%20Azerbaijan%27s%20performance%20in%20PISA%202006%20%28Eng%29.pdf.

Coalition for Clean Universities. 2009: "The University Integrity Contest—An Integrity System for the Romanian Higher Education." Online publication of the Romanian Academic Society (SAR), Bucharest. http://www.sar.org.ro/files/366_CUC%20report.pdf.

Commander, Simon, and János Köllö. 2004. "The Changing Demand for Skills: Evidence from the Transition." IZA Discussion Paper 1073, Institute for the Study of Labor, Bonn.

Contreras, D., L. Flores, and F. Lobato. 2003. "Monetary Incentives for Teachers and School Performance: The Evidence for Chile." Department of Economics, University of Chile, Santiago.

Crostat (Republic of Croatia Central Bureau of Statistics). 2007. Raw dataset from Croatia 2007 Labor Force Survey, Crostat, Zagreb, Croatia.

CVTS (Continuing Vocational Training Survey) (dataset). 1995, 2005. Eurostat, Luxembourg. http://epp.eurostat.ec.europa.eu/portal/page/portal/education/introduction.

Czech Republic, Government of. 2007. "The Strategy of Lifelong Learning in the Czech Republic." Government Decree 761/2007, Prague.

Dahlman, Carl. 2009. "Different Innovation Strategies, Different Results: Brazil, Russia, India, China, and Korea (the BRICKs)." In *Innovation and Growth: Chasing a Moving Frontier*, ed. Vandana Chandra, Deniz Eröcal, Pier C. Padoan, and Carlos A. P. Braga, 131–68. Paris: Organisation for Economic Co-operation and Development and World Bank.

Dar, Amit, Sudharshan Canagarajah, and Paud Murphy. 2003. "Training Levies: Rationale and Evidence from Evaluations." World Bank, Washington, DC.

Dearden, Lorraine, Leslie McGranahan, and Barbara Sianesi. 2004. *An In-Depth Analysis of the Returns to National Vocational Qualifications Obtained at Level 2*. London: Centre for the Economics of Education.

Dearden, Lorraine, Howard Reed, and John van Reenen. 2000. "Who Gains When Workers Train? Training and Corporate Productivity in a Panel of British Industries." CEPR Discussion Paper 2486, Centre for Economic Policy Research, London.

Denhardt, Janet V., and Robert B. Denhardt. 2003. *The New Public Service: Serving, Not Steering.* New York: M. E. Sharpe.

Duke, Chris, Abrar Hasan, Paul Cappon, Werner Meissner, Hilary Metcalf, and Don Thornhill. 2008. *OECD Reviews of Tertiary Education: Croatia*. Paris: Organisation for Economic Co-operation and Development.

EBRD (European Bank for Reconstruction and Development)–World Bank. 2006. "Life in Transition Survey 2006." EBRD, London, and World Bank, Washington, DC. Data available on the EBRD website, http://www.ebrd.com/pages/research/analysis/publications/transition/data.shtml.

EC (European Commission). 2008. "New Skills for New Jobs. Anticipating and Matching Labour Market and Skill Needs." Commission Staff Working Document accompanying the Communication from the Commission to the European Parliament, the Council, the European Economic and Social Committee, and the Committee of the Regions. EC, Brussels.

Edstats (database). World Bank, Washington, DC. http://go.worldbank.org/ITABCOGIV1.

Ercan, Hakan. 2008. "The Evolution of Demand for Skills in Turkey." Background paper for *Skills—Not Just Diplomas: Managing for Results in Education Systems in Eastern Europe and Central Asia*, ed. Lars Sondergaard and Mamta Murthi (Washington, DC: World Bank, forthcoming). Unpublished; available upon request.

Estermann, Thomas, and Terhi Nokkala. 2009. *University Autonomy in Europe I. Exploratory Study*. Brussels: European University Association.

ETF (European Training Foundation). 2007. "Kyrgyzstan: ETF Country Plan 2007." ETF, Turin.

EU (European Union). 2008. "Recommendation of the European Parliament and of the Council of 23 April 2008 on the Establishment of the European Qualifications Framework for Lifelong Learning." *Official Journal of the European Union* C (111): 1–7. http://eur-lex.europa.eu/LexUriServ/LexUriServ.do?uri=oj:c:2008:111:0001:0007:en:pdf.

Eurofound (European Foundation for the Improvement of Living and Working Conditions). 2007. "Fourth European Working Conditions Survey" (EWCS 2005). Eurofound, Dublin, Ireland. The EWCS 2005 dataset is accessible via the UK Data Archive (UKDA) of the University of Essex at www.esds.ac.uk.

European Integration Consortium. 2009. "Labour Mobility within the EU in the Context of Enlargement and the Functioning of the Transitional Arrangements." Employment, Social Affairs, and Equal Opportunities Directorate General, European Commission, Nuremberg.

Eurostat SD (Statistics Database). Education and Training. Eurostat, Luxembourg. http://epp.eurostat.ec.europa.eu/portal/page/portal/education/data/database.

———. Labour Market. Eurostat, Luxembourg. http://epp.eurostat.ec.europa.eu/portal/page/portal/labour_market/introduction.

Fielden, J. 2008. "Global Trends in University Governance." Education Working Paper Series 9. Education Unit, Human Development Network, World Bank, Washington, DC.

Flabbi, Luca, Stefano Paternostro, and Erwin R. Tiongson. 2007. "Returns to Education in the Economic Transition: A Systematic Assessment Using Comparable Data." Policy Research Working Paper 4225, World Bank, Washington, DC.

Fleisher, Belton M., Klara Sabirianova, and Xiaojun Wang. 2005. "Returns to Skills and the Speed of Reforms: Evidence from Central and Eastern Europe, China, and Russia." *Journal of Comparative Economics* 33 (2): 351–70.

Glazerman, Steven, Eric Isenberg, Martha Bleeker, Amy Johnson, Julieta Lugo-Gil, Mary Grider, and Sarah Dolfin. 2009. "Impacts of Comprehensive Teacher Induction: Results from the First Year of a Randomized Controlled

Study." NCEE 2009-4072, National Center for Education and Evaluation, U.S. Department of Education, Washington, DC.

Godfrey, Martin. 2003. "Youth Employment Policy in Developing and Transition Countries—Prevention as well as Cure." Social Protection Discussion Paper Series 0320, World Bank, Washington, DC.

Gorodnichenko, Yuriy, and Klara Sabirianova Peter. 2005. "Returns to Schooling in Russia and Ukraine: A Semi Parametric Approach to Cross-Country Comparative Analysis." *Journal of Comparative Economics* 33 (2): 324–50.

Gunny, Madeleine, and Evelyn Viertel. 2007. *Designing Adult Learning Strategies: the Case of South Eastern Europe*. Turin: European Training Foundation.

Hanushek, Eric A. 2006. "The Single Salary Schedule and Other Issues of Teacher Pay." Paper prepared for the University of Arkansas Department of Education Reform Technical Board of Advisors Conference Agenda, Fayetteville, October 19–21.

Hanushek, Eric A., and M.E. Raymond. 2005. "Does School Accountability Lead to Improved Student Performance?" *Journal of Policy Analysis and Management* 24 (2): 297–327.

Hanushek, Eric A., and Ludger Wößmann. 2008. "The Role of Cognitive Skills in Economic Development." *Journal of Economic Literature* 46 (3): 607–68.

Harmon, Robert, and Keith MacAllum. 2003. "Documented Characteristics of Labor Market-Responsive Community Colleges and a Review of Supporting Literature." U.S. Department of Education, Washington, DC.

Hazan, Mihails. 2009. "Latvian Teachers: Underpaid and Over-Regulated?" Background study for the World Bank project, "Latvia Development Policy Lending: Social Sectors and Public Administration Reform," World Bank, Washington, DC.

Herbst, Mikołaj, Jan Herczyński, and Anthony Levitas. 2009. *Finansowanie Oświaty w Polsce—Diagnoza, Dylematy, Możliwości* (Financing of Education in Poland—Diagnosis, Dilemmas, Opportunities)." Warsaw: Wydanie Pierwsze.

Heckman, James J. 1999. "Policies to Foster Human Capital." NBER Working Paper 7288, National Bureau of Economic Research, Cambridge, MA.

Heyneman, Stephen P., Kathryn H. Anderson, and Nazym Nuraliyeva. 2008. "The Cost of Corruption in Higher Education." *Comparative Education Review* 52 (1): 1–25.

Holdsworth, Nick. 2009. "Czech Republic: Degree Audit Follows Corruption Claims." *University World News*, November 8.

Huitfeldt, Henrik, Jens Johansen, and Irena Kogan. 2008. "An Analysis of Labour Market Entry in Serbia and Ukraine." In *Transition from Education to Work in EU Neighboring Countries*. Turin: European Training Foundation.

Hungary, Ministry of Education and Culture. 2006. "Recognition of Non-Formal and Informal Learning; OECD RNFIL Project: Country Background Report—Hungary." Ministry of Education and Culture, Budapest.

IEA (International Association for the Evaluation of Educational Achievements). 1995, 1999, 2003, and 2007. "Mathematics Teacher Background Data Almanac." In "Trends in International Mathematics and Science Study (TIMSS)." TIMSS International Study Center, Boston College, Chestnut Hill, MA.

———. 1995, 1999, 2003, and 2007. "Science Teacher Background Data Almanac." In "Trends in Mathematics and Science Study (TIMSS)." TIMSS International Study Center, Boston College, Chestnut Hill, MA.

IES (International Center for Data Statistics). 2001, 2006. "PIRLS (Progress on International Reading Literacy Study) Results." IES, U.S. Department of Education Institute of Education Sciences, Washington, DC. http://nces.ed.gov/surveys/pirls/.

IFF Research. 2008. "Understanding the Impact of the Adult Learning Grant." Learning and Skills Council, London.

ILO (International Labour Organization). Bureau of Statistics. 1988. *International Standard Classification of Occupations (ISCO-88)*. 3rd rev. ILO: Geneva. http://www.ilo.org/public/english/bureau/stat/isco/isco88/index.htm.

Ireland, National Qualifications Authority of. 2003. "The Role of National Qualification Systems in Promoting Lifelong Learning. Background Report for Ireland." OECD, Paris.

Ivaschenko, Oleksiy. 2008. "The Survey of Skills, Labor Demand and Job Vacancies in Kazakhstan. Main Findings." PowerPoint presentation, European and Central Asia Region, World Bank, Washington, DC, March 11.

Jakubowski, Maciej, Harry Anthony Patrinos, Emilio Ernesto Porta, and Jerzy Wiśniewski. 2010. "The Impact of the 1999 Education Reform in Poland." Policy Research Working Paper 5263, World Bank, Washington, DC.

Jongbloed, Ben. 2008. "Strengthening Consumer Choice in Higher Education." In *Cost-Sharing and Accessibility in Higher Education: A Fairer Deal?* ed. Pedro N. Teixeira, D. Bruce Johnstone, Maria J. Rosa, and J. J. Vossensteijn, 19–50. New York: Springer.

Juhn, Chinhui, Kevin M. Murphy, and Brooks Pierce. 1993. "Wage Inequality and the Rise in Returns to Skill." *Journal of Political Economy* 101 (3): 410–42.

Kang, Seoghoon, and Dong-Pyo Hong. 2002. "Technological Change and Demand for Skills in Developing Countries: An Empirical Investigation of the Republic of Korea's Case." *The Developing Economies* 40 (2): 188–207.

Kapelyushnikov, Rostislav. 2008. "Russia's Human Capital: An Assessment." Background Paper for *Skills—Not Just Diplomas: Managing for Results in Education Systems in Eastern Europe and Central Asia*, ed. Lars Sondergaard and

Mamta Murthi (Washington, DC: World Bank, forthcoming). Unpublished; available upon request.

Kehm, Barbara M., and Bjørn Stensaker, eds. 2009. *University Rankings, Diversity, and the New Landscape of Higher Education.* Global Perspectives on Higher Education, Vol. 18. Rotterdam: Sense Publishers.

Kheyfets, Igor, Massimo Mastruzzi, Dino Merotto, and Lars Sondergaard. 2011. "A New Data Tool to BOOST Public Spending Efficiency." Europe and Central Asia Knowledge Brief Vol. 43 (September 2011), World Bank, Washington, DC.

Korka, Mihai. 2008. "Implementing the Modern Approach of Quality Assurance in Romanian Higher Education." Paper presented at the "Income Convergence" Conference, Bucharest, April 8.

Kouznetsova, Tatiana. 2009. "Strengths and Weaknesses of Reading Activity of Primary School Graduates in Russia according to PIRLS: 2006 Results." *Education Issues* (1) [State University Higher School of Economics, Moscow].

Krstić, Gorana, and Peter Sanfey. Forthcoming. "Earnings Inequality and the Informal Economy: Evidence from Serbia." *Economics of Transition.*

Kertesi, Gabor, and Janos Kollo. 1999. "Economic Transformation and the Return to Human Capital. The Case of Hungary, 1986-1996." Budapest Working Paper on the Labour Market 9907, Institute of Economics, Hungarian Academy of Sciences, Budapest.

———. 2001. "Economic Transformation and the Revaluation of Human Capital —Hungary 1986–1999." Budapest Working Paper on the Labour Market 0104, Institute of Sciences, Hungarian Academy of Sciences, Budapest.

Leinbach, D. Timothy, and Davis Jenkins. 2008. "Using Longitudinal Data to Increase Community College Student Success: A Guide to Measuring Milestone and Momentum Point Attainment." CCRC (Community College Research Center) *Research Tools* 2 (January).

Leitch Review of Skills. 2006. *Prosperity for All in the Global Economy: World Class Skills.* London: HM Treasury.

Levy, Frank, and Richard J. Murnane. 2004. *The New Division of Labor: How Computers are Creating the Next Job Market.* Princeton: Princeton University Press.

LFS (Labour Force Survey) (database). Eurostat, Luxembourg. http://epp.eurostat.ec.europa.eu/portal/page/portal/labour_market/introduction.

Linden, Tony, Nina Arnhold, and Kirill Vasiliev. 2008. "From Fragmentation to Cooperation: Tertiary Education, Research, and Development in South Eastern Europe." Education Working Paper 13, World Bank, Washington, DC.

Martin, Rob, Frank Villeneuve-Smith, Liz Marshall, and Ewan McKenzie. 2008. *Employability Skills Explored.* London: Learning and Skills Network.

Machin, Stephen, and John Van Reenen. 1998. "Technology and Changes in Skill Structure: Evidence from Seven OECD Countries." *Quarterly Journal of Economics* 113 (4): 1215–44.

Mansoor, Ali, and Bryce Quillin, eds. 2007. *Migration and Remittances: Eastern Europe and the Former Soviet Union.* Washington, DC: World Bank.

McKinsey & Company. 2007. "How the World's Best-Performing School Systems Come Out on Top." McKinsey & Company, Social Sector Office, New York. http://www.mckinsey.com/clientservice/Social_Sector/our_practices/Education/Knowledge_Highlights.aspx.

———. 2008: "An Introduction to the McKinsey Report and What It Means for Education in Australia." Presentation, McKinsey & Company, New York. Cited with permission.

———. 2010. "Closing the Talent Gap: Attracting and Retaining Top-Third Graduates to Careers in Teaching—An International and Market Research-Based Perspective" Byron Auguste, Paul Kihn, and Matt Miller, McKinsey & Company, Social Sector Office, New York. http://www.mckinsey.com/clientservice/Social_Sector/our_practices/Education/Knowledge_Highlights.aspx.

Mitra, Pradeep, Marcelo Selowsky, and Juan Zalduendo. 2010. *Turmoil at Twenty: Recession, Recovery, and Reform in Central and Eastern Europe and the Former Soviet Union.* Washington, DC: World Bank.

Mungiu-Pippidi, Alina. 2009. "Assessing Corruption in the Romanian Higher Education System: The Coalition for Clean Universities." Photocopy, Hertie School of Governance, Berlin.

Munich, Daniel, Jan Svejnar, and Katherine Terrell. 1999. "Returns to Human Capital under the Communist Wage Grid During the Transition to a Market Economy." *Review of Economics and Statistics* 87 (1): 100–127.

Nastasescu, Vasile. 2006. "Romania: Higher Education System and Its Quality Assurance." Paper presented at The Third Europe and Central Asia (ECA) Education Conference, "Quality and Relevance of Education," St. Petersburg, October 4–6.

Newell, Andrew, and Barry Reilly. 1997. "Rates of Returns to Educational Qualifications in the Transitional Economies." Discussion Paper in Economics 03/97, University of Sussex, Brighton.

Newell, Andrew, and Mieczyslaw W. Socha. 2007. "The Polish Wage Inequality Explosion." IZA Discussion Paper 2644, Institute for the Study of Labor, Bonn.

OECD (Organisation for Economic Co-operation and Development). 1994. *The OECD Jobs Study: Facts, Analysis, Strategies.* Paris: OECD.

———. 1999a. *Measuring Student Knowledge and Skills: A New Framework for Assessment.* Paris: OECD.

———. 1999b. *OECD Employment Outlook: Giving Youth a Better Start.* Paris: OECD.

———. 2004a. "Improving Skills for More and Better Jobs: Does Training Make a Difference?" In *OECD Employment Outlook 2004,* 183–224. Paris: OECD.

———. 2004b. "Raising the Quality of Educational Performance at School." Policy Brief, OCED, Paris. http://www.oecd.org/publications/Pol_brief.

———. 2005a. *Attracting, Developing, and Retaining Effective Teachers—Final Report: Teachers Matter.* Paris: OECD.

———. 2005b. "The Definition and Selection of Key Competencies—Executive Summary." OECD, Paris.

———. 2005c. *Modernizing Government: The Way Forward.* Paris: OECD.

———. 2005d. *Promoting Adult Learning.* Paris: OECD.

———. 2005e. "Thematic Review of Adult Learning: Poland Country Note." OECD, Paris.

———. 2006. "OECD Economic Surveys: Netherlands." OECD, Paris.

———. 2007a. *Analysis.* Volume 1 of *PISA 2006: Science Competencies for Tomorrow's World.* Paris: OECD.

———. 2007b. *Education at a Glance: OECD Indicators.* Paris: OECD.

———. 2007c. *Performance-Based Budgeting in OECD Countries.* Paris: OECD.

———. 2007d. "PISA 2006: Science Competencies for Tomorrow's World; Executive Summary." OECD, Paris.

———. 2008. *Education at a Glance 2008: OECD Indicators.* Paris: OECD.

OECD Education At a Glance Database. OECD, Paris. http://www.oecd.org/document/30/0,3343,en_2649_39263238_39251550_1_1_1_1,00.html.

OECD and World Bank. 2007. *Reviews of National Policies for Education: Higher Education in Kazakhstan.* Paris: OECD.

Ok, Wooseok, and Peter Tergeist. 2003. "Improving Workers' Skills: Analytical Evidence and the Role of the Social Partners." OECD Social, Employment, and Migration Working Papers 10, Organisation for Economic Co-operation and Development, Paris.

Orazem, Peter, and Milan Vodopivec. 1994. "Winners and Losers in Transition: Returns to Education, Experience, and Gender in Slovenia." Policy Research Working Paper 1342, World Bank, Washington, DC.

Osborne, David, and Ted Gaebler. 1992. *Reinventing Government: How the Entrepreneurial Spirit is Transforming the Public Sector.* Reading, MA: Addison-Wesley Publishing Company, Inc.

OSI (Open Society Institute). 2007. *Equal Access to Quality Education for Roma.* Vol. 1. Monitoring Report. Budapest: OSI/EU Monitoring and Advocacy Program.

Pachuashvili, Maria. 2007. "Changing Patterns of Private-Public Growth and Decline: The Case of Georgian Higher Education." PROPHE Working Paper 10, Program for Research on Private Higher Education, Albany, NY.

Patrinos, Harry Anthony. 2008. "Labor Markets and Education and Training in Ukraine." Photocopy, World Bank, Washington DC.

Patrinos, Harry Anthony, Tazeen Fasih, Juliana Guaqueta, Emilio Porta, Kevin Macdonald, and Plamen Danchev. 2010. "A Review of the Bulgaria School Autonomy Reforms." Report 54890-BG, World Bank, Washington, DC.

Peter, Klara Sabirianova. 2003. "Skill-Biased Transition: The Role of Markets, Institutions, and Technological Change." IZA Discussion Paper 893, Institute for the Study of Labor, Bonn.

PISA Database. 2000, 2003, 2006, 2009. Organisation for Economic Co-operation and Development, Paris. http://www.oecd.org/edu/pisa/2009.

Poland, Government of. 2007. Raw dataset from Poland 2007 Labor Force Survey, Central Statistical Office, Warsaw.

Poland, National Bank of. 2008. "Yearly Survey of Enterprises, 2008." National Bank of Poland, Warsaw.

Pricopie, Remus, Valeriu Frunzary, Nicoleta Corbu, and Ivan Loredana. 2010. "Arguments for a New Policy Dialog on Access and Equity." *Romanian Journal of Communication and Public Relations* 12 (2): 9–25.

Psacharopoulos, George, and Harry A. Patrinos. 2004. "Returns to Investment in Education: A Further Update." *Education Economics* 12 (2): 111–34.

Rauhvargers, Andrejs, Cynthia Deane, and Wilfried Pauwels. 2009. "Bologna Process Stocktaking Report 2009." Report from working groups appointed by the Bologna Follow-up Group to the Ministerial Conference in Leuven/Louvain-la-Neuve, Lifelong Learning Programme, European Commission, Brussels.

Romania, Government of. National Institute of Statistics. 2008. *Romanian Statistical Yearbook 2008*. Bucharest: National Institute of Statistics.

———, Ministry of Education, Research and Innovation. 2009. "Report on the State of the National Education System 2009." Ministry of Education, Research and Innovation, Bucharest.

Russian Federation, Government of. 2007. Raw dataset from 2007 Russian Federation Labor Force Survey, Federal State Statistics Service, Moscow.

Rutkowski, Jan. 1996a. "Changes in the Wage Structure during Economic Transition in Central and Eastern Europe." World Bank Technical Paper 340, World Bank, Washington, DC.

———. 1996b. "High Skills Pay-off: The Changing Wage Structure during Economic Transition in Poland." *Economics of Transition* 4 (1): 89–112.

———. 2001. "Earnings Inequality in Transition Economies of Central Europe: Trends and Patterns During the 1990s." Social Protection Discussion Paper 0117, World Bank, Washington, DC.

———. 2007. "From the Shortage of Jobs to the Shortage of Skilled Workers. Labor Markets in the EU New Member States." IZA Discussion Paper 3202, Institute for the Study of Labor, Bonn.

———. 2008a. "Does the Labor Market Support Croatia's EU Convergence?" Photocopy, World Bank, Washington, DC. Unpublished background paper for World Bank, 2009, "Croatia's EU Convergence Report: Reaching and Sustaining Higher Rates of Economic Growth." Report 48879-HR, 2 vols., Europe and Central Asia Region, World Bank, Washington, DC.

———. 2008b. "Labor Market in Georgia: Lack of Jobs or Structural Mismatches?" Photocopy, World Bank, Washington, DC. Unpublished background paper for Georgia Country Economic Memorandum, World Bank, Washington, DC.

———. 2010. "Demand for Skills in FYR Macedonia." Photocopy. Report supported by the Multidonor Trust Fund, "Labor Markets, Job Creation, and Economic Growth," through funding of the German, Norwegian, Austrian, and Korean governments. World Bank, Washington, DC.

Rutkowski, Jan, and Stefano Scarpetta. 2005. *Enhancing Job Opportunities: Eastern Europe and the Former Soviet Union.* With Arup Banerji, Philip O'Keefe, Gaëlle Pierre, and Milan Vodopivec. Washington, DC: World Bank.

Salmi, Jamil. 2009. "The Growing Accountability Agenda in Tertiary Education: Progress or Mixed Blessing?" *World Bank Education Working Paper Series* 16. Document 47760, Education Unit, Human Development Network, World Bank, Washington, DC.

———. 2011. "Review of Student Learning Assessment Experiences in Higher Education." Unpublished paper, World Bank, Washington, DC.

Santiago, Paulo, and Karine Tremblay. 2008. "Setting the Right Course, Steering Higher Education." With Marie-Claire Duguay and Thomas Weko. In *Special Features: Governance, Funding, Quality*, Volume 1 of *Tertiary Education for the Knowledge Society*, P. Santiago, K. Tremblay, E. Basri, and E. Arnal, 67–162. Paris: OECD.

Scarpetta, Stefano, and Milan Vodopivec. 2005. "Restructuring, Productivity, and Job Creation." In *Enhancing Job Opportunities: Eastern Europe and the Former Soviet Union*, ed. Jan J. Rutkowski and Stefano Scarpetta, 125–54. Washington, DC: World Bank.

Silova, Iveta. 2009. "The Crisis of the Post-Soviet Teaching Profession in the Caucasus and Central Asia." *Research in Comparative and International Education* 4 (4): 367–84.

Slantcheva, Snejana, and Daniel Levy, eds. 2007. *The Search for Legitimacy: Private Higher Education in Central and Eastern Europe.* Basingstoke: Palgrave-MacMillan.

Steiner-Khamsi, Gita, and Christine Harris-Van Keuren. 2008. "The Pendulum of Decentralization and Recentralization Reforms: Its Impact on Teacher

Salaries in the Caucasus, Central Asia, and Mongolia." With Iveta Silova and Ketevan Chachkhiani. Background paper for *Education for All Global Monitoring Report 2009: Overcoming Inequality: Why Governance Matters.* Paris: UNESCO; London: Oxford University Press.

Steiner-Khamsi, Gita, and Iveta Silova. 2007. *How NGOs React: Globalization and Education Reform in the Caucasus, Central Asia and Mongolia.* West Hartfield, CT: Kumarian Press.

Stensaker, Bjørn, Jürgen Enders, and Harry de Boer. 2006. "Comparative Analysis and Executive Summary." Part One of "The Extent and Impact of Higher Education Governance Reform Across Europe." Final report to the Directorate-General for Education and Culture of the European Commission, Center for Higher Education and Policy Studies, University of Twente, Enschede, The Netherlands.

Tan, Hong. 2001. "Do Training Levies Work? Malaysia's HRDF and Its Effects on Training, and Firm-Level Productivity." Working Paper, World Bank Institute, Washington, DC.

Tan, Hong, and Gladys Lopez Acevedo. 2005. "Evaluating Training Programs for Small and Medium Enterprises, Lessons from Mexico." Policy Research Working Paper 3760, World Bank, Washington DC.

Tan, Hong, Yevgeniya Savchenko, Vladimir Gimpelson, Rostislav Kapelyushnikov, and Anna Lukyanova. 2007. "Skills Shortages and Training in Russian Enterprises." Policy Research Working Paper 4222, World Bank, Washington, DC.

Tumeneva, Yulia. 2006. "Analysis of Russian Education Features as Correlates with Student Achievements in PISA." In *Russian Schools: From PISA 2000 to PISA 2003*, ed. Anatolii Kasprjak, 110–76. Moscow: Logos.

UIS (UNESCO Institute for Statistics). Data Centre (various databases). UIS. Montreal. http://stats.uis.unesco.org/unesco/TableViewer/document.aspx?ReportId=143&IF_Language=eng.

UNECE (United Nations Commission for Europe) SD (Statistical Database), Labour Force and Wages. UNECE, Geneva, Switzerland. http://w3.unece.org/pxweb/database/STAT/20-ME/3-MELF/?lang=1.

UNICEF (United Nations Children's Fund). 2007. *Education for Some More than Others?* Geneva: UNICEF.

United Kingdom, DFES (Department for Education and Skills). 2003. "The Role of National Qualification Systems in Promoting Lifelong Learning. Background Report for the United Kingdom." Organisation for Economic Co-operation and Development, Paris.

United Nations. 2006. "World Population Prospects—the 2006 Revision." Department of Economic and Social Affairs, Population Division, United Nations, New York.

Usher, Alex. 2009. "Ten Years Back and Ten Years Forward: Developments and Trends in Higher Education in Europe Region." Paper presented at the UNESCO Forum on "Higher Education in the Europe Region: Access, Values, Quality and Competitiveness," Bucharest, May 21–24.

Usher, Alex, and Jon Medow. 2009. "A Global Survey of University Rankings and League Tables." In *University Rankings, Diversity, and the New Landscape of Higher Education*, ed. Barbara M. Kehm and Bjørn Stensaker, 3–18. Vol. 18 of Global Perspectives on Higher Education. Rotterdam: Sense Publishers. The university rankings of the Center for Higher Education Development (CHE) in Gütersloh, Germany, can be accessed at http://www.che-ranking.de/cms/?getObject=615&getLang=en.

Vegas, Emiliana, and Jenny Petrow. 2008. *Raising Student Learning in Latin America: the Challenge for the 21st Century*. Washington, DC: World Bank.

Vincze, Maria, and Janos Kollo. 1999. "Economic Transformation and the Return to Human Capital. The Case of Hungary, 1986–1996." Budapest Working Papers on the Labour Market 9907, Institute of Economics, Hungarian Academy of Sciences, Budapest.

World Bank. 2003a. Raw dataset from 2003 Tajikistan Living Standards Measurement Survey, World Bank, Washington, DC.

———.2003b. "Project Appraisal Document on a Proposed Loan in the Amount of $60 Million to Romania for a Rural Education Project." Report 25101-RO, World Bank, Washington, DC.

———. 2003c. *The World Development Report 2004: Making Services Work.* Washington, DC: World Bank.

———. 2005a. *Expanding Opportunities and Building Competencies for Young People. A New Agenda for Secondary Education*. Washington, DC: World Bank.

———. 2005b. Raw dataset from 2005 Uzbekistan Regional Panel Survey, World Bank, Washington, DC.

———. 2007a. "Azerbaijan Efficiency Issues in General Education: Results from a Public Expenditure Tracking and Service Delivery Survey (PETSDS) of General Education in Azerbaijan." Draft report, World Bank, Washington, DC.

———. 2007b. "Accelerating Bulgaria's Convergence: The Challenge of Raising Productivity." Report 38570, Poverty Reduction and Economic Management Unit, World Bank, Washington, DC.

———. 2007c. "The Labor Market and Education and Training in the Western Balkans." Draft policy note, World Bank, Washington, DC. http://siteresources.worldbank.org/EXTECAREGTOPEDUCATION Resources/444607-11926 36551820/Labor_Market_and_Education_Note_Western_Balkans .June_28a.pdf.

———. 2007d. "Turkey—Higher Education Policy Study." Report 9674, Human Development Sector Unit, World Bank, Washington, DC.

———. 2008a. "Czech Republic: Improving Employment Chances for the Roma." Report 46120, Human Development Sector, World Bank, Washington, DC.

———. 2008b. "Introducing a Student Loan Scheme in Romania. A Discussion Paper." Report 46206, World Bank, Washington, DC.

———. 2008c. "Investing in Turkey's Next Generation: The School-to-Work Transition and Turkey's Development." Report 44048, Human Development Sector Unit, World Bank, Washington, DC.

———. 2008d. "Ukraine—Improving Intergovernmental Fiscal Relations and Public Health and Education Expenditures Policy: Selected Issues." Report 42450, Poverty Reduction and Economic Management Unit, Europe and Central Asian Region, World Bank, Washington, DC.

———. 2009a. "Croatia's EU Convergence Report: Reaching and Sustaining Higher Rates of Economic Growth." 2 vols. World Bank, Washington, DC.

———. 2009b. "Slovak Public Expenditure Review." World Bank, Washington, DC.

———. 2009c. "Ukraine Labor Demand Study." Human Development Sector Unit, Europe and Central Asia Region, World Bank, Washington, DC.

———. 2010a. "Azerbaijan: Living Conditions Assessment Report." Report 52801, Human Development Sector Region, World Bank, Washington, DC.

———. 2010b. "Europe 2020—Poland; Fueling Growth and Competitiveness in Poland—Through Employment, Skills, and Innovation." Draft report, World Bank, Washington, DC.

———. 2011a. "Improving the Quality and Equity of Basic Education in Turkey—Challenges and Options." Policy Note 54131-TR, World Bank, Washington, DC.

———. 2011b. "Strengthening Skills and Employability in Peru." Report No. 61699-PE, World Bank, Washington, DC.

World Development Indicators (database). World Bank, Washington, DC. http://data.worldbank.org/data-catalog/world-development-indicators.

Yemtsov, Ruslan G., Stefania R. Cnobloch, and Cem Mete. 2006. "Evolution of the Predictors of Earnings during Transition." Unpublished manuscript, World Bank, Washington, DC.

Zeigele, Frank. 2009. "How to Ensure Equity, Quality and Efficiency: Performance-Based Budgeting." Presentation delivered at the Fifth World Bank ECA Education Conference, Budva, Montenegro, October 27–29.

ECO-AUDIT
Environmental Benefits Statement

The World Bank is committed to preserving endangered forests and natural resources. The Office of the Publisher has chosen to print *Skills, Not Just Diplomas: Managing Education for Results in Eastern Europe and Central Asia* on recycled paper with 50 percent postconsumer fiber in accordance with the recommended standards for paper usage set by the Green Press Initiative, a nonprofit program supporting publishers in using fiber that is not sourced from endangered forests. For more information, visit www.greenpressinitiative.org.

Saved:
- 6 trees
- 1.7 million BTUs of total energy
- 534 pounds of net greenhouse gases
- 2,567 gallons of waste water
- 175 pounds of solid waste

www.ingramcontent.com/pod-product-compliance
Lightning Source LLC
Chambersburg PA
CBHW050436240426
43661CB00055B/2402